CONTEMPORARY ISSUES IN FINANCE AND INSOLVENCY LAW VOLUME 2

There is increasing regulatory interdependence amongst Central, East and South East Asia, European and North American financial markets, and these markets account for over one-third of the world's population and global financial markets. As these Asian markets become more integral to global financial economy, more cohesive, compatible and integrated insolvency and restructuring laws are essential. This two-volume work reviews why we should internationalise current cross-border insolvency and how we could restructure laws to address inadequacies.

The two-volume work evaluates international regulatory reforms directed at detecting and managing cross-border insolvency and restructuring crises across the entire economy including financial markets. The authors call for schemes of arrangements and letters of comfort to be formally accepted as international legal tools. The work also assesses recent, but as yet unregulated developments in financial agreements, namely, the use of close-out netting provisions. They are a significant preventative legal mechanism, protecting debtors, creditors and employees among others, before a declaration of insolvency. The book discusses international arbitration, data protection and artificial intelligence in cross-border insolvency and restructuring. Finally, it seeks a meaningful balance between self-regulation through financial contracts and other party practices, and regulation imposed by governments and international financial regulators.

This extensive work will be a useful reference for legal practitioners, policy makers and scholars working on financial regulation and international financial laws.

Leon Trakman is UNSW Emeritus Professor and Former Dean of Law at the University New South Wales in Sydney, Australia. He has held professorial appointments in the United States, at Wisconsin, University of California (Davis) and Tulane; in Canada at McGill and Dalhousie; and in Australia at UNSW. He is author of ten books and over 150 journal articles including on topics that are addressed in this book. A barrister and international commercial arbitrator, he serves on international commercial arbitration panels of global arbitration centres. A panellist under the NAFTA, he was regularly appointed by the US, Canadian and Mexican Governments to resolve trade and investment disputes. He currently serves on the Remedies Panel of the United States Mexico Canada Agreement (USMCA). He holds both Master and Doctorate degrees from Harvard University.

Robert Walters, Lecturer, Victoria University, Melbourne, Australia. Dr. Walters is also Adjunct Professor of Law, European Faculty of Law, New University, Slovenia, Europe, and admitted to practice law in Australia. Robert is a qualified International Arbitrator. He is a member of ASEAN Law Association – Singapore, Asia Pacific Scholar (Privacy/Data Protection) Network. His work on cross-border data flows in the new digital economy has been recognised globally, and in 2021 he was engaged by the British Government to undertake a project on determining data adequacy across commonwealth countries. Dr. Walters specialises in transnational commercial and private law (data protection, cyber security, artificial intelligence, trade, finance and investment including cross-border insolvency, contracts and arbitration).

"Cross-border insolvency necessarily involves multiple jurisdictions. But, as this important new work demonstrates, it also routinely necessitates multiple perspectives – economic and legal, of course, but also social, political, and medical. A particular strength is the manner in which the book focuses on the digital economy, where data is a source of value but doesn't fall neatly into existing categories: Is it a good? Is it a service? Is it something else? At the same time, the authors ground their research in the practical and the pragmatic, offering concrete proposals in support of regulatory convergence and harmonisation that, they argue, will better enable the global economy to navigate increasingly choppy waters. For practitioners, scholars, and students it will be of great interest – and of great use."

Simon Chesterman, *Dean and Provost's Chair Professor of the National University of Singapore Faculty of Law and Senior Director of AI Governance at AI Singapore*

"In this innovative new book, Trakman and Walters make the case for urgent reform of cross border corporate insolvency and restructuring law. Their account covers, but goes beyond, challenges with the existing enforcement and recognition regime, to call for 'internationalisation' of various legal tools and mechanisms, including several rarely discussed in a cross-border insolvency and restructuring context such as letters of comfort, data protection, and artificial intelligence. This impressive scope is matched by engagement with an impressive number of jurisdictions: Australia; India; Indonesia; China; Singapore; UK; US; and the European Union. The result is a book which deserves a place on the bookshelves of anyone interested in this important field."

Sarah Paterson, *Professor of Law, London School of Economics*

"As the world continues to grapple with the COVID-19 pandemic and economic downturn, this is a most timely and impressive study of cross-border insolvency. A particular strength is its extensive research. The authors cover not only technical substantive laws concerned with transnational insolvency, but also complicated private international law issues such as jurisdiction and international commercial arbitration, which are rarely discussed in the literature. It further identifies key emerging areas of international commercial law such as data protection and artificial intelligence that will form part of cross-border insolvency and restructuring. Specifically the book calls for nations to collaborate at the internationalisation level for current and future economic shock. One of the finest works on cross-border insolvency, this book is essential reading for everyone interested in the insolvency law, international commercial law, private international law and international dispute resolution."

Weixia Gu, *Associate Professor, The University of Hong Kong Faculty of Law and Co-Chair, American Society of International Law Asia-Pacific Interest Group (2018–2021)*

"Throughout the COVID-19 pandemic the world has experienced various levels of financial stress. However, in this context of a global crisis some crucial aspects of financial infrastructural stress, such as cross border insolvency and restructuring, have not often been spoken or written about. Against the backdrop of a period of growth, internationally, nevertheless a comparatively large number of entities have had to restructure or declare insolvency. With many entities based in multiple locations and in different countries, this book provides partitioners, scholars, and students with a highly sophisticated comparative legal analysis. The authors make an important point – that national and international regulators need to take a preventative approach, to ensure or minimise as far as possible future economic shocks, and ensure a high level of certainty. As the digital economy expands, the authors also highlight the importance of data and artificial intelligence technology to future cross border restructuring and insolvency. In calling for greater internationalisation of these area of law and of close out netting provisions, the authors embrace the roles of international organisations such as UNCITRAL-UNICTAD which can have a positive effect. I highly recommend this book to anyone with an interest in cross border insolvency or restructuring."

Michael Stuckey, *Professor and Dean of School of Law, University of Tasmania, Australia*

"Insolvency law and its practice sits within a country's legal system. The book explains how insolvency law and its various mechanisms – preventive and reconstructive, often 'multi-layered' – are applied to businesses under financial stress. The book's particular merit is its coverage of a broader range of insolvency laws and their intersections than we generally see, beyond the UNCITRAL Model Law and schemes of arrangement to close out and netting arrangements, keepwell agreements, arbitrations, data control and artificial intelligence. In comparing and contrasting different national approaches, this text makes a valuable and timely contribution to international insolvency law."

Michael Murray, *Principal at Murrays Legal, Sydney, Australia and Director, Australian Academy of Law*

CONTEMPORARY ISSUES IN FINANCE AND INSOLVENCY LAW

Volume 2

Leon Trakman and
Robert Walters

Routledge
Taylor & Francis Group
LONDON AND NEW YORK

First published 2023
by Routledge
4 Park Square, Milton Park, Abingdon, Oxon OX14 4RN

and by Routledge
605 Third Avenue, New York, NY 10158

Routledge is an imprint of the Taylor & Francis Group, an informa business

British Library Cataloguing-in-Publication Data
A catalogue record for this book is available from the British Library

Library of Congress Cataloging-in-Publication Data
A catalog record for this book has been requested

ISBN: 978-1-032-31916-2 (hbk)
ISBN: 978-1-032-31913-1 (pbk)
ISBN: 978-1-003-31202-4 (ebk)

DOI: 10.4324/9781003312024

Typeset in Bembo
by Apex CoVantage, LLC

CONTENTS

FIGURES

FOREWORD

Over the course of 2020 and 2021, the world was affected by, and attempted to come to terms with the COVID-19 pandemic. The impact was very different from prior economic and geopolitical shocks such as the 2008 Global Financial Crisis (GFC). No nation was spared from the pandemic. It had an obvious and terrible effect on the lives of many people, not only in loss of life and on-going medical problems, but also on their jobs and livelihoods and the economies of the countries in which they lived. The movement of people ground to a halt nationally and internationally. Borders were closed; economic production stalled. Unlike the GFC, where economic production remained largely untouched, the pandemic forced millions of people out of work. There was a significant rise in cross-border insolvencies, offset to a degree by a rise in local and transnational restructuring. At the same time there was a decline in cross-border mergers and acquisitions as businesses responded to the pandemic by looking inwards, due to the uncertain global economic outlook.

In these circumstances, it is perhaps not a surprise that cross-border insolvency and restructuring are garnering more attention. A rise in transnational trade and investment preceded the pandemic and will be likely to rise again as the world learns to live with the pandemic. Companies are again looking at ways in which to maximise profits, while ensuring they operate with certainty with the result that increasingly they are establishing offices and branches in other countries. This international growth has led to an increase in cross-border insolvency and restructuring and to international and national legal frameworks adapting to accommodate this activity. Such developments provide some legal certainty for entities under financial stress, as well as for their creditors and related parties. However, legal developments across borders can be and are somewhat variable in nature and so not always amenable to consistent application in practice. The current international legal framework, coupled with domestic legislative, administrative and judicial regulatory measures, provides a foundation upon which to base and enhance global insolvency and reconstruction measures. However, there is scope to do more to harmonise cross-border insolvency and restructuring laws.

The lack of universal implementation or consistent application of the 1997 UNCITRAL Model Law on Cross-Border Insolvency has created challenges. Some states have not adopted the UNCITRAL Model Law, while others have construed and applied it restrictively. In contrast, the jurisdictions which are the subject of discussion and comparative analysis in this book have generally adopted a universalist approach to cross-border insolvency and have implemented the UNCITRAL Model Law. In order to meet the needs of future development, consideration needs to be given to a convergence of approaches by nation states by adopting a more universalist approach. While the authors of this book have only undertaken a limited comparison of the approaches of Australia, the European Union, China, Indonesia, India, Singapore, the United Kingdom and the United States of America, they have identified many similarities in the respective cross-border insolvency and restructuring legal regimes of those jurisdictions. But more work can be done to achieve a higher level of legal convergence.

This book is timely. Its recommendations may strengthen the current international framework for cross-border insolvency and restructuring. The authors' analysis is thought provoking and demonstrates that the principles, concepts and tools available in private international law may not be sufficient to resolve the potential challenges and conflicts that are likely to arise in cross-border restructuring and insolvency in the future. Their proposals constitute a real contribution to the debate as to how to develop and entrench more effective mechanisms of cross-border insolvency.

The Honourable Justice Brigitte Markovic
Federal Court of Australia

PREFACE

Deglobalisation has been well underway for some time. The recent pandemic has in the eyes of some international organisation contributed to this. The World Economic Forum in 2020 summarised the current deglobalisation activity insightfully as follows:

> With coronavirus (COVID-19) raising concerns around globalization and world trade, global value chains are beginning to fray, as countries look inwards for economic growth, write two experts. Since the early 1990s until recently, the world had been witnessing an economic 'convergence,' whereby poor countries were beginning to catch up with rich ones. Hyper-globalization drove the global export-to-GDP ratio from 15% to 25% over the two decades leading up to the 2008 global financial crisis. This export boom fuelled rapid growth in developing countries. There is every reason to worry that a historic process of deglobalization is underway, threatening to scuttle the growth models of poor countries that previously used trade as a path to prosperity. Worst of all, this disturbing shift has been met by silence or even encouragement by those who should know better. The intellectual response to deglobalization and the reversal of the historic process of convergence has been a near-deafening silence. Very few academics or policymakers in advanced economies have spoken up in defense of an open global order on behalf of poorer countries. Cosmopolitan elites who previously had been loud and enthusiastic champions of globalization have sat on their hands.[1]

1 World Economic Forum, *How Deglobalisation Is Hurting the World's Emerging Economies*, https://www.weforum.org/agenda/2020/09/convergence-threatened-by-deglobalization-covid19/.

However, in the new digital economy, the globalisation of commercial and personal data increases annually. Data, while often not thought of as an issue in cross-border insolvency, has continued to emerge as being challenging and problematic, due to the fragmented approach to regulating cross-border data flows of personal data. While this book is not an explicit call to assist poorer countries directly, it defends the rules-based rule of law to assist emerging and developing countries, not only developed ones. In other words, by strengthening the global legal framework for transnational insolvency and restructuring, in our view, no one nation state should be disadvantaged, so long as the benefits in international economic growth are shared. We identify those benefits with the harmonisation and convergence of transnational law and policy governing cross-border restructuring and insolvency. The book does so by addressing the comparative and interdisciplinary research of the United Nations Commission on International Trade Law (UNCITRAL) Model Law on Cross-Border Insolvency and the International Institute for the Unification of Private Law (UNIDROIT) Principles on Close Out Netting. Arguably these institutions have been instrumental in bringing together the nations of the world to establish a global framework that has sought to harmonise cross-border insolvency law. The book digresses slightly to the emerging areas of law that challenge those previously mentioned, such as data protection and artificial intelligence.

This work is intended to make a significant step forward, in promoting a global regulatory environment that provides a significant layer of certainty in regulating cross-border insolvency and corporate restructuring. However, there continues to be an urgent need to address immediate threats to global commerce, resulting from the pandemic, trade sanctions and other sources of international commercial disruption. Sustaining the harmonisation and convergence of divergent national laws is necessary going forward. However, in practice it is difficult to achieve. Promoting these developments is an essential mandate of both the UNCITRAL and UNIDROIT to undertake at the earliest possible time. This book is intended to advance these central goals in pursuing and attaining such harmonisation in relation to transnational insolvency and restructuring law. This is a priority for the international business community, and governments to ensure the economy has another layer to shield itself for the next economic shock.

Professor, Dr. Leon Trakman
Dr. Robert Walters

ACKNOWLEDGEMENT

The authors extend particular thanks to Justice Brigitte Markovic, Federal Court of Australia, and Chair, United Nations Commission on International Trade Law – Coordinating Committee, for her valuable insight in reviewing draft Chapters 1, 2 and 3, and for her kind support and endorsement.

This book draws upon the work undertaken by global law forms that include but are not limited to Baker Mckenzie, Clifford Chance and Jones Day.

The authors thank Erazem Bohinc (Banking & Capital Markets, Frankfurt), from Clifford Chance, for providing legal opinions contained in the Firm's book on International Swaps and Derivatives. Thanks to Mr. Michael Murray, Sydney Australia from Murray's Legal and to Neil Hammon for their work on domestic and cross-border insolvency and restructuring arrangements.

The book benefitted from the contributions of a number of academics. Among these, Professor Arne *Mavčič* of the European Faculty of Law, New University, Slovenia, Europe was instrumental in connecting the authors with European experts in this field. Researchers in the field of finance and insolvency at Gujarat National Law University in India, notably Professor Dr. Mamata Biswal, Assistant Professor Harsha Rajwansh, provided valuable input on the law of insolvency in India. Associate Professor Sinta Dewi Rosadi at Universitas Padjadjaran, Indonesia kindly verified information on Indonesia.

Importantly, the authors thank their respective partners for their support throughout the research and writing stages of this book. Leon Trakman is indebted to Lynne-Marie Wade for her caring and for kindly proofreading selected book chapters. Robert thanks his wife Catherine Tan for providing him with the time and space to complete the work.

7

INTERNATIONAL ARBITRATION

International trade and investment have provided significant economic and social benefits to countries across the globe. However, it has not come without its own complex disputes. This chapter explores some of the issues and benefits of using international commercial arbitration (ICA) to address disputes arising in cross-border insolvency. With the implementation of the UNCITRAL Model Law on Cross-Border Insolvency 1997, and the push for a universalist approach to cross-border insolvency, international commercial disputes have inevitably resulted. As highlighted in Chapter 2, an important principle that derived from the Model Law was the need to identify the COMI (centre of main interest) in the insolvency or other proceedings. Coupled with identifying COMI is the importance of promoting greater cooperation among states in regulating cross-border insolvency. Included in that cooperation is the value of states and their courts recognising and enforcing arbitration awards. So impelled, the International Insolvency Institute has called upon the UNCITRAL to establish a dedicated arbitration commission. The intended purpose of that commission is to extend the global authority of the International Convention on the Recognition and Enforcement of Foreign Arbitration Awards (NY Convention) in resolving complex cross-border insolvency disputes.[1] The pervasive virtue attributed to international commercial arbitration is its international dimensions. That is, the commercial expertise of the arbitrators; the reliance on expeditious proceedings; the lower cost of ICA proceedings on average than domestic judicial proceedings, particularly at global commercial hubs. The further benefit of ICA relates to its recognition by multiple state signatories to the New York Convention and its enforcement by courts in those states. This benefit contrasts with the limited recognition and

1 United Nations Commission on International Trade Law, *Model Law on Cross-Border Insolvency*, 1997, https://uncitral.un.org/en/texts/insolvency/modellaw/cross-border_insolvency.

DOI: 10.4324/9781003312024-1

enforcement of foreign judicial decisions under the Hague Convention on the Recognition and Enforcement of Foreign Judgements in Civil or Commercial Matters (Hague Convention on Foreign Judgements.[2] This chapter will examine the arbitrability of cross-border insolvency disputes. It will also examine when and why specific disputes are exempted from ICA.

7.1 Introduction

The recent global pandemic has had a catastrophic effect on the stability of businesses around the world and facilitated the expansion of cross-border disputes over the growing debt of financially unstable companies. As the business world emerges incrementally from the pandemic but inflation has increased, the case for more unified methods for resolving cross-border dispute relating to debt, and insolvency, has grown more pressing.[3] This has been further heightened by the recent conflict in Ukraine. Increasingly needed are global institutions and processes through which to resolve disputes over the repayment of debts, the restructuring and reorganising of corporate assets, and failing that, corporate insolvency. Even as nation states localise global trade and investment, they still need to recognise viable institutions through which to resolve disputes over cross-border debts and their legal sequelae.

ICA is an important means of resolving such disputes. It can also serve as a functionally efficient method of resolving international commercial disputes according to the choice of law adopted by the parties. It can also consolidate cross-border proceedings in which the debtors and creditors are located in different jurisdictions. Arbitrators can also apply flexible rules of procedure to expedite hearings efficiently.[4] The choice of arbitration is also party driven in that it proceeds according to the direction agreed to by the parties from the outset. Applied to cross-border insolvency proceedings, the objectives of ICA are to resolve disputes between creditors and debtors transparently, equitably and efficiently, without which creditors would be unable to collect on their claims. In the absence of orderly procedures, the rights of debtors (and their employees) would be inadequately protected, while creditors would be treated disparately and unequally.[5] In essence, the use of ICA in cross-border insolvency proceedings can promote the effective resolution of disputes across financial and market sectors as well as legal jurisdictions.

2 The Hague, Netherlands, 2 July 2019.

3 Kiran Nasir Gore, Charles H. Camp, The Interplay Between Insolvency Proceedings and Parallel International Arbitration Proceedings in the Post-Pandemic World, *The World Financial Review* (2020), 1–2.

4 Andrew Chan, Jonathan Chan, Jo Tay, Alexander Lawrence Yeo, Cross-Border Insolvency and Its Impact on Arbitration, *Singapore Academy Law Journal* 26, 999 (2014), 998–1004.

5 Orderly & Effective Insolvency Procedures, *Key Issues, Legal Department, International Monetary Fund*, 1999, https://www.imf.org/external/pubs/ft/orderly/.

The policy objectives underlying ICA potentially conflict with cross-border insolvency proceedings before domestic courts. National insolvency laws are often designed to achieve uniquely domestic and often mandatory public policies for the benefit of debtors and creditors.[6] The objective of ICA is generally to resolve insolvency disputes in light of the intention of the disputing parties and subject to their choice of law. Robert Kovac[7] highlights the key distinctions between courts regulating insolvency nationally and ICA doing so transnationally:

> Insolvency regulation, the emphasis is on the equality of creditors, centralisation of claims, rescue of the insolvent party, State control, a transparent and accountable process, a coordinated distribution of assets and authority usually derived from statute; whereas arbitration regulation, the authority derives from a contractual relationship of the parties (party autonomy that is autonomous from State) and the emphasis is on the resolution of a particular dispute between (usually two) parties and is generally private and confidential.[8]

Viewed this way, international commercial arbitration seeks to provide the parties with, the ability to choose the applicable procedure and law governing their contractual relationship.[9] Two key purposes underlie their intentions in relation to the conduct of arbitration. The first is to ensure that the arbitration tribunal complies with the choice of law, jurisdiction and seat of arbitration selected by the parties. The second is that the award is recognised and enforceable in multistate jurisdictions, not only in the forum. These are elaborated upon later.

What formally distinguishes domestic insolvency proceedings and ICA proceedings is that, while domestic proceedings apply by operation of the law, ICA applies by the choice of the parties. Domestic judicial decisions bind the parties by operation of the law. The parties to ICA are bound by the decisions of transnational arbitrators whom they choose, according to procedures administered by party-selected arbitration institutions, rules and procedures. Functionally, however, even though the parties to ICA, insolvency proceedings can influence the application of insolvency laws, by adopting contract clauses that provide for terminating or restructuring an entity, they are bound by the law they have chosen. In effect, if the parties choose domestic law to resolve their disputes, they are bound by that law, not unlike domestic courts being so bound. The procedures adopted by domestic

6 Kiran Nasir Gore, Charles H. Camp, The Interplay Between Insolvency Proceedings and Parallel International Arbitration Proceedings in the Post-Pandemic World, *The World Financial Review* (2020), 1–3.

7 Robert Kovacs, A Transnational Approach to the Arbitrability of Insolvency Proceedings in International Arbitration, *Journal of Bankruptcy Law and Practice* 21, 3 (2012), 5.

8 Ibid.

9 Ibid., 1–3.

courts and international arbitrators may diverge, such as when the parties choose to be bound by the institutional rules of an international arbitration association as distinct from domestic legal procedures. The common denominator, in the case of both judicial decisions and arbitration awards, is that they are legally binding upon the parties.

This chapter compares insolvency proceedings before courts and ICA, focusing on different domestic jurisdictions that, to varying degrees, function as legal and financial hubs. It also discusses those areas that remain exempt from ICA, or when the dispute is not subject to an agreement to arbitrate, primarily, when it is not arbitrable. The chapter briefly draws on recent court decisions in selected jurisdictions that address tensions between ICA and insolvency proceedings before courts of law. Considered further are the tension between arbitration clauses in insolvency disputes, and the ongoing management of debt and arbitration. Additionally considered will be insolvency proceedings that are conducted after the finalisation of arbitration but before the issuance of the arbitration award.

Central to the tension between arbitration and insolvency is the autonomy of the parties to choose the process of arbitration. This process is compared to the mandate of the court to direct the process of insolvency. Judicial oversight of ICA ordinarily occurs only after the arbitration award, that is, in judicial enforcement proceedings at which a court determines whether the arbitration proceedings had complied with the law chosen by the parties. This oversight relates, *inter alia*, to the appointment of the arbitrator(s), their compliance with the applicable law in the conduct of proceedings and in rendering an Interim or Final award.

In contrast, courts of law that deal with insolvency cases are bound by the law governing their appointment which is ordinarily provided for by statute in the appointing state. Judges are not appointed by the parties. Their authority to review arbitration proceedings and/or an arbitration award is also determined by that law or statute. It ordinarily accords the judge or judges full oversight over insolvency proceedings. This could also include reviewing the relevant winding up or related proceedings. Judges are also empowered to determine whether the parties have complied with the judicial mandate imposed on them.

In adopting this multilateral approach to ICA, the chapter will also examine the UNCITRAL Model Law on International Commercial Arbitration[10] and its particular benefit when used to resolve cross-border insolvency. When coupled with the UNCITRAL Model Law on Cross-Border Insolvency, it will be argued that recourse to ICA can sometimes have advantages over resorting to courts in resolving such disputes. This is on the basis of the parties agreeing to arbitrate.

10 UNCITRAL, *Model Law on International Commercial Arbitration (1985), with Amendments as adopted in 2006*, https://uncitral.un.org/sites/uncitral.un.org/files/media-documents/uncitral/en/19-09955_e_ebook.pdf.

7.2 The Recognition and Enforcement of International Commercial Arbitration

The impact of insolvency proceedings, orders, resolutions *per se* on the substantive validity of an arbitration agreement are challenging.[11] They pose a number of questions, such as whether an arbitration agreement in one jurisdiction can prevent the initiation of insolvency proceedings and procedures (including orders and resolutions) in another jurisdiction.[12] This section will demonstrate that the answer to these questions depends on a number of variables. Arguably, these answers also depend on the success attributed to ICA in providing a viable transnational method of resolving cross-border insolvency disputes.

In 2007, the International Insolvency Institute recommended that the UNCITRAL Working Group on Cross-Border Insolvency adopt the New York Convention on the Recognition and Enforcement of International Commercial Arbitration Awards[13] (NY Convention). The Institute also recommended use and application of the NY Convention to cross-border insolvency disputes.[14] Additionally, the Institute contended that it would be sound public policy to use ICA in many, and possibly all insolvency proceedings. Furthermore, the International Insolvency Institute encouraged UNCITRAL to establish a Commission consisting of insolvency and arbitration experts to examine and propose changes in either insolvency or arbitration law. The proposal was aimed at improving the effective use of international arbitration in cross-border bankruptcy matters.[15] More than a decade later, no Commission has been established. However, ICA has continued to play a considerable role in regulating cross-border insolvency. The further reality is the likelihood of a geometric increase in international financial disputes leading to insolvency, given the economic instability resulting from trade wars, pandemics and tensions between global and domestic governance of cross-border business relationships. Reliance on arbitration is likely to expand in regulating such disputes particularly as inflation and the prospects of a global recession escalate.

Recent developments in cross-border insolvency have been shifting in recognition of continuing global financial fragility, such as in distinguishing between main and non-main foreign insolvency proceedings. As Chapters 2 and 3 in Volume 1 have highlighted, the UNCITRAL Model Law on Cross-Border Insolvency identifies the 'main' foreign proceedings as proceedings that take place at the debtor's 'centre of main interests' ('COMI'). In contrast, non-main proceedings ('COM2') take

11 Andrew Chan Chee Yin, Jonathan Chan Tuan San, Jo Tay Yu Xi, Alexander Lawrence Yeo Han Tiong, Cross-Border Insolvency and Its Impact on Arbitration, *Singapore Academy of Law Journal* 26 (2014), 999–1002.

12 Ibid., 1000–1002.

13 New York Convention on the Recognition and Enforcement of International Commercial Arbitration Awards, 1958, http://www.newyorkconvention.org/11165/web/files/original/1/5/15432.pdf.

14 Zack Clement, *Greater Use of International Arbitration in Cross-Border Insolvency Cases*, Address to UNCITRAL Congress Vienna, 12 July 2007, https://www.iiiglobal.org/sites/default/files/Zack-ClementUNCITRAL.pdf.

15 Ibid.

place anywhere else where the debtor has an 'establishment', which is defined as a place of operations and where the debtor carries out non-transitory economic activity.[16] The Model Law establishes that the insolvent debtor's COMI provides the primary law to govern cross-border proceedings. Its rationale is that a single distribution of the worldwide assets of an enterprise is preferable to the separate distribution of assets in each of multiple jurisdictions.[17] The organisational benefit is to provide greater uniformity and efficiency through centralised control over insolvency proceedings. The functional purpose is to facilitate the reorganisation or sale of the enterprise as a whole, leaving its worldwide assets largely intact. The operational goal is to avoid piecemeal dismemberment of that enterprise and the likelihood of it being liquidated at a significantly reduced value.[18]

The intended benefit of the Model Law on Cross-border Insolvency is therefore to provide a more universalised framework to regulate cross-border insolvency. This is achieved by codifying the general principle of cooperation and communication when cross-border insolvency proceedings are commenced in two or more states.[19] However, the dichotomy between COMI and COM2 proceedings has not been fully resolved under cross-border insolvency law, notwithstanding the Model Law. As Alan Gropper argues, 'the application of the COMI principle in cross-border cases has neither simplified the law regulating cross-border insolvency, nor provided a structure through which a single court can control the insolvency proceedings of a multinational enterprise'.[20] For Gropper, international commercial arbitration can improve the outcomes derived from cross-border insolvency law by two means. The first is by enabling the debtor and its financial creditors to benefit from speedier and less expensive dispute resolution procedures. The second is by allowing the parties to exercise a choice of the law in the event of the debtor's default.[21] Specifically, the parties can choose international commercial arbitration to bring all relevant subsidiaries and affiliates into the same proceedings. They can also obtain an ICA award that is presumptively recognised and enforceable in all states that are signatories to the NY Convention.[22]

The Model Law on Cross-Border Insolvency does provide for the recognition and enforcement of a foreign main proceeding, consistent with the 1958 NY Convention.[23] However, Article 20 of the Model Law places limits on the enforcement

16 United Nations Commission on International Trade Law, *Model Law on Cross-Border Insolvency*, 1997, Part One, art. 2(f), Part Two, 30–31. See also, Allan L. Gropper, The Arbitration of Cross-Border Insolvencies, *American Bankruptcy Law Journal* 18 (2012), 205–206.

17 Ibid.

18 Ibid.

19 Ibid.

20 Ibid., 207.

21 Ibid., 222.

22 Ibid. There were 161 state signatories to the NY Convention. All domestic jurisdictions studied in this book have acceded to it. However, EU Member States, not the EU itself, have done so. It is out of scope to assess the conditions under which different states have acceded to the Convention.

23 United Nations Commission on International Trade Law, Model Law on Cross-Border Insolvency, 1997, Article 20, Effects of Recognition of a Foreign Main Proceeding 1.

of various kinds of insolvency actions, including the enforcement of an ICA award. This limitation restricts the freedom of the parties in agreeing to adopt ICA, to also agree on the enforcement of the award. Thus, maintaining the parties' lack of capacity to so agree on enforceability, or that the issues in dispute are not arbitrable, needs to be managed carefully. These limitations are most significant when it is not possible to implement an automatic stay of arbitral proceedings. For example, if the arbitration does not take place in either the enacting State, or in the State of the main proceeding, it may be difficult to enforce the stay of arbitral proceedings. Moreover, the interests of the parties may be a reason for allowing an arbitral proceeding to continue and be determined by the law of the enacting State.[24]

The NY Convention affirms the recognition and enforcement of arbitration awards that involve multiple parties engaged in legal relationships that extend across national jurisdictions and laws. Article I provides specifically for 'the recognition and enforcement of arbitral awards made in the territory of a State other than the State where the recognition and enforcement of such awards are sought'.[25] While the Convention limits the scope of that recognition and enforcement, such as in providing for a signatory state to decline to enforce an ICA award on grounds of public policy, its primary purpose is to facilitate recognition by states.[26] The inferred result is that the NY Convention discourages states from staying insolvency actions (ISA) where insolvency proceedings have commenced elsewhere.

Moreover, given the distinctive attributes of ICA, in particular its frequent diversion from the legal system of the State at which the arbitral proceeding takes place, it is not always practical for courts to stay an arbitration. This is especially so where insolvency proceedings have already commenced elsewhere. For instance, if the arbitration does not take place in either the enacting State, or in the State of the main insolvency proceeding, it may be difficult to enforce the stay. Apart from that, the interests of the parties may also be a reason for allowing arbitration proceedings to continue. Paragraph 2 of Article II of NY Convention provides that the term 'agreement in writing' shall include an arbitral clause in a contract or arbitration agreement signed by the parties or contained in letters or telegrams.[27] Paragraph 2 of Article 20 of the Model Law on Cross-Border Insolvency, in turn, provides for the modification or termination of a stay and suspension of the recognition of a foreign proceeding. Apart from these provisions, the interests of the parties may be a reason for allowing an arbitral proceeding to continue, as envisaged by paragraph 2 of that Article, as determined by the law of the enacting State.[28] The next section

24 Ibid., Article 20(1).

25 Ibid., Article 1.

26 Ibid., Article III. See also, Leon Trakman, Aligning State Sovereignty with Transnational Public Policy, *Tulane Law Review* 93 (2018).

27 Ibid., Article II.

28 United Nations Commission on International Trade Law, Model Law on Cross-Border Insolvency, 1997, Article 20, Paragraph 180–181, Subparagraph 1 (a) refers not only to 'individual actions' but also to 'individual proceedings' in order to cover, in addition to 'actions' instituted by creditors in a court against the debtor or its assets, enforcement measures initiated by creditors outside the court

will discuss unresolved tensions within international commercial arbitration that relate to cross-border insolvency.

7.3 Tension Between Arbitration and Cross-Border Insolvency

Due to the extensive issues that can arise from tensions between the law governing insolvency and arbitration, this section will examine only selected judicial decisions in Australia, the United Kingdom (UK), Singapore and the United States (US). The section will examine issues relating to the annulment of arbitration agreements and clauses. It will also examine the management of debt and arbitration and entering insolvency after commencing arbitration and the issuance of an arbitration award. Further, this section will discuss disputes over assets of an insolvent entity that are located in different jurisdictions. It will also discuss the notion of arbitrability and its current status amongst the previously mentioned states.

Generally, issues arise when the parties have commenced insolvency proceedings prior to commencing ICA. If an insolvency proceeding unfolds before or during an arbitration, the procedural considerations in both cases are ordinarily similar.[29] It is possible that the local law guiding the insolvency proceedings will require other dispute resolution proceedings to be stayed. This approach allows the bankruptcy administrator to consolidate the insolvent business's debts and assets. In parallel, the arbitration tribunal will often need to decide, not only which state's law governs, but also how its domestic courts are likely to construe that law.[30] As a result, the conflict between domestic insolvency proceedings and ICA is often difficult to reconcile. The judicial interpretation of the law may diverge in applying it to contract provisions between debtors and creditors. The arbitrator's construction of that law may add to that divergence in interpretation of the contract. At the extreme, insolvency proceedings may undermine the agreement to arbitrate itself, by invalidating it or severely narrowing its scope of application.[31]

---

system, being measures that creditors are allowed to take under certain conditions in some States. Sub-paragraph 1 (b) has been added to make it abundantly clear that executions against the assets of the debtor are covered by the stay.

29 Kiran Nasir Gore, Charles H. Camp, The Interplay Between Insolvency Proceedings and Parallel International Arbitration Proceedings in the Post-Pandemic World, *The World Financial Review* (2020), 1–3.

30 Ibid.

31 Ibid. An example highlighted by the authors, in 2007, Elektrim filed for insolvency in Poland. Under Polish bankruptcy law, the arbitration agreements were considered invalid and the arbitrations were required to be discontinued. The Warsaw court revoked Elektrim's powers of self-administration. The arbitral tribunals maintained the discretion to determine their own jurisdiction. The LCIA arbitral tribunal determined that English law governed the arbitration, despite the guidance of Polish bankruptcy law. The ICC tribunal determined that Polish law governed it lacked jurisdiction. These contrasting arbitral decisions were reviewed by the UK and Swiss courts, respectively, and were upheld as valid. It demonstrates the complex competing legal and policy implications of parallel insolvency and arbitration proceedings.

7.3.1 Arbitration Clauses – Insolvency Disputes

This sub-section concentrates on the evaluation of arbitration clauses as they relate to insolvency disputes under EU and US law. It focuses, too, on the interface between the domestication of such clauses through EU regulations and case law in both EU and US jurisdictions, while demonstrating movement towards multilateralism in their interpretation. The section initiates discussion of how legislatures and courts are adopting international instruments that support such multilateralism, such as through the Model Law on Cross-Border Insolvency, the New York Convention on the Recognition and Enforcement of International Commercial Arbitration Awards (1958) (NY Convention), and the UNCITRAL Rules. This sub-section will initiate discussion of the significance of the EU and US's adoption of these Rules and Conventions and apply them to the enforcement of arbitration awards relating to cross-border insolvency.

Subsequent sections will explore how domestic courts interpret and apply arbitration clauses in cross-border contracts. It will examine interpretative divergence in their decisions whether to enforce awards relating to insolvency due, in part, to disparate legal traditions, such as civil and common law legal systems, and divergence among courts over literal versus contextual methods of interpreting such clauses. It will also demonstrate how domestic courts diverge in their construction of the binding force of arbitration awards due to disparate interpretations of international laws, rules and conventions, such as the Model Law and NY Convention. Among those disparities are interpretative differences among courts in the same jurisdiction.

A domestic court, in determining whether to recognise and enforce an ICA, will often need to decide, not only which country's law governs, but also how insolvency proceedings will be regulated by that law. It will also need to decide on whether the arbitral tribunal erred in its construction of that law. Such determinations will entail the judicial assessment of competing constructions of law in applying arbitration clauses in contracts to ensuing insolvency disputes. In *Syska (Elektrim SA) v. Vivendi Universal SA and Ors*,[32] the English Court of Appeal highlighted the technical issues that arise from the interrelationship between cross-border insolvency proceedings and ICA. The case resulted in an appeal to the High Court from the judgement of Christopher Clarke J. sitting in the Commercial Court.[33] It raised questions about the legal consequences arising from an arbitration proceeding in one EU Member State in which a party to the reference became insolvent in another EU Member State. In issue was the effect on ICA of the law of the Member State in which insolvency proceedings had been instituted, compared to the effect on ICA of the law of the Member State at which the reference was taking place.[34] The Court concluded that it was incorrect to characterise the dispute as a conflict between the provisions of Article 4 and Article 15 of Council

32 [2009] EWCA Civ 677, http://www.bailii.org/ew/cases/EWCA/Civ/2009/677.html.
33 [2008] EWHC 2155 (Comm) now reported at [2008] 2 Lloyd's Rep 636.
34 Ibid., 1.

Regulation (EC) No 1346/2000 on Insolvency Proceedings. Article 4 of the Regulation provided that the applicable law to insolvency proceedings and their effects shall be that of the Member State within the territory of which such proceedings are opened. On the other hand, Article 15 provided that the effects of insolvency proceedings on a pending lawsuit concerning an asset or a right of which the debtor has been divested shall be governed solely by the law of the Member State in which that lawsuit is pending.[35] The case demonstrated how the EU focused on the place where arbitral proceedings commenced, which will determine the law that is to be applied to the dispute. It also reinforced how the EU has generally left it to Member States to govern cross-border insolvency matters within the Union.

The material facts of the case in *Elektrim SA* were as follows. In 2001, a Polish mobile telephone company, Elektrim, entered into an agreement with two Vivendi companies (Vivendi) pursuant to which Vivendi was to acquire an interest in Elektrim's PTC holdings. The agreement contained a dispute resolution clause providing for arbitration in London under the Rules of the London Court of International Arbitration (LCIA Rules).[36] The parties agreed that, while the agreement itself was governed by Polish law, the arbitration clause was subject to English law.[37] In 2003, Vivendi commenced arbitration against Elektrim, claiming EUR1.9 billion for breach of the obligation under the Third Investment Agreement (TIA) by interfering with or failing to secure the interest that Vivendi was supposed to obtain in PTC. In August 2007, two months prior to the liability hearing in the arbitration, Elektrim was declared bankrupt by the Warsaw District Court.[38] At the arbitral hearing in London on 15 October 2007, the Tribunal heard arguments from both parties as to whether the arbitration agreement had been annulled. In an Interim Partial Award, the Tribunal, by majority, rejected Elektrim's challenge to jurisdiction and found for Vivendi. On 20 March 2008, a Partial Interim Award was issued. The Tribunal ruled the Elektrim breached the TIA. In February 2009, the Final Award was issued by the Tribunal.

The award was subject to judicial review in the UK. In issue at the trial in 2008 was whether the legal consequences were to be determined by the law of the Member State where the insolvency has been declared, here Poland, or the law in the Member State where the arbitration was conducted in the UK. Clarke J. found that there was a conflict between the general provisions of Article 4 of the EC Regulation on Insolvency Proceedings providing for the choice of law, and the particular provision of Article 15 providing that an asset or right of which the debtor has been divested shall be governed solely by the law of the Member State in which that lawsuit is pending.[39] Clarke J. ruled that 'the latter provision [Article 15]

35 Ibid., Council Regulation (EC) No 1346/2000 of 29 May 2000 on insolvency proceedings OJ L 160, 30 June 2000, 1–18.
36 Ibid., London Court of International Arbitration 1998, 2014, 2020.
37 Ibid., 4–10.
38 Ibid.
39 *Syska v. Vivendi Universal SA & Ors* [2009] 1 ALL ER (Comm) 244, Christopher Clarke J. sitting in the Commercial Court [2008] EWHC 2155 (Comm) now reported [2008] 2 Lloyd's Rep 636.

prevailed and that English law should determine the effect of the insolvency on the arbitration. There was no provision under English law annulling the arbitration agreement and the award stood'.[40]

The Court of Appeal dismissed the appeal. It maintained that Regulation No. 1346/2000 sought to coordinate the operation of cross-border insolvency proceedings within the EC, not only by restricting the opening of secondary insolvency proceedings, but also by regulating which system of law should govern the main insolvency proceedings. In construing Article 15 in conjunction with Article 4, it held that Article 4(1) established the general rule that the law applicable to insolvency proceedings and their effect shall be that "of the Member State in which such proceedings are first opened. Specific examples are contained in Article 4(2) of aspects of such insolvency proceedings which fall within this general rule".[41]

The Court of Appeal focused its reasoning on the particular provisions of Article 15 in light of the general choice of law provisions in Article 4, stating:

> It is accepted for the purposes of this appeal that an existing arbitration is a pending lawsuit within the meaning of Article 15 and Article 4(2)(f). In most cases this is likely to be decisive of the issue as to which system of law should govern the arbitration proceedings because the law of the State of the opening of the proceedings (*lex concursus*) will itself be purely procedural. This led to the argument that it moves the case from the choice of law rule specified in Article 15 into the territory covered by the general rule under Article 4(1). Support for this is said to be found in Article 4(2)(e) which confirms that the general rule applies to 'current contracts' to which the debtor is party.[42]

40 Ibid.

41 Ibid., 27–28. Article 4 of the Regulation provides:

> Save as otherwise provided in this Regulation, the law applicable to insolvency proceedings and their effects shall be that of the Member State within the territory of which such proceedings are opened, hereafter referred to as the 'State of the opening of proceedings'. The law of the State of the opening of proceedings shall determine the conditions for the opening of those proceedings, their conduct and their closure.

Article 4.2 then gives a non-exclusive list of examples of matters which the law of the state of the opening of proceedings is to determine. Two of those examples are: (e) the effects of insolvency proceedings on current contracts to which the debtor is party; (f) the effects of insolvency proceedings on proceedings brought by individual creditors, with the exception of lawsuits pending. Articles 5 to 15 of the Regulation then identify the cases which come within the words save as otherwise provided at the beginning of Article 4.1.

42 Ibid., 30–31. An example of this would be a provision of domestic insolvency law similar to s.130(2) or Schedule B1, paragraph 43 of the Insolvency Act 1986, both of which impose an automatic stay on the continuation of legal proceedings except with the permission of the court. Assuming that the relevant provision of the *lex concursus* does apply to arbitration proceedings, there will be nothing in a law of that kind which would take the case outside Article 4(2)(f). In the case of pending proceedings, Article 15 would therefore apply.

The result was that, even though the law of the State where proceedings were opened is 'purely procedural', it is nevertheless a forum of convenience in coordinating multi-jurisdictional insolvency proceedings. An obstacle in determining the law governing the validity of an insolvency claim arises over whether insolvency proceedings commencing before insolvency should be stayed once arbitration is subsequently initiated. In addressing this obstacle, the Court needed to determine the status of the claim itself. As highlighted by Longmore J., 'if litigation or arbitration has begun before insolvency occurs the natural expectation of businesses would be that it should be that law that should determine whether the proceedings should continue or come to a shuddering halt'.[43] Longmore J. went further by maintaining that a 'lawsuit (including a reference to arbitration) becomes necessary when there is a need to determine the existence or validity of a particular claim which (if valid) will then be permitted to participate in the insolvency proceedings'.[44] Until the validity of that particular claim is ascertained, it has no status in, nor relevance to, the pre-existing insolvency proceedings. Longmore J. concluded, it was clear that the majority of the arbitrators came to the correct conclusion and the trial judge was also correct to decline to set aside the award. He determined that the appeal should be dismissed, in which the remaining Justices, Patten and Mummery concurred.[45]

This case highlights some important considerations relating to the relationship between arbitration and insolvency proceedings. It informs practitioners and legal scholars of the importance of clearly determining the relationship between arbitration and insolvency in their contracts and dispute resolution clauses. If the contract is unclear on the applicable law, the arbitral tribunal appointed by contract needs to consider domestic insolvency laws including the law in the third country in which the insolvency arose. The case further highlights the complexity of applying foreign law rules, even between Member States of the EU. Therefore, arbitration tribunals will need to consider how foreign law rules affect the insolvent party, particularly following the destabilising 2020 pandemic.

Significantly, in its interpretation of Regulation No. 1346/2000, the *Syska* decision underpins the EU's movement towards a functional regulatory pathway towards resolving cross-border insolvency disputes through international commercial arbitration. However, this case does not bely perfect symmetry in resolving insolvency disputes internationally. Illustratively, the Regulation does not encompass all prospective areas of commercial insolvency. It excludes insurance undertakings, credit institutions, investment undertakings holding funds or securities for third parties and collective investment undertakings from its scope. Such exclusions are likely to be replicated in other jurisdictions, based on their localised economic, political and legal policies. The likely result is that attempts to reconcile a cross-border arbitration proceeding with insolvency proceedings conducted in different

43 Ibid., 16.
44 Ibid.
45 Ibid., 25.

jurisdictions, will be encumbered by the exclusion of different industries, among other exclusions, in those jurisdictions.

The Court in *Syska* adopted an interpretation of the EU Regulation which provides clarity over the jurisdictional scope of insolvency proceedings beyond stipulating for the law at the place of the main insolvency proceedings. Still, the Court's conclusion is mechanical, by concluding that both main and secondary insolvency proceedings are determined by the law of the Member State at which insolvency proceedings first commenced. However, that mechanical construction is well advised in providing interpretative clarity that facilitates the resolution of transnational insolvency disputes across EU Member States in that case. The Court's reasoning also reflects the theme underlying this book, in valuing consistency amongst arbitrators resolving cross-border insolvency disputes under English law. Insofar as the regulation of transborder insolvency proceedings in member states vary from the EU regulatory structure, it is uncertain whether Member State courts will adopt comparable constructions to the Court in *Syska*.

An illustration of an attempt to reconcile arbitration and insolvency proceedings, including in the construction of an arbitration clause in the applicable contract, is evident in the decision of the US Bankruptcy Court in *Re Servicos de Petroleo Constellation SA*[46] There the Court ruled that 'foreign debtors, members of an integrated enterprise group, satisfied debtor eligibility requirements under the Bankruptcy Code, and at the location of the parent holding company's center of main interests (COMI), namely, Luxembourg'.[47] Regarding arbitration, the Court pointed out that:

> at the Recognition Hearing, the Court also questioned Alperton's (Alperton Capital Ltd being contingent creditor of one of the ten Chapter 15 Debtors (Constellation Overseas)) standing to object to recognition of Chapter 15 of the Bankruptcy Code,[48] Debtors other than Constellation Overseas, an entity with which it is a contingent creditor based on a pending arbitration claim.[49]

46 In *Re Servicos de Petroleo Constellation SA* United States Bankruptcy Court, S.D. New York, 9 May 2019, 600 B.R. 237, Case No. 18–13952 (MG) 2019.

47 Ibid., although ultimate parent holding company's COMI was Luxembourg, the debtor-parent had sufficient ties with Brazil for recognition of the Brazilian reorganisation as a foreign nonmain proceeding; the location of the holding company's COMI was Brazil; and the location of the COMI for certain members of the integrated enterprise group was Brazil.

48 Note, Chapter 15 is a new chapter added to the Bankruptcy Code by the Bankruptcy Abuse Prevention and Consumer Protection Act of 2005. It is the US domestic adoption of the Model Law on Cross-Border Insolvency promulgated by the United Nations Commission on International Trade Law ('UNCITRAL') in 1997, and it replaces Section 304 of the Bankruptcy Code. Because the UNCITRAL is the source of Chapter 15, the US interpretation must be coordinated with the interpretation given by other countries that have adopted it as internal law to promote a uniform and coordinated legal regime for the resolution of cross-border insolvency cases. See United States Court, https://www.uscourts.gov/services-forms/bankruptcy/bankruptcy-basics/chapter-15-bankruptcy-basics.

49 Ibid., 245–246.

On the issue of arbitration between the parties, the Court specifically addressed the shareholder agreements that included specific arbitration clauses. The clauses provided that the shareholders agree to binding arbitration in New York under the Rules of the International Chamber of Commerce.[50] In April 2019, the arbitration tribunal issued an Interim Award that: "prevented Constellation Overseas from taking actions that would effectively destroy Alperton's potential interest in the Disputed Companies prior to the ultimate resolution of the arbitration".[51]

On 6 December 2018, each of the Chapter 15 Debtors initiated bankruptcy proceedings in Brazil by filing a judicial recovery (JR) (*recuperação judicial*) Petition with the Brazilian Court. The JR Petition requested that the Brazilian Court substantially consolidate the judicial reorganisation of the entire group. The request was made with the support of creditors. The Court further highlighted that foreign debtors seeking relief under Chapter 15 must satisfy the debtor eligibility requirements set forth in Section 109(a) of the Bankruptcy Code. Section 109(a) provided that 'only a person that resides or has a domicile, a place of business or property in the United States, or a municipality, may be a debtor under the Bankruptcy Code'. Courts in this Circuit held that Section 109(a) could be satisfied through bank accounts in the US, including by an undrawn retainer.[52] More importantly, the Court elaborated that it had 'previously held that a debtor's contract rights, including rights pursuant to debt that contains a New York governing law and forum selection clause, constitute intangible property of the debtor in New York for purposes of Section 109(a)'.[53] Therefore, it concluded that the presence of the New York choice of law and forum selection clauses satisfied the requirements of Section 109(a). As such, the Court held that all of the principal documents setting forth Parent/Constellation's prepetition debt obligations were governed by New York law and generally contemplated New York as the venue for disputes.

Subsequently, Alperton filed a motion seeking an order granting Alperton leave to seek relief from the US District Court for the Southern District of New York to confirm and enforce the Interim Award. The Court determined that the Interim Award was designed only to provide interim relief prior to the Final Award. At the time of writing this book, no final arbitration award had been handed down, which had precluded the Court from examining it. The Court at that time had decided only on the recognition of

50 Ibid., 251.
51 Ibid.
52 Ibid., 269.
53 Ibid., 269.

foreign main and non-main proceedings.[54] However, it reached no decision on COMI, but decided that this issue could be revisited when the parties provided new evidence of changed circumstances of any of the Chapter 15 debtors.

What is notable at this time is that the Court decided that the dispute was governed by New York law and generally contemplated New York as the venue for disputes. That determination was based on the US Bankruptcy Code, not unlike the English Court in *Syska* basing its decision on EU Regulation No. 1346/2000. What is seemingly unavoidable is that domestic courts will base their decisions on an interpretation of domestic laws and regulations. Even through courts are bound by their states' adoption of international laws such as the Model Law and conventions such as the NY Convention, their courts are likely to base the scope of choices of law and forum on internally generated statute and case law.

7.3.2 Managing Debt and Arbitration

Courts are also challenged in managing debt either prior to, during or following an arbitration award. This is especially so where an entity has declined to fulfil its debt obligations under an arbitration award and the matter is subsequently raised in judicial proceedings. Such a scenario occurred in 2017, in the case of *Taurus Petroleum Ltd v. State Oil Marketing Company of the Ministry of Oil, Republic of Iraq (SOMO)*,[55] where the UK Supreme Court adopted a distinctive approach in reconciling the ongoing management of debt and arbitration. The appeal related to a contract between the Complainant, Taurus Petroleum Ltd, a Swiss domiciled oil trading company, and the Respondent, State Oil Marketing Company of Iraq ('SOMO'), for the sale of crude oil and liquified petroleum gas (LPG).

At issue in this case were disputes that arose between the parties that were referred to UNCITRAL arbitration as provided for in a series of crude oil contracts. Although the seat of the arbitration was Baghdad, by agreement all hearings took place in London before Mr. Ian Hunter QC as sole arbitrator. It was nevertheless agreed that the seat would remain in Baghdad. A Partial Final Award was issued on 23 October 2012 and the Final Award was rendered on 13 February 2013, whereby SOMO was ordered to pay Taurus US$8,716,477.[56]

54 Ibid., 243, Chapter 15 Debtors in either a foreign main proceeding or in a foreign non-main proceeding, pursuant to Chapter 15 of title 11 of the United States Code.

55 *Taurus Petroleum Ltd v. State Oil Marketing Company of the Ministry of Oil, Republic of Iraq (SOMO)* [2017] UKSC 64, https://www.supremecourt.uk/cases/docs/uksc-2015-0199-judgment.pdf.

56 Ibid., 1–4.

SOMO declined to honour the award and paid nothing to satisfy it, except that the debt had been reduced by the set off of orders for costs made in favour of SOMO by the Court of First Instance and in the Court of Appeal. SOMO applied to have the Partial Final Award set aside. The Supreme Court dismissed the application on the ground that the application was premature because the Partial Final Award did not deal with all the issues between the parties. The application was also dismissed because neither SOMO nor Taurus had asked the Iraqi court to ratify the award.[57]

Thereafter, neither SOMO nor Taurus took steps to have either award ratified in Iraq; and SOMO had made no further challenge to either award. However, the Court stressed that Taurus was seeking to enforce the award in England and not in Iraq where the proceedings had been held. At issue was whether Taurus was entitled to enforce the award or the judgement of the Iraq court by combining third-party debt orders and/or receivership orders to recover moneys owed to Taurus.[58] In a three to two majority decision, the appeal was allowed. For the claim to be successful, the Court concluded that it was necessary to determine that the debt was incurred within the jurisdiction.[59] The Supreme Court then considered whether there was a 'debt due or accruing due to the judgment debtor [SOMO] from the third party [Credit Agricole]' for the purposes of CPR Part 72, which regulated Third Party Debt Orders. In responding, the Court noted that this issue

> depends on the construction of a most unusual form of letter of credit. For all its unusual features, however, the instrument must be construed as a whole, and as far as possible in such a way as to make each part of it consistent with every other part.[60]

A letter of credit was issued by a bank as a form of guarantee by which the buyer agreed to purchase particular goods from the seller at an agreed price. Further, the letters of credit were intended to provide a degree of certainty and security. However, the debt orders posed obstacles. Lord Mance noted in dissent:

> As to the principles governing third party debt orders, the majority judgments raise a more general concern. They fail in my view to give proper effect to the governing principles, they risk creating confusion and, on the facts of this case, they prejudice, without justification, the deliberately agreed rights of a fourth party (CBI).[61]

57 Ibid.
58 Ibid.
59 Ibid., Lord Clarke (paras. 19 to 26), Lord Sumption (paras. 61 to 65) and Lord Hodge (paras. 74 to 78).
60 Ibid., 61.
61 Ibid., 85.

While not specifically related to the arbitration, the Supreme Court stressed that the other options that were available in resolving the dispute, had not been followed. It stated:

> Firstly, it determined that the issuance of a receivership order would be an appropriate step because English law would apply. Secondly, it opined that both domestic and international policies favoured the efficient recognition and enforcement of arbitration awards. Thirdly, the Court noted that it would be inconsistent to treat the arbitration award as a judgment of the English courts for enforcement purposes, whilst limiting the available enforcement methods for having an insufficient connection to this jurisdiction [English jurisdiction].[62]

The Supreme Court concluded, by a majority of three to two, that the Appeal should proceed insofar as it challenged the refusal of the Court of Appeal to make a receivership order. In hearing the Appeal,[63] the Court agreed that maintaining successful international commerce depended on the enforcement of contracts, the arbitration awards and judgements.[64] It noted further that the 1958 NY Convention and the UNCITRAL Model Law and Rules, and the domestic legal framework together, ensured the efficient recognition and enforcement of arbitration awards. The Supreme Court ultimately upheld and reinforced a uniform approach towards both international arbitration and cross-border insolvency. It further highlighted the subtle but important issues that arise from cross-border insolvency, where arbitration proceedings and awards may intervene, such as, when managing party obligations to repay debts.

The benefit of courts seeking to establish greater uniformity in the enforcement of arbitration awards is to establish both more coherence and cohesiveness in the application of international institutions such as the NY Convention and Model Law and domestic laws to resolving trans-border insolvency disputes. These benefits are accentuated by the increasing justification, in unstable economic times to incorporate both arbitration and insolvency clauses in cross-border finance agreements, specifically in anticipation of disputes over rising corporate debt. As is commonly argued within the scientific community in responding to the outbreak of disease, prevention is better achieved through an effective advance plan rather than having no plan at all. In applying this analogy to cross-border insolvency, legal practitioners need to carefully prepare and draft both insolvency and arbitration clauses in order to resolve subsequent disputes relating to debt, or failing that, to provide greater clarity to a determining arbitral tribunal or court.

62 Ibid., 54–55.
63 Ibid., On appeal from: [2015] EWCA Civ 835.
64 Ibid., 54.

7.3.3 Entering into Insolvency Following Conclusion of Arbitration – but Before Award is Issued

A further judicial challenge in reconciling cross-border insolvency and arbitration laws arises when insolvency proceedings commence before the conclusion of an arbitration. In other words, how will courts deal with parties who enter into insolvency proceedings after the conclusion of an arbitration, but before the issuance of the award? In the US, there have been ongoing disputes over the legal relationship between arbitration and insolvency proceedings. Chapter 15 of the US Bankruptcy Code facilitates the cross-border administration of insolvency proceedings. Pertinently, it allows foreign representatives in corporate bankruptcy proceedings in the US to seek the cooperation of American courts to access an insolvent business's assets. However, Chapter 11 bankruptcy proceedings in the US are designed to require a stay of other pending judicial and arbitration proceedings, to allow the bankruptcy court to fully administer and oversee all of a Chapter 11 debtor's debts and assets.[65]

In *Re JSC BTA Bank*,[66] the US District Court made an order under Chapter 15 of the American Bankruptcy Code, granting a Petition to the foreign representative of JSC BTA Bank who was Chairman of the Management Board of BTA. The Petition sought recognition of the Bank's proceedings pending before a Specialized Financial Court in Kazakhstan. At issue was the alleged violation of a stay order granted by the Kazakhstan Court resulting from the arbitration of the dispute between BIC-BRED and BTA Bank.[67] The US District Court case highlights how complex issues arise in relation to the administration of all the debtor's assets. In this case, BIC-BRED commenced arbitration proceeding against BTA Bank in Switzerland on 29 October 2009. BIC-BRED sought a determination that BTA Bank had breached a loan agreement and was liable for the amount of the loan, including damages and interest.[68] On 19 July 2010, the arbitrator issued an award that included the Recognition Order and its impact on the Arbitration Proceedings.[69] The US District Court maintained that:

> After careful review of Section 1520(a)(1) [of the Bankruptcy Code] in context, continued prosecution by BIC-BRED of the Arbitration Proceeding in Switzerland did not violate the automatic stay. The Arbitration Proceeding relates to an entirely distinct foreign financing transaction that has no direct or indirect impact upon property within the territorial jurisdiction of the United States. The bankruptcy court, at least in the setting of an ancillary

65 Ibid., 11 U.S.C. §362(a).

66 In *Re JSC BTA Bank*, 434 B.R. 334, 336 (S.D.N.Y. Bankr. 2010).

67 Ibid., 336.

68 Ibid.

69 Ibid. On 2 March 2010, the Court entered an order in this Chapter 15 case (the '*Recognition Order*') granting the Petition for recognition of the foreign main proceeding of JSC BTA Bank ('*BTA Bank*') currently pending in the Specialized Financial Court of Almaty City, Republic of Kazakhstan (the '*Kazakh Court*').

> Chapter 15 case, should not stand in the way of a foreign arbitration process when the outcome will have no foreseeable impact on any property of the foreign debtor in the United States.[70]

The Court dealt with the protection of the assets of a foreign debtor under Chapter 15 and addressed claims brought by and against the debtor that could be brought before it.[71] Importantly, the Court rejected the argument made by the foreign representative for the extra-territorial application of the automatic stay of proceedings against the debtor in a foreign arbitration, based on the language and context of Section 1520(a)(1) and the ancillary nature of a Chapter 15 case. However, the Court exempted situations in which the foreign financial transaction 'has no direct or indirect impact upon property within the territorial jurisdiction of the United States'.[72] The Court limited the jurisdiction of a bankruptcy court under Chapter 15, explaining that:

> [t]he bankruptcy court, at least in the setting of an ancillary Chapter 15 case, should not stand in the way of a foreign arbitration process when the outcome will have no foreseeable impact on any property of the foreign debtor in the United States.[73]

Noteworthy too, the Court recognised the obligation of domestic courts to adopt an international approach to cross-border insolvency in accordance with Chapter 15. It stated that the 'international origins of Chapter 15 are the dominant and consistent theme that underlies the various specific provisions of this Chapter and that distinguishes Chapter 15 from all other chapters within the Bankruptcy Code'.[74] The Court identified this as the 'one' Chapter of the Bankruptcy Code that is predicated on international coordination and cooperation. It encourages bankruptcy courts to rely on law beyond the US for interpretative guidance. That is, 'Chapter 15 invokes the jurisdiction of the bankruptcy court to assist in the administration of a foreign insolvency or restructuring proceeding'.[75] The Court concluded that Chapter 15 deals with the protection of assets of a foreign debtor in the US in relation to claims brought by and against the debtor. However, based on its reliance on the language of Section 1520(a)(i) and the ancillary nature of the Chapter 15 case, it rejected the foreign representative's application for a stay based on extra-territorial proceedings. Yet, this exception was in a specific context, namely, when there is a demonstrated relationship between those proceedings and the debtor's property in the US.[76]

70 Ibid., 340.
71 Ibid., 348.
72 Ibid., 340.
73 Ibid.
74 Ibid.
75 Ibid.
76 Ibid., 348.

The Court further concluded that the automatic stay that came into effect upon entry of the Recognition Order did not apply to the Arbitration Proceedings. On this basis, the BIC-BRED did not violate the stay order in Switzerland. The Court denied the motion and maintained that a further order was required by BIC-BRED.

The case highlights that Chapter 15 allows the US to determine the nature and scope of a foreign insolvency proceeding when the debtor and assets are located in the state. It also demonstrates limitations inhering in purporting to apply Chapter 15 internationally. Still, the Court did note that consideration of the UNCITRAL Model Law is important in the US. It also stressed that, when a debtor's assets are threatened by creditor collection efforts, the debtor can seek injunctive relief from the courts of the host state. However, such a process of internationalisation sought by the Court is not straightforward, particularly in countries that have not adopted the Model Law.

7.3.4 Assets Located in Separate Jurisdictions

A further challenge for cross-border insolvency proceedings occurs where the assets of a debtor company are located in two different jurisdictions. Allan Gropper argues that, 'when assets are located in two different jurisdictions, those assets are then subject to two different insolvency laws: this, in turn, increases the likelihood that they will be subject to competing insolvency administrators'.[77] Where this occurs, it is very difficult to identify comprehensively the choice of law or jurisdiction, presupposing the absence of clear agreement between the parties on how to resolve the matter, by arbitration or otherwise.[78] Gropper's response, with which we agree, is that, where parties seek to resolve disputes in which assets are located in multiple jurisdictions, their agreement to arbitrate should be prepared with care and skill. It should make clear choice of law and jurisdiction to avoid both uncertainty and conflict at a later time of financial stress for the debtor.

7.3.5 Arbitrability – Australia and Singapore

Arguably, while judicial power is the essential prerogative of states, the parties may expressly accord jurisdiction to arbitrators to settle their disputes.[79] However, the state retains the power to prohibit the settlement of certain categories of disputes outside the jurisdiction of its courts.[80] Thus, the question arises whether there are

77 Allan L. Gropper, The Arbitration of Cross-Border Insolvencies, *American Bankruptcy Law Journal* 18 (2012), 223.

78 Ibid.

79 Bernard Hanotiau, What Law Governs the Issue of Arbitrability? *Arbitration International* 12 4 (1996), 391–404, https://doi.org/10.1093/arbitration/12.4.391.

80 Ibid.

areas of cross-border insolvency law that cannot be arbitrated, or in effect, are not arbitrable.

Centrally an objective determination of arbitrability, concerns the types of issues that cannot be submitted to arbitration. This extends to specific classes of disputes that are exempt from arbitration proceedings and belong exclusively within the domain of national courts.[81] Lawrence Shore emphasises that:

> internationally, arbitrability refers to whether specific classes of disputes are barred from arbitration either because of public policy or because they are outside the scope of the arbitration agreement. . . . [A]rbitrability refers to whether the specific claims raised are of [a] subject matter capable of settlement by arbitration, and are not subject to the exclusive jurisdiction of . . . courts.[82]

Articles II (1) of the New York Convention,[83] as well as Articles 34(2)(b)(i) and 36(1)(b)(i) of the Model Law on International Commercial Arbitration 1985 with amendments in 2006[84] have substantive functions in the recognition and enforcement of arbitration agreements and awards. However, neither the Model Law nor the NY Convention have left the categories of disputes that are arbitrable to national legislatures and court systems to determine.[85] Robert Kovacs elaborates that national laws often directly address specific subject matter, such as insolvency, competition/anti-trust regulation and intellectual property law, in determining which disputes are not arbitrable. He maintains that, under the NY Convention:

> Article II (1) provides that 'each Contracting State shall recognize an agreement in writing under which the parties undertake to submit to arbitration all or any differences which have arisen or which may arise between them in respect of a defined legal relationship, whether contractual or not, concerning a subject matter that is capable of resolution though arbitration'. (2) The term 'agreement in writing' shall include an arbitral clause in a contract or an arbitration agreement, signed by the parties or contained in an exchange of letters or telegrams. (3) The court of a Contracting State, when seized of an action

81 Robert Kovacs, A Transnational Approach to the Arbitrability of Insolvency Proceedings in International Arbitration, *Journal Bankruptcy Law & Practice* 5, Art. 21, 3 (2012), 32–36.

82 Lawrence Shore, The United States' Perspective on 'Arbitrability', in L. A. Mistelis, S. L. Brekoulakis, *Arbitrability: International & Comparative Perspectives*, Kluwer Law International, 2009; in Robert Kovacs, *A Transnational Approach to the Arbitrability of Insolvency Proceedings in International Arbitration, Journal Bankruptcy Law & Practice* 5, Art. 21, 3 (2012), 32–36.

83 Convention on the Recognition and Enforcement of Foreign Arbitral Awards, New York 1958.

84 Resolution adopted by the General Assembly, 40/72. Model Law on International Commercial Arbitration of the United Nations Commission on International Trade Law, 11 December 1985, 1994, https://uncitral.un.org/sites/uncitral.un.org/files/media-documents/uncitral/en/19-09955_e_ebook.pdf.

85 Robert Kovacs, A Transnational Approach to the Arbitrability of Insolvency Proceedings in International Arbitration, *Journal Bankruptcy Law & Practice* 5, Art. 21, 3 (2012), 35–36.

> in a matter in respect of which the parties have made an agreement within the meaning of this Article, shall, at the request of one of the parties, refer the parties to arbitration, unless it finds that the said agreement is null and void, inoperative or incapable of being performed. Article II does not contain a rule as to what law governs the question of arbitrability at the pre-award stage which has given rise to a number of divergent views in national court practices.[86]

In further elaborating on the nature and scope of arbitrability, the Federal Court of Australia held in the case of *WDR Delaware Corporation v. Hydrox Holdings Pty Ltd* that:[87]

> [T]he issue of arbitrability goes beyond the scope of an arbitration agreement. It involved consideration of the inherent power of a national legal system to determine what issues are capable of being resolved through arbitration. The issue of arbitrability therefore goes beyond the will or the agreement of the parties.[88]

More recently, in *Reinhart v. Hancock Prospecting*,[89] the High Court of Australia emphasised how 'commercial arbitration is ordinarily based upon the agreement of the parties to a form of alternative dispute resolution'.[90] It added that an arbitration clause, 'in which parties consent to the resolution of their disputes by arbitration, will often be part of a package of rights and duties upon which they have agreed'.[91] As a general rule, therefore, the High Court highlighted that 'third parties who do not incur the burdens of other provisions in the contract, should not be entitled to take the benefit of the arbitration clause'.[92]

However, not all issues giving rise to disputes under Australian commercial law fall within the confines of arbitration. Arbitration will not apply to insolvency when the arbitration conflicts with the regulatory framework. For instance, Section 11 of *Carriage of Goods by Sea Act 1991* (Cth)[93] declares an arbitration agreement void in relation to a bill of lading, unless the place of arbitration is in Australia. Further exemptions to arbitration in Australia arise under tax, intellectual property and some insurance contracts.[94] Cross-border tax disputes are also subject to special arrangements provided for in tax treaties. Disputes over the application of either Part IVA of the *Income Tax Assessment Act 1936* (ITAA 1936) or Section 67 of the *Fringe Benefits*

86 Ibid., 34.
87 [2016] 245 FCR 452, 124.
88 Ibid.
89 [2019] HCA 13, 87.
90 Ibid., 87.
91 Ibid., 87–88.
92 Ibid.
93 Carriage of Goods by Sea Act 1991 No. 160, 1991, Section 11.
94 Insurance Contracts Act 1984 (Cth), Section 43.

Tax Assessment Act 1986 (FBTAA), in turn, are excluded from being regulated by arbitration.[95] What unifies most national laws is that a commercial dispute involving third parties, typified by a cross-border insolvency dispute, will not be arbitrable if it conflicts with the law that applies to the dispute. If the regulatory authority, usually a domestic court, decides that there is no such conflict, or that the conflict has been resolved, then arbitrability will no longer be in issue. The insolvency in dispute will be arbitrable.

In applying the rules of the Australian International Arbitration Act 1974 (IAA), the New South Wales Supreme Court in the case of *Infinite Plus Pty Ltd*[96] ordered that, in accordance with Section 7(2) of the IAA, any claim between the first plaintiff and first defendant would be stayed until further ordered.[97] The Court also ordered a stay pending the outcome of the arbitration.[98] These orders exemplify the discretion accorded to an Australian tribunal to rule on its own jurisdiction. This jurisdiction is comparable to Article 16 of the UNCITRAL Model Law on International Commercial Arbitration which provides for the competence of an arbitral tribunal to rule on its jurisdiction without denying the power of a court to reassess that competence in enforcement proceedings.[99] As a result, under Australian law, arbitration awards are not absolute. Australian courts are afforded some discretion in resolving conflicts over the arbitrability of insolvency disputes in different national legal systems. However, Australia's multi-layered approach in reconciling insolvency proceedings and arbitration, is far from clear. In particular, following a party entering liquidation, an Australian court needs to determine the effect of the *Corporations Act 2001* on liquidation proceedings.[100] According to an interpretation of Section 471B of the Corporations Act, an arbitration would be stayed pending a judicial determination on liquidation, empowering the court to then decide whether to enforce the arbitration award. Subsequently, the arbitrability

95 Australian Tax Office, https://www.ato.gov.au/Business/International-tax-for-business/In-detail/Mutual-agreement-procedure/?page=7.

96 [2017] NSWSC 470.

97 The Court excepted from this stay the first plaintiff's claim for relief that the second plaintiff purchase the first defendant's shares in the company.

98 Ibid., 81.

99 UNCITRAL Model Law on International Commercial Arbitration adopted by the United Nations Commission on International Trade Law on 21 June 1985 and amended by the United Nations Commission on International Trade Law on 7 July 2006. Article 16, 'Competence of Arbitral Tribunal to Rule on Its Jurisdiction'. It provides that:
'The arbitral tribunal may rule on its own jurisdiction, including any objections with respect to the existence or validity of the arbitration agreement. For that purpose, an arbitration clause which forms part of a contract shall be treated as an agreement independent of the other terms of the contract. A decision by the arbitral tribunal that the contract is null and void shall not entail ipso jure the invalidity of the arbitration clause.'

100 Corporations Act, Section 471B, provides for a stay of proceeding and suspension of the enforcement process.

of the dispute over liquidation would remain stayed if and until the Australian court lifts that stay. As a result, uncertainty over the scope of arbitrability in relation to cross-border insolvency remains material in Australia.

The tension between arbitration and insolvency also arose under Singapore law. In the case of *Larsen Oil and Gas Pte Ltd v. Petroprod Ltd*,[101] the Singapore Supreme Court reasoned that 'arbitration and insolvency processes embody, to an extent, contrasting legal policies'.[102] On the one hand, arbitration embodies the principles of 'party autonomy and the decentralisation of private dispute resolution'.[103] On the other hand, the 'insolvency process is a collective statutory proceeding that involves the public centralisation of disputes so as to achieve economic efficiency and optimal returns for creditors'.[104] Notably, insolvency proceedings under Singapore law do not, *per se*, affect the validity of arbitration agreements entered into prior to the commencement of insolvency proceedings. In personal bankruptcies, Section 148A of the Singapore Bankruptcy Act[105] gives the Official Assignee the option to either disclaim or adopt a contract containing an arbitration agreement. There is no statutory equivalent to Section 148A of the Bankruptcy Act in corporate insolvencies.

Notwithstanding its interpretation of the provisions above, the Supreme Court of Singapore, in *Larsen*,[106] regarded arbitrability as central in its distinction between private remedy claims and avoidance claims made by a liquidator or judicial manager. The Court maintained that:

> it makes sense to draw a line between private remedial claims (either common law or statutory), about which the company's pre-insolvency management have good reason to be concerned; and claims that can only be made by a liquidator/judicial manager of an insolvent company, to which they are completely indifferent.[107]

The Supreme Court added: 'We therefore hold that arbitration clauses should not ordinarily be construed to cover avoidance claims in the absence of express language to the contrary and that the Arbitration Clause did not cover Petroprods claims against Larsen'.[108] Arguably, the Supreme Court was making the point that private claims assist in construing the scope of an arbitration clause, and are

101 [2011] 3 SLR414, 1. In Andrew Chan, Jonathan Chan, Jo Tay, Alexander Lawrence Yeo, Cross-Border Insolvency and Its Impact on Arbitration, *Singapore Academy Law Journal* 26 (2014), 999.
102 Ibid., 1.
103 Ibid.
104 Ibid.
105 Bankruptcy Act Cap 20, 2009 Rev Ed.
106 [2011] 3 SLR414, 1. In Andrew Chan, Jonathan Chan, Jo Tay, Alexander Lawrence Yeo, Cross-Border Insolvency and Its Impact on Arbitration, *Singapore Academy Law Journal* 26 (2014), 999.
107 [2011] 3 SLR 414.
108 [2011] 3 SLR414, 21.

therefore arbitrable, whereas avoidance claims fall within the domain of liquidators and company directors. The Court elaborated that the:

> question of the arbitrability of insolvency-related claims has never been raised in the local [Singapore] courts, and would certainly be of great importance to arbitration and insolvency practitioners, we consider it appropriate for us to explicate our views on what would be the proper judicial approach towards an arbitration agreement that expressly includes insolvency-related claims such as avoidance claims.[109]

In applying its views, the Court ruled that 'Petroprod's claims against Larsen do not fall within the scope of the Arbitration Clause. Even if they do, these claims are non-arbitrable because they are in essence insolvency claims'.[110]

Singapore's International Arbitration Act 1994 provides specific circumstances in which the High Court of Singapore can set aside an award.[111] These include circumstances in which the award was subject to inducement or deception, affected by fraud or corruption, or breached the rules of natural justice in a manner that prejudices the rights of any party.[112]

Andrew Chen et al. have adopted a fourfold distinction to summarise the challenges between arbitration and insolvency in relation to Singapore. The first challenge posed is the operation of the proper law of the contract, coupled with the normal conflict of law rules. The second is that insolvencies in one jurisdiction may have extended beyond jurisdictional borders due to their statutory recognition and application. Third, and pertinent to Singapore, is the recognition and facilitation of insolvency law and ICA through the common law. Fourth, parties to an arbitration may be affected by the commencement of parallel insolvency proceedings at the jurisdiction of the seat of the arbitration.[113]

The illustrative cases in Australia and Singapore explain that arbitrability is important in determining the types of disputes that can be settled by arbitration and when the subject matter of a claim is to be determined by a domestic court according to the applicable law. Exercising their sovereign powers, domestic statutory authorities continue to choose what types of matters, not limited to cross-border insolvency, can be settled outside the domestic jurisdiction. Once a court in that jurisdiction makes this choice, it determines when those matters become arbitrable.

Notwithstanding these jurisdictional constraints on the recognition and enforcement of ICA in domestic insolvency proceedings, it is important for parties negotiating and drafting contract clauses to expressly address the seat and jurisdiction of

109 Ibid., 22.
110 Ibid., 59.
111 International Arbitration Act Chapter 143A, 1994, Section 24.
112 Ibid., Section 24.
113 Andrew Chan, Jonathan Chan, Jo Tay, Alexander Lawrence Yeo, Cross-Border Insolvency and Its Impact on Arbitration, *Singapore Academy Law Journal* 26, 999 (2014), 1035.

arbitration. The extent to which domestic law and courts recognise the autonomy of parties to self-regulate through a contract that includes an agreement to arbitrate, diverges across jurisdictions. Such variations pose challenges to cross-border insolvency and arbitration involving assets, debts and creditors in multiple jurisdictions, as is discussed in the next section.

This section has briefly highlighted the ongoing tension between arbitration and cross-border insolvency proceedings before domestic courts. It has illustrated that the courts identified in the section have permitted ICA primarily on a case-by-case basis, according to the discretion granted to them by the applicable statutory law governing insolvency. In exercising that discretion, courts have set aside arbitration awards under their respective national statutory regimes. However, this judicial practice is dependent, *inter alia*, on whether the agreement to arbitrate, the arbitration proceedings and award preceded the initiation of insolvency or other debt management proceeding. In exercising their discretion differently, significant challenges continue to arise in how domestic courts resolve conflicts between cross-border insolvency and arbitration. The next section will briefly highlight issues that arise when courts applying concepts such as the seat, jurisdiction, restructuring, consent and winding up proceedings.

7.3.6 Seat and Jurisdiction

Arguably, a key requirement in adopting arbitration is to determine the arbitral seat and jurisdiction. The seat is critical in providing a pathway for determining the law that, will be applied to govern the arbitration and enforce the award. Jurisdiction is equally important in enabling a court to exercise exclusive jurisdiction over a dispute, including over the recognition and enforcement of an arbitration award. By and large, these important elements to arbitration can be addressed through specifically drafted arbitration clauses within contracts.

The recent UK High Court case of *Riverrock* demonstrates the importance of drafting contractual agreements to ensure that the seat and forum (*forum conveniens*) of the arbitration is clearly chosen.[114] The Court cites Clause 8.4 of the London Court of International Arbitration Agreement ('the LCIA Arbitration Agreement') which provides that:

> Any dispute under the Agreement or in connection with it shall be referred to and finally resolved by arbitration under the LCIA Rules, which Rules are deemed to be incorporated by reference into this clause. The number of arbitrators shall be three (3). The Seller shall appoint one arbitrator, the Purchaser shall appoint the second arbitrator, and arbitrators nominated by the Parties shall appoint the third arbitrator that shall be the

114 *Riverrock Securities Limited v. International Bank of St Petersburg (Joint Stock Company)* [2020] EWHC 2483 (COMM), 2020 WL 05658172.

> chairman of the arbitration. The seat, or legal place, of arbitration shall be London, England. The language to be used in the arbitral proceeding shall be English.[115]

The High Court maintained that the:

> parties having agreed to submit to the jurisdiction of the English court in respect of the exercise of such powers as the choice of seat confers (which include the power to grant anti-suit relief), the argument that the English court is not the appropriate court to grant such relief is an extremely challenging one.[116]

Furthermore, the Court, in referring to the 2020 case of *Enka Insat*,[117] reinforced the long-held conception of the *forum conveniens*, by stating that:

> [T]he English court as the court of the seat of the arbitration is necessarily an appropriate court to grant an anti-suit injunction and questions of *forum conveniens* do not arise. This judicial reasoning follows two essential principles. Firstly, the choice of the seat of the arbitration is embodied in an agreement between the parties to submit to the jurisdiction of the court at that seat empowering it to excising such powers as the choice of seat confers. Secondly, the grant of an anti-suit injunction to restrain a breach or threatened breach of the arbitration agreement is an exercise of such powers.[118]

While the complaint in *Enka Insat* case was dismissed, it reaffirmed the position that arbitration in England is an effective alternative to domestic insolvency proceeding that prevails over extra-territorial arbitration proceedings. The Court concluded in favour of deciding the claim according to the arbitration agreement itself, construed in accordance with the applicable law of England.

In Australia, the position of a foreign party to an insolvency proceeding in relation to an arbitration with its seat in Australia falls within Schedule 1 of the Australian Cross-border Insolvency Act 2008,[119] which coincides with Article 21 of the UNCITRAL Model Law on Cross-Border Insolvency. The Federal Court of Australia in *Pink v. MF Global UK Limited (In Special Administration)*[120] noted that:

> Article 21 of the Model Law provides that, upon recognition of a foreign proceeding, where necessary to protect the assets of the debtor or the

115 Ibid., 7.

116 Ibid., 29.

117 Ibid., *Enka Insaat Ve Sanayi v. OOO Insurance Co Chubb and Others* [2020] EWCA Civ 574, 42.

118 Ibid., 42.

119 No. 24, 2008, as amended by Act No. 33 2016 and registered on 3 March 2017, https://www.legislation.gov.au/Details/C2017C00063.

120 [2012] FCA 260.

> interests of the creditors, the Federal Court may, at the request of the foreign representative, grant any appropriate relief. Article 21(1) then specifies types of relief that may be granted. Under art 21(1)(e), the relief includes entrusting the administration or realisation of all or part of the debtor's assets located in Australia to the foreign representative or another person designated by the Federal Court. It is appropriate, in the present case, to order that the administration or realisation of all of the assets of Global UK in Australia be entrusted to the Administrators.[121]

The Court further confirmed that, under the Model Law as adopted by the Australian Cross-Border Insolvency Act, the powers of a registered liquidator to grant additional relief were extended to the Administrator. It stated:

> Article 21(1)(g), as applied by Section 11 of the Australian Cross-border Insolvency Act 2008, provides that the Federal Court may grant any additional relief that may be available, relevantly here, to a registered liquidator within the meaning of Section 9 of the Corporations Act 2001. The Court argued that it was disposed to accede to the application by the Administrators to make an order that, subject to the provisions of the Corporations Act, all powers normally available to liquidators appointed under the provisions of the Corporations Act be made available to the Administrators.[122]

Accordingly, the Court in *Pink* does not confirm whether an Australian court will automatically stay proceedings until foreign insolvency issues arising from the agreement to arbitrate are settled. However, any pending court action will be stayed where the issues are subject to an arbitration agreement entered into in another signatory state to the New York Convention, or where proceedings under Section 7(1) of the IAA are capable of resolution by arbitration in accordance with Section 7(2).[123] In contrast, an Australian court is unlikely to stay domestic

121 Ibid., 17.

122 Ibid., 18.

123 International Arbitration Act 1974, Section 7 provides for the enforcement of foreign arbitration agreement. Where:
(a) the procedure in relation to arbitration under an arbitration agreement is governed, whether by virtue of the express terms of the agreement or otherwise, by the law of a Convention country; (b) the procedure in relation to arbitration under an arbitration agreement is governed, whether by virtue of the express terms of the agreement or otherwise, by the law of a country not being Australia or a Convention country, and a party to the agreement is Australia or a State or a person who was, at the time when the agreement was made, domiciled or ordinarily resident in Australia; (c) a party to an arbitration agreement is the Government of a Convention country or of part of a Convention country or the Government of a territory of a Convention country, being a territory to which the Convention extends; or (d) a party to an arbitration agreement is a person who was, at the time when the agreement was made, domiciled or ordinarily resident in a country that is a Convention country; this Section applies to the agreement.

proceedings if the arbitration agreement is null and void, inoperative or incapable of being performed under Section 7(5) of the IAA.

7.3.7 Winding Up

A further challenge in reconciling international commercial arbitration and cross-border insolvency proceedings relates to a winding up application. Winding up enables the assets of a company to be sold in order to repay a debt. Generally, winding up is undertaken in two ways. The first is voluntary and the second is compulsory. Compulsory winding up is undertaken by the court, although the process of winding up may vary between jurisdictions.

An application for winding up was considered by the Singapore Court of Appeal in *AnAn.*[124] There, the Court ruled that, where a winding up application was premised on a debt which was subject to arbitration, the debtor needed simply to show that there was a dispute over the debt which was the subject of an arbitration agreement.[125] At issue in *AnAn* was the:

> applicable standard of review – whereas a debtor seeking to resist a winding-up application would ordinarily be required to raise triable issues relating to the disputed debt, AnAn argued that because the global master repurchase agreement (GMRA) contained an arbitration agreement, the applicable standard was to demonstrate a *prima facie* dispute which fell within the scope of that arbitration agreement.[126]

Applying this *prima facie* standard of review, the Singapore Court allowed the appeal and set aside the order for winding up the appellant's business.

According to the Global Market Repurchase Agreement (GMRA), AnAn was required to maintain sufficient collateral under the agreement, with the level of collateral being measured by an indicator known as the Repo Ratio. The Repo Ratio in the case was essentially calculated on the basis of the purchase price of the Global Depository Receipts (GDRs] plus accrued interest and divided by the prevailing value of the GDRs. According to this Ratio, as the value of the GDRs

124 *AnAn Group (Singapore) Pte Ltd v. VTB Bank (Public Joint Stock Company)* [2020] SGCA 33.

125 Ibid.

126 Ibid., para. 14. In that case, the Appellant, AnAn Group (Singapore) Pte Ltd ('AnAn'), was a Singapore holding company, while the Respondent was VTB Bank (Public Joint Stock Company) ('VTB'), a state-owned Russian bank. On 3 November 2017, AnAn and VTB entered into a global master repurchase agreement ('GMRA') under which AnAn agreed to sell VTB global depository receipts ('GDRs') of shares in EN+ Group PLC ('EN+') and then repurchase those GDRs from VTB at a later date at pre-agreed rates. The pre-agreed rates that AnAn would pay VTB at the date of repurchase amounted, in essence, to the original purchase price paid by VTB plus interest and other costs. Despite the structure of the transaction as a sale and repurchase, this agreement was, in substance, a loan from VTB to AnAn.

dropped, the Repo Ratio would rise accordingly.[127] The GMRA contained both a choice of law and an arbitration clause. Clause 15(a) of Annex 1 to the GMRA provided that the GMRA was governed by English law. Clause 15(b) contained the following arbitration clause:

> [A]ny dispute arising out of or in connection with this Agreement, including any question regarding its subject matter, existence, negotiation, validity, termination or enforceability, shall be referred to arbitration and finally settled on the following terms: (i) the arbitration shall be conducted in accordance with the Arbitration Rules of the Singapore International Arbitration Centre which Rules are deemed incorporated into this Clause.[128]

Given these background facts, the Court in *AnAn* evaluated the circumstances in which a Singapore court was expected to stay or dismiss insolvency proceedings in order to enable arbitration to proceed:

> If a company wishes to obtain a stay of winding-up proceedings on the basis that the underlying debt upon which the statutory notice is founded is disputed, it must establish in the normal way that there is a bona fide dispute on substantial grounds. If it has not satisfied the court as to the bona fides and substantial nature of its claim it can only expect a short adjournment to enable it to commence the arbitration and then, if sufficient evidence to establish a genuine dispute is still absent it can expect to have to give an undertaking to proceed with the arbitration with all due dispatch.[129]

Importantly, the Court maintained that:

> By dismissing the winding-up application on the basis that the dispute is governed by an arbitration agreement and that the prima facie standard of review is satisfied, subject to other applications to wind up the company, the potentially insolvent company would be given unrestrained freedom to continue trading and incurring ordinary business and legal expenses until the conclusion of the arbitration of the dispute.[130]

The Court in *AnAn* recognised the tension that arose when a debtor-company faced multiple claims, with larger claims being subject to arbitration, but not smaller claims. Should the creditor of a substantial claim for a winding up application, the debtor-company could stave off the application by demonstrating, on a *prima facie* standard,

127 Ibid., 5.
128 Ibid., 7.
129 Ibid., 38.
130 Ibid., 105.

that there is a dispute relating to the debt. In the meantime, the debtor-company could elect to pay off the smaller debts which are not subject to arbitration.[131]

The Singapore Court of Appeal identified a further tension between a debtor securing the stay of a winding up order pending the outcome of an arbitration in order to avoid insolvency proceedings, and a creditor relentlessly seeking an insolvency order to bypass arbitration agreed to by the parties. As the Court opined:

> Nonetheless, in our judgment, the difficulties presented by the examples related to the *prima facie standard*, are not insignificant. However, any misuse of the prima facie standard to stay or dismiss winding up proceedings can be addressed by the abuse of process control mechanism. Furthermore, any possible misuse of the prima facie standard must be contrasted with the real possibility of abuse by creditors unilaterally choosing the insolvency route to bypass their obligation to refer the dispute to arbitration.[132]

Based on this, the Court viewed the ensuing tension between the process of winding up and the contractual clauses for any dispute to be resolved by the statutory requirements of national laws. In *AnAn*, the Court went further, arguing that:

> arbitration and insolvency processes embody, to an extent, contrasting legal policies. On the one hand, arbitration embodies the principles of party autonomy and the decentralisation of private dispute resolution. On the other hand, the insolvency process is a collective statutory proceeding that involves the public centralisation of disputes so as to achieve economic efficiency and optimal returns for creditors.[133]

Most states, particularly those compared in this book, have grounded their respective 'insolvency obligations in national laws',[134] whereby their courts interpret and apply the domestic insolvency statute.

While out of scope of this chapter to compare all statutory requirements, a national court will generally rule over contracts, property, stays, amongst other categories of disputes, according to legislative requirements. On the other side, the regulation of ICA, while still being subject to statutory requirements, is less prescriptive given the consensual nature of ICA agreements. Generally, statute regulating international commercial arbitration are developed to assist in facilitating the process of arbitrating. More specifically, court intervention is limited to the legality of an agreement to arbitrate and the enforcement of ICA awards. Thus, statutory regulations governing cross-border insolvency generally apply more pervasively in judicial proceedings than in international commercial arbitration.

131 Ibid., 106.
132 Ibid., 107.
133 Ibid., 68.
134 Julian Ellis, A Comparative Law Approach: Enforceability of Arbitration Agreements in American Insolvency Proceedings, *American Bankruptcy Law Journal* 92, 141 (2018), 145.

Unless contractual/dispute resolution clauses specifically require arbitration to resolve cross-border insolvency disputes, the court, as in the Singapore case of *AnAn*, will ordinarily have legal authority and oversight of a winding up or insolvency proceeding. The case of *AnAn* highlighted that, where contractual arrangements for resolving any dispute are clear, a court should not digress from those arrangements and attempt to apply the statutory provisions of insolvency to obtain a preferred outcome.

In seeking to establish middle ground, the Singapore Court in *AnAn* maintained that a prompt resolution was necessary, notably during the period of uncertainty stemming from the pandemic.[135] The case highlights that, where the applicant creditor can show that the continuing solvency of the debtor company is an ongoing concern, the court can decline to grant a winding up application. Any concern over the balance sheet of the company that is subject to insolvency or winding up proceedings, will arise when the debtor-company relies on an arbitration clause to delay payment of the debt. Where a stay of winding up is granted, the creditor can apply to the court to wind up the company, provided it can be shown that no steps have been taken to have the matter arbitrated.

Arguably, the territorial scope of national insolvency laws has had a considerable impact on the legal capacity to resolve cross-border disputes. What has emerged, outside the UNCITRAL Model Law on Cross-Border Insolvency, are fragmented national laws and decisions on the recognition and enforcement of arbitration awards in insolvency proceedings. The 2020 Singapore case highlights to the international business community that the current transnational approach to cross-border insolvency is functional; and indirectly, that its functionality supports further internationalisation of cross-border insolvency law. The case also underscores the subtle, but important role of national courts in providing economic stability in relation to cross-border insolvency. In our view, the approach adopted in *AnAn* needs to be carefully considered in other jurisdictions, in the absence of comparable decisions in those jurisdictions at the time of writing.

The significance of international commercial arbitration in trans-border insolvency proceedings is nevertheless not self-evident. If arbitration is to be recognised in insolvency proceedings, much depends on the agreement reached by the parties at the outset. Their arbitration agreements need to be specific and clear, as do their choices of law and jurisdiction. For arbitration proceedings to be effective in cross-border insolvency disputes, much will also depend on the ability and willingness of the parties to make fitting choices of both substantive and procedural law. Much will hinge on the willingness of states to adopt the Model Law, and their courts being willing to construe that Law uniformly in reaching decisions that have transnational legal and economic consequences. In issue is more than national

135 Ibid.

courts endorsing universalism as an abstraction in resolving cross-border insolvency disputes. In issue is how they effectuate a uniform Model Law that responds effectively to the financial implications of insolvency, notably in an era of global economic instability. Much also depends on expansive cross-border recognition of that uniform law, and the capacity of ICA rules and procedures to resolve insolvency disputes in an expeditious, cost-effective and sustainable manner.

7.4 Conclusion

International commercial arbitration can serve as an effective mechanism to expedite transnational insolvency disputes. However, divergence between insolvency and arbitration proceedings has led to the appreciation, among jurists and academics, that reconciling insolvency proceedings with arbitration 'presents a conflict of near polar extremes'.[136]

These limitations notwithstanding, international commercial arbitration is both legally and commercially instrumental in resolving disputes over debts. However, this chapter only addressed one of the ongoing tensions between the nature and application of the law governing cross-border insolvency and international commercial arbitration. For an arbitration agreement to operate effectively in resolving cross-border insolvency disputes, both the debtor and often multiple creditors must consent to the form and operation of arbitration. Such consent will ordinarily unify the process of arbitration; it will benefit creditors who are parties to arbitration, and minimise the impairment of debts owed to them. For international commercial arbitration to be fully effective, insolvency practitioners will need to better understand its benefits in resolving disputes over debts. Debtors and creditors will be best advised to agree on an insolvency process before the arbitration commences. They will want to agree upon a clear arbitration plan that takes account of prospective disputes over the nature of debt and the distribution of assets to offset that debt on insolvency. They will also need to ensure that their arbitration plan reconciles the pre-existing and modified legal obligations owed by the debtor to the creditor prior to the commencement of arbitration. The arbitration agreement should also provide clearly and from the outset for the influence, if any, of local laws upon the process of arbitration.

An ongoing tension exists between the applicable arbitration institution and the statutory framework in which insolvency proceedings are conducted. Central to a statutory insolvency scheme is the ability to devise legal mechanisms that enable creditors to recover debts from an insolvent entity. That entails recognition that the parties that were legally responsible to manage the debtor entity under a

136 *Re United States Lines Inc*, 197 F 3d 631, 640; see also S. M. Kröll, L. A. Mistelis, S. L. Brekoulakis, *Arbitrability: International & Comparative Perspectives*, Kluwer Law International, 2006, 358.

pre-existing insolvency plan, are often not the parties to a subsequent arbitration. A further and often unavoidable outcome is that insolvency proceedings may lead to results that differ significantly from arbitration proceedings. A related problem is that national courts are likely to recognise and enforce arbitration awards in trans-border insolvency cases according to an applicable law that diverges from jurisdiction to jurisdiction, and from state to state. National courts will be relied upon to construct the scope and process of arbitration disparately according to the statutory insolvency regime in which they are appointed. Arbitration tribunals will construe rules and process of arbitration according to choices of law and jurisdiction adopted by the parties. A tension for courts to address is that, in deciding that the insolvency should proceed in accordance with an arbitration agreement, they can prevent the debtor or a creditor from continuing insolvency proceeding through the courts. Yet, the consent to arbitrate that preserves the right of parties to proceed by arbitration, does not provide assurance that courts will prioritise that right over the applicable statutory law of insolvency. Based on this, in some jurisdictions like Australia, when arbitration proceedings are ongoing where insolvency proceedings have been commenced elsewhere such as in the UK, resolving this tension may not be straightforward.

Recent judicial decision in Australia and Singapore have also demonstrated the willingness of their courts to uphold a transnational approach to cross-border insolvency that includes promoting the use of arbitration as a viable process in resolving such disputes. Apart from such general benefits as cost and time efficiency, confidentiality and informality, an arbitration over cross-border insolvency arbitration is ordinarily conducted before an arbitration tribunal that, understandably, has greater expertise than a court of general jurisdiction. Arbitration proceedings can also accommodate disputes over debtor assets and creditor rights in multiple jurisdictions. Furthermore, an International Commercial Arbitration Award is likely to be binding and enforceable across multiple jurisdictions under the NY Convention to which most states are signatories. The result is that an arbitration agreement chosen by the parties will ordinarily lead to an award that is enforceable across national boundaries, unless it is nullified, inoperable or incapable of being performed. That enforceability provides creditors and debtors with greater certainty and predictability that their rights will be enforceable in multiple jurisdictions with dissimilar legal systems. This is something that domestic judicial decisions cannot assure.

The proposition is not that arbitration operates as a panacea for restructuring or otherwise resolving disputes over cross-border debts or the distribution of assets. Notwithstanding the multiple commercial benefits attributed to international commercial arbitration, the terms of arbitration agreements, from the outset, are often dictated by creditors with greater bargaining power than debtors. A dominant creditor can often ensure that the arbitration agreement reflects its preferred choices of law and jurisdiction. That creditor can often afford the cost and time to arbitrate, even though arbitration is touted as more cost effective and expeditious than domestic litigation.

However, domestic litigation relating to cross-border insolvency is increasingly the subject of international cooperation among states. That cooperation extends beyond international institutions such as UNCITRAL and UNIDROIT to transnational judicial networks. The Judicial Insolvency Network (JIN)[137] now produces 'Guidelines for Communication and Cooperation between Courts in Cross-Border Insolvency Matters'. Even though the current membership of the JIN is limited to six albeit primarily significant jurisdictions,[138] it arguably serves as a foundation upon which to build a global network of judges collaborating over cross-border insolvency law. Pertinently, the JIN recognises the value of arbitration as an efficient and effective alternative in resolving cross-border insolvency matters outside of busy court schedules.

In contrast, the shift from judicial to arbitral resolution of cross-border insolvency is evident in the work of INSOL, an anacronym for When 'Where' Matters: Anchoring Jurisdiction in Insolvency (INSOL).[139] In April 2019, INSOL, UNCITRAL and the World Bank collaborated in producing a report on the legal and broader economic policies impacting on cross-border insolvency. In 2015, INSOL released a Special Report titled 'When "Where" Matters: Anchoring Jurisdiction in Insolvency', in which it formally recognised the importance of insolvency arbitration. It stated that courts in most jurisdictions enforce contractual agreements that specify when, where and how the allocation of debts and assets in insolvency disputes should be determined. The Report recognised that, underlying the presumption of enforceability of arbitration awards across jurisdictions, is the policy that party autonomy entitles contractual counterparties to decide 'where' to litigate or arbitrate.[140] Additionally, the International Bar Association (IBA)[141] has supported the idea that arbitration is an effective alternative process to litigation in cross-border insolvency.

However, if the ICA is to serve as a viable option in resolving cross-border insolvency claims, it needs to be developed and adopted skilfully. Arbitration clauses need to be clear in selecting arbitration as the primary, or as a supplementary means of resolving debtor-creditor disputes. Arbitrators need to understand the complex

137 The Judicial Insolvency Network, http://www.jin-global.org/news-events.html.

138 Ibid., membership include, United States Bankruptcy Court for the Southern District of New York, United States Bankruptcy Court for the District of Delaware, the grand Court of the Cayman Islands, Supreme Court of Bermuda, Court of Appeal of England and Wales, Federal Court of Australia, Supreme Court of New South Wales, Seoul Bankruptcy Court, Supreme Court of Singapore.

139 INSOL, *When 'Where' Matters: Anchoring Jurisdiction in Insolvency*, 2015, https://www.insol.org/emailer/May_2015_downloads/Special%20Report%20Jurisdiction.pdf.

140 Ibid., ii.

141 International Bar Association, file:///C:/Users/ROB/Downloads/Insolvency_UNCITRAL_July2013.pdf. See also UNCITRAL Working Group V 49th Session, May 2016. Note by the International Bar Association Observer Delegation: International Insolvency Convention: Issues, Options and Feasibility Considerations, file:///C:/Users/ROB/Downloads/IBA%20Submission%20UNCITRAL%20re%20Insolvency%20Convention%20May%202016.pdf, point 25.

nature of cross-border debt disputes, as well as competing national insolvency laws. They also need to adopt procedures and make awards that meet the expectations of the parties in agreeing to arbitrate and in choosing the arbitrators.

There are few attributes of commercial litigation across a plethora of jurisdictions that international commercial arbitration cannot replicate functionally. Nor is litigation, inferentially, unable to replicate the attributes of expertise, speed, informality and cost-effective proceedings attributed to arbitration. What international commercial arbitration offers is a supplementary, if not alternative, method of resolving disputes involving large-scale corporate debts that transcend domestic boundaries.

8

CROSS-BORDER INSOLVENCY AND DATA PROTECTION LAW

The economy over the past decade has seen a significant shift from the traditional industrial base to trade in the use of personal data. The growth in the collection and use of personal data has resulted in nation states developing comprehensive privacy and data protection laws. These legal protections accorded to personal data flows will inevitably find their way into cross-border insolvency and restructuring proceedings. Yet and similar to cross-border insolvency and restructuring, the internationalisation of transnational data flow and protection laws is significantly deficient. The resulting effect has seen nation states adopting very different laws because of the way the right of privacy is adopted and applied. This chapter highlights how the current private international law approach taken to regulate personal data is significantly fragmented. In other words, personal data in some jurisdictions is comprehensively regulated, whereas in other jurisdictions data protection is an emerging area of law. Due to the varied approaches taken by nation legal systems to such protection, this chapter will briefly compare the laws of Australia, European Union (EU), China and United States (US).[1] It will demonstrate how each jurisdiction has taken similar, but still distinctive approaches to defining personal data.

1 This work builds and draws on the work undertaken by Leon Trakman and Robert Walters who have written extensively on data protection law. See also Robert Walters, Insolvency and Data Protection, *Business Law Review* 11, 42 (2020), Wolter Kluwer. For a further comparative analysis of data protection laws, see also Robert Walters, Leon Trakman, Bruno Zeller, *Data Protection Law: A Comparative Analysis of Asia-Pacific and European Approaches*, Springer, 2019; Robert Walters, Marko Novak, *Cyber Security, Artificial Intelligence and Data Protection Law*, Springer, forthcoming. This chapter differs from the previous work as it discusses storage limitations and data portability as these legal concepts impact or otherwise on cross-border insolvency and restructuring.

DOI: 10.4324/9781003312024-2

8.1 Introduction

Personal data has been described as the new oil by experts in the area.[2] The new digital economy is developing at a rapid pace and the economic output is yet to be fully realised. The phrase 'data are the new oil' is increasingly heard in discussions on competition in the digital era, particularly since the publication of a widely referenced article by *The Economist* in 2017.[3] A key difference between the protection of oil and personal data is that, while oil is a finite and non-reusable resource, data can be infinite and reused, and complicated by the recognition given to ownership and access to rights in data including personal data. Moreover, the international bandwidth usage is increasingly shifting towards content providers, such as Amazon, Google, Facebook and Microsoft, among others.[4] The ability of many of these large digital firms to acquire and analyse large quantities of data, including across a wide range of products and markets, highlights a central dichotomy of how to handle personal data when an entity becomes insolvent.

The trade in personal data is not confined to any single state and knows no national borders. The actual transnational flow of this data is also only beginning to be fully understood. Importantly, the flow of data in international trade has expanded over the last several decades. However, an inevitable result of recent trade destabilisation is that companies engaged in trans-border data flows that are threatened with insolvency or need to restructure as a consequence of financial stress. That need is likely to be accentuated by the extension of data flows to such sectors as agriculture, the environment, health and education, transport, and infrastructure (ITC). Data flows underpinning a vibrant trade in personal data, are also increasingly pervading supply chains, logistics, tourism and maritime sectors. These flows underly expanding commercial and legal mechanisms that are used to facilitate lucrative transnational trade in such data.[5] These developments require that regulators take more account of how such data flows are managed throughout a cross-border restructuring or insolvency. The regulatory complexity of differences in cross-border laws will not be easy to overcome, particularly where a company has offices located in several third countries that have based their collection and use of law on the local laws. It will necessitate an understanding of data protection laws, along with the emerging area of cross-border data flows and adequacy. Importantly, it will necessitate a level of understanding in relation to where the data is stored and whether that data is subject to localisation arrangements, or specific definitions of

2 Marcin Szczepański, *Is Data the New Oil? Competition Issues in the Digital Economy*, European Parliament, 2020, https://www.europarl.europa.eu/RegData/etudes/BRIE/2020/646117/EPRS_BRI(2020)646117_EN.pdf.

3 Ibid.

4 Ibid., in Organisation for Economic Cooperation and Development, *Measuring the Digital Transformation: A Roadmap for the Future*, 2019, https://www.oecd-ilibrary.org/sites/9789264311992-en/1/2/1/1/index.html?itemId=/content/publication/9789264311992-en&mimeType=text/html&_csp_=32da5d2095ef596b16d96b0367b9d519&itemIGO=oecd&itemContentType=book.

5 Leon Trakman, Robert Walters, Bruno Zeller, Trade in Personal Data: Extending International Legal Mechanisms to Facilitate Transnational Trade in Personal Data?, *European Data Protection Law Review*, 6 (2020) 243, 258; Robert Walters, *Cross-Border Data Flows – an Evolving Multilayered Regulatory Approach Required!*, Victoria University, forthcoming.

sensitive personal data. Furthermore, it will demand requisite knowledge about the operation of key concepts such as consent and disclosure.

Bob Wessels stresses that many changes will be required in the digital economy in managing cross-border insolvency and restructuring. He emphasises the 'need for greater understanding of the challenges faced in providing data protection by national associations of turnaround managers, accountants and insolvency lawyers, to understand the challenges faced in providing effective data protection'.[6] Wessels elaborates by demonstrating that data protection will necessarily play a greater part in their future efforts, leading to the establishment of national insolvency registers and a centralised search engine modelled on the European framework.[7] He provides an example of where and how capital structures of companies in the 21st century will be different from those in the 20th century. Specifically, businesses that were once driven by hard assets, such as real estate, natural resources and machinery, will become increasingly dependent upon, and valued on the basis of, intangible assets such as data, claims, licenses, know-how and goodwill.[8] Their key application in the new digital economy, will be through the growing value of personal information as data assets (e.g. customers' databases) in the insolvent estates of debtors. The expansion of processes to digitise and collect data, especially big data, will also bring data protection issues in the forefront of legal and insolvency practice. This chapter will emphasise how data protection laws need to give greater attention to the impact of data on the overall management and conduct of cross-border insolvency. In issue is the security of personal data, including security of persons engaged in trans-border dealings in which the disclosure of personal information can have ramifications upon them in states beyond where the disclosure is made. A related issue is the risks of social ostracisation, ethnic persecution and sexual harassment of those whose personal data is disclosed, extending beyond the economic risks posed to the entity's continuing business in that state.

The personal harm in insolvency and restructuring, is to the individual data subject. They are the essential targets, and victims, of abuse of their personal data. Important, too, in disputes over the collateral harm is to those with whom the individual associates, such as employer entity, its suppliers, customers and other employees. Beyond personal harm to the individual, therefore, is threatened harm to the commercial activities and persons with whom that individual is associated and ultimately, to the public at large. At risk is the largely uncontrolled transmission of the personal data of those persons who are associated, with the commercial entity, not limited to the data subject. In further issue is the realisation that, beyond the individual, these classes of persons are also impacted by the disclosure of such personal data. The benefit of such protection extends yet further to a public interest in both the private and data security of individuals including those who are engaged in cross-border trade and investment.

6 Bob Wessels, *Cross-Border Cooperation and Communication: How to Comply with Data Protection Rules in Matters of Insolvency and Restructuring*, Chase Cambria Company (Publishing) Ltd, 2019, 1–2, https://www.ibbi.gov.in/uploads/resources/c3593c9f41984c6f31f278974de3cf37.pdf.

7 Ibid.

8 Ibid.

These assertions do not purport to present data protection as unlimited in their scope of application. Nor should such protection be so extended that it renders business activities wholly insulated from public scrutiny. What is asserted is that, with advanced technologies, exposing individual data to ever widening public scrutiny, the protection of such data ought to be subject to at least some commensurable protection, not limited to protection in insolvency proceedings. The telling issue is how far this commensurability should extend in a world in which personal data is hoarded by collectors, processors and other users that have, at least technologically, a seemingly boundless ability to use and abuse that data.

The converse risk arises when data protection becomes over-extensive, and when it borders on the virtually infinite protection of personal data. This, too, is a pressing challenge for data regulators in establishing limits in the protection of personal data in the insolvency and restructuring of financially embattled entities. Under scrutiny here are these seminal further facts. The activities of data subjects and entities with which those entities are associated are engaged in multilateral trade and investment. Data protection laws vary across jurisdictions in which such trade and investment is conducted. The nature of such protection must necessarily take account of the need to effectively regulate the use of personal information across jurisdictions that are embroiled in insolvency and restructuring proceedings. The challenge is to regulate personal data in a single jurisdiction that has a single data protection law but is subject of disparate interpretations including in other jurisdictions. It is ever more challenging to do so across multiple jurisdictions in which data protection laws not only differ, but are sometimes absent.

In determining how to frame cross-border insolvency laws in light of such wider issues of data protection and data flows, it is therefore necessary to address the interface between regulating and conducting a cross-border insolvency with managing personal data under disparate national laws. In issue will be how to reconcile the regulatory approach adopted in an insolvency proceeding with the management of that data. In seeking such reconciliation, it will be necessary to decide whether the protection of personal data is, or ought to be, treated as a priority in managing cross-border corporate insolvency. An obstacle in doing so at this time is the relatively limited development of data protection laws to date. For example, corporate legislation in Australia does not specifically refer to data protection, although businesses must comply with the Privacy Act 1988, that embodies Privacy Principles.[9] The US Bankruptcy Code is comparable to the Australian insolvency legislation in not specifying any requirement for the collection and use of personal data, including in relation to bankruptcy proceedings. In contrast, the EU is assiduous in protecting personal data on human rights grounds to which a free market in data subserves. These developments, and deficiencies, will be analysed in this chapter.

9 Australian Privacy Principles, APP 11 requires organisations to take active measures to ensure the security of personal information that it holds. In practice, this means that organisations must take reasonable steps to protect the information from misuse, interference, as well as unauthorised access, modification or disclosure.

Central to the collection and collation of personal data today, is how national privacy laws have been established to regulate the use of that data. Understanding the definition of personal data is arguably the starting point to know where and how that data will impact upon, or be impacted by, a cross-border insolvency or restructure. However, what has emerged globally are different legal frameworks that have been developed in response to these concerns. In responding to this divergence, nation states have begun to view the EU as a benchmark for establishing national data protection laws. Yet, others have opted to diverge and set their own pathway. These developments will become evident throughout this chapter.

The chapter will also highlight how the laws in jurisdictions discussed later have regulated the concept of consent for the transfer or sale of personal data in very different ways. Such divergence becomes important when an entity is subject to an insolvency, restructure or merger-acquisition proceeding. Specifically, data subjects may not have consented that their personal data can be transferred or sold to a third party, while the requirements for and extent of consent diverges across jurisdictions. Such divergence is also challenging in cross-border insolvencies involving personal data where the laws in some jurisdictions do not specifically address personal data in restructuring, while others do so disparately. As a result, the protection of personal data will need to be managed in light of such legal diffusion in which insolvency or restructuring is being managed by a person or entity other than the entity facing insolvency or restructuring.

This chapter will also discuss whether jurisdictions have established regulations for the use of a controller, processor or other officer within an entity that is subject to insolvency, restructure or merger-acquisition. It will highlight the importance of understanding their roles and responsibilities in handling personal data, particularly in cross-border transfer of the data. Their familiarity with differences in data protection laws is necessary for them to respond effectively to challenging insolvency and restructuring issues including the legality of their responses.

The chapter will highlight further whether the relevant jurisdictions compared have established data localisation laws for data storage and in addition, have provided for data portability. Data portability allows data subjects to request that their personal data that is stored by one organisation be transferred to another organisation. This has implications where the other organisation has established an office in a third country. Most noteworthy, this has significant implications where data is transferred to a state with little or no data protection laws. In contrast, storage restrictions through data localisation is a new addition to the data protection legal framework in which states require that the data of their respective citizens be stored only in the country of that citizen. Data controllers and processors also need to be familiar with the varied legal approaches to defining personal data to comply with the level of consent that is required for the collection and use of that data in cross-border insolvency and restructuring proceedings.

8.2 Data Protection Versus Privacy

Protecting people's personal data is a necessary response to an Internet that has a significant influence upon our daily lives. A related result is the formidable growth in personal details that are captured daily on the Internet, particularly across international borders. For instance, a data subject who resides in Sydney, Australia, makes online purchases of goods and services from an entity located in Myanmar. That data subject's personal data may have crossed, in virtual space, several international borders in order to reach Myanmar. Materially, that entity may have access to that person's personal data including, significant data. The result is that millions of people are, often unwittingly, subject to the transnational flow of their personal and financial data. That data, in turn, is being stored, processed and otherwise used by data collectors and processors for often economically motivated reasons. Typically, a person's financial data may be particularly significant in a corporate insolvency in which that person is a director or officer of that entity. Pertinent, too, is the collection and processing of personal data of a mass of people, typically consumers, to demonstrate their views about the services and the sustainability of that entity.

Problematic, are the challenges over how data protection laws have been developed in different states to regulate the user of personal data by corporate entities. First, states increasingly regulate organisations that acquire personal data by requiring them to appoint a controller, processor or some other officer to manage the collection, use and storage of that data. Secondly, for such personal data to be identified, it must be defined. The challenge is how domestic regulatory regimes define personal data. Thirdly, states provide that the use of personal data is subject to the consent of the person whose data is being used. The regulatory challenge for the regulatory state, here, is to ensure that consent is reasonably obtained, given its importance to organisations seeking to use or sell that data to third parties. Fourthly, states need to regulate the storage of personal data, by placing additional controls over where and how the data can be stored. Fifthly, states need to regulate the portability of data by which organisations transfer data from one entity to another.

A primary means by which states protect data subjects from organisations that collect, process, transfer and otherwise mine their data is through data protection laws. These laws are best described as tools of privacy. In other words, a person is afforded a level of privacy through the controls exercised by data protection laws. The challenge is to develop data protection laws that are consistent with, or are at least mutually reconcilable, and that transcend divergent conceptions of privacy. On the positive side, 120 states have now adopted, or are considering adopting, data protection based somewhat on EU standards.[10] The problem is that the notion of privacy over the Internet is very differently conceived from jurisdiction to jurisdiction. For instance, some jurisdictions, such as the EU, view privacy over the Internet and data protection as a fundamental right.[11] However, China and Singapore have not recognised privacy as a fundamental right in the same way as some of their

10 Graham Greenleaf, Global Analysis of Data Privacy Laws and Bills, *Privacy Law and Business International Report* 145 (2017), 14–24.

11 Robert Walters, Leon Trakman, Bruno Zeller, *Data Protection Law: A Comparative Analysis of Asia-Pacific and European Approaches*, Springer, 2019, 45–81.

regional or international counterparts.[12] Other states, such as Indonesia, have struggled with the concept of privacy over the Internet, because the citizens of those state largely view privacy as communal and not individual in nature. A comparable narrative has evolved in India, due in part to linguistic and cultural divergence throughout the country. While principles of privacy alone are unlikely to determine the scope of data protection in cross-border commerce, such as in corporate reorganisation or insolvency, data protection laws will be determinative.

The different positions that states have adopted towards privacy have, by and large, have influenced how states and regional organisations have developed their respective data protection laws. In 2018, the EU implemented the 2018 General Data Protection Regulation (GDPR),[13] which protects personal data as a fundamental right. Walters and Novak[14] acknowledge that, at the opposite end to the maximalist the data protection framework such as is associated with the GDPR, is the perception of China taking a minimalist approach to protecting personal data as a human right; however, there is evidence that China has adopted a data protection regime.[15]

In between these two inferred models of data protection law in China as distinct from the EU, are the laws of Singapore, the US and Australia that adopt a predominantly business friendly or consumer-based model, or a hybrid of the two. In further contrast, India and Indonesia that have adopted a sectorial approach, do not yet adequately regulate the use of personal data. The US has also developed a sectorial approach to individual rights. In these respects, the US's individual rights approach to data protection, based on privacy rights, diverges from the GDPR's social rights approach. The sectorial approach taken by the US also separates the many rights afforded to data subjects under specific legislation, whereas the EU has aggregated all the data rights into a single statute. On this basis, it could be argued that the EU has taken a more social rights-based approach, rather than an individual sector-based approach as can be seen in the US.

Leon Trakman and Robert Walters note that a further and more complicated consideration could arise if personal data is afforded an intellectual property right.[16]

12 Simon Chesterman, *Data Protection Law in Singapore, Privacy and Sovereignty in an Interconnected World*, Academic Publishing, 2018, 4.

13 Regulation 2016/679 of the European Parliament and the Council of 27 April 2016 on the protection of natural persons with regard to the processing of personal data and on the free movement of such data, and repealing Directive 95/46/EC, Official Journal of the European Union L 119/1.

14 Robert Walters, Marko Novak, *Cyber Security, Artificial Intelligence and Data Protection Law*, Springer, 2021, Ch 15.

15 Ibid. On October 21, 2020, the National People's Congress ('NPC'), China's top legislative body, released its first draft of the Personal Information Protection Law. There are notable similarities to the European Union's ('EU') General Data Protection Regulation ('GDPR') and other recent privacy legislation in major jurisdictions in some important areas; the draft law introduces a number of provisions that are consistent with recent trends in other Chinese laws in the areas of data and technology, such as the draft Data Security Law and the newly enacted Export Control Law. Covington, https://www.cov.com/-/media/files/corporate/publications/2020/10/china_releases_first_draft_of_personal_information_protection_law.pdf.

16 Leon Trakman, Robert Walters, Bruno Zeller, Is Privacy and Personal Data Set to Become the New Intellectual Property, *International Review of Intellectual Property and Competition Law* (2019), 937–970.

Should this be realised, the need for its consideration during insolvency proceedings will pose further challenges as to how personal data is protected. To date, there has been little appetite for personal data to be afforded a property right. The next section discusses some of the recent case law from selected jurisdictions pertaining to personal data and insolvency.

Case Law

This section highlights selected cases from the jurisdictions compared in this chapter that have considered personal data in cross-border insolvency. Beginning in 2015, when *RadioShack Corporation*[17] went bankrupt and Chapter 11 bankruptcy had commenced in the US, it was reported that, if RadioShack was to be liquidated, it would almost certainly sell off its massive cache of customer data.[18] That data included the social security numbers, emails, home addresses and telephone numbers of 67 million customers. Under US law, if a debtor's privacy policy prohibits the sale or transfer of personal data, Section 332 of the Bankruptcy Code provides that the data may still be sold, but only under the supervision and with the approval of a 'consumer privacy ombudsman' and the Bankruptcy Court.[19] Subsequently, the Federal Trade Commission recommended that conditions be placed on the sale of the personal information of consumers in order to protect their privacy.[20] The matter highlights the many issues relating to the protection of personal data when an entity like RadioShack becomes insolvent in the US and seeks to sell its commercial information and data that includes consumers' personal data, to its global customer base. In response, the FTC placed conditions of the sale of RadioShack customer personal data that included:

- Customer information should not be sold as a standalone asset but bundled with other assets.
- Customer information should be sold only to another entity that is in the same line of business as RadioShack.
- The buyer should agree to be bound by RadioShack's privacy policies at the time of data collection.
- The buyer should notify customers and obtain consent to use data in any way that differs from the conditions set by RadioShack.[21]

17 *RadioShack Corporation et al.* No. 15-10197 (BLS) (Bankr. D. Del.) In Robert Walters, Insolvency and Data Protection, *Business Law Review* 11, 42 (2020), 4–10.

18 Ibid.

19 Ibid.

20 Ibid.

21 Federal Trade Commission, Radioshack, https://www.ftc.gov/news-events/press-releases/2015/05/ftc-requests-bankruptcy-court-take-steps-protect-radioshack. See also, Letters from FTC to Radioshack, https://www.ftc.gov/system/files/documents/public_statements/643291/150518radioshac kletter.pdf.

The US Regulator placed conditions on the sale of personal data,

> By restricting what personal data could be sold to be only email addresses, it highlighted the importance of personal data in trade, and the potential pitfalls entities, and their creditors, will face when facing insolvent.[22]

These pitfalls are further compounded when entities have to navigate the various data protection laws of different states. This is readily demonstrated today. As the sequel to COVID-19 pandemic continues to impact upon global trade and investment, states have resorted to business lockdowns that expose commercial sectors to continuing financial stress and insolvency. Nor has the perceived economic recovery of some states like the US, Singapore and Australia, reversed the rise in cross-border insolvency proceedings at the time of writing this book. The prospective threat is of insolvency and restructuring proceedings to extend into 2022–2023 and beyond. Those threats compound the risk of exposing personal data to abuse, not limited to the collection and sale of the data of the insolvent entity.

The challenges and prospective results identified earlier, are highlighted in a 2019 UK High Court case of *Green v. Group Ltd & Others*.[23] There, the Court considered whether to appoint joint administrators of companies within the Cambridge Analytica group (liquidators), and whether they had breached the relevant data protection laws. The Court also considered whether the appointment of the joint administrators as liquidators would undermine public confidence in the insolvency process. The structure of the company was complex. Firstly, the holding company was Emerdata Ltd ('Emerdata'). Emerdata's majority shareholder was a Delaware corporation (Cambridge Analytica Holdings LLC). One of Emerdata's subsidiaries was SCL Group Ltd ('Group'), a non-trading holding company. Secondly, the group also consisted of SCL Analytics Ltd ('Analytics'), which was also a non-trading company. At one time the Group had a minority interest in another company, SCL Insight Limited ('Insight'). Thirdly, the trading subsidiaries of Analytics were (1) SCL Commercial Limited ('Commercial') which provided data analysis to commercial customers; (2) SCL Social Limited ('Social') which provided campaign management and communications services to political customers; and (3) SCL Elections Limited ('Elections') which was the main trading company. Elections itself had one dormant subsidiary, Cambridge Analytica (UK) Ltd ('Cambridge UK').[24] The insolvency was of Cambridge UK. Thus, strictly speaking, this was not a cross-border insolvency, but rather a domestic insolvency. Yet, the case demonstrates that the same issues will arise in a cross-border insolvency matter.

The facts of this well publicised case were that, on 23 March 2018, the Information Commissioner's Office (ICO) raided the offices of Cambridge Analytica

22 Robert Walters, Insolvency and Data Protection, *Business Law Review* 11, 42 (2020), 6–15.
23 *Green v. Group Ltd & Others* [2019] EWHC 954 (Ch), https://www.bailii.org/ew/cases/EWHC/Ch/2019/954.html.
24 Ibid., 9–2.

in the UK and seized several servers and a significant quantity of evidence. That seizure also included the accounting books and records of Cambridge Analytica. In July 2018, the ICO was continuing to examine these materials to ascertain whether the law had been broken and whether regulatory action needed to be taken against Cambridge Analytica, given significant concerns that it had breached data protection laws through its acquisition, storage and usage of personal data. In November 2018, the ICO considered that it had identified serious breaches of data protection principles which justified its imposing a fine on Cambridge Analytica. It did not, however, commence any criminal proceedings relating to the general conduct of Cambridge Analytica business, although it did bring an action on one specific failure, as is discussed later.[25] The UK Court went onto say that:

> As to the case for an independent investigation in the widest sense into the activities of the Cambridge Analytica business in acquiring, aggregating and analysing personal data, I certainly agree that there is a strong case for it. I simply do not accept that an insolvency process is the appropriate machinery to use. Administration is about the collection of assets and the ascertainment of claims, about realisation and distribution in some cases and about re-organisation in others. It is about businesses and unpaid creditors and jobs: and administrators are given the tools appropriate to that task. Liquidation is not in substance different. Whilst each entails performance of statutory reporting duties (an important interest of the community at large) neither process is a free-floating public enquiry into possible unlawful activity implicit in the business model of the insolvent company (be that unlawful activity a contravention of some licence condition or a breach of food hygiene requirements or health and safety at work regulations or data protection rules).[26]

The consequences of these comments by the High Court in *Green* highlight that data protection laws are becoming increasingly important before and during insolvency. This development, in our view, will grow, not recede. The need for practitioners to be fully conversant with the relevant data protection laws of more than one state will be required. Administrators and liquidators will also need to be across the relevant data protection laws to understand what if any data is being collected and stored by the entity, and where it is being stored.

The Court in *Green* also reinforced its reasoning by citing the High Court (Chancery Division) in *Re Southern Pacific Personal Loans*[27] maintaining that:

> where a company holds and processes data then it is the company alone (and not the company and its directors together) which is the data controller; and

25 Ibid., 8.
26 Ibid., 85.
27 Ibid., 71, Ltd [2014] Ch 426.

> the fact that the company becomes subject to an insolvency process does not of itself make the office holder a 'data controller'. The office holder will only become a 'data controller' if he takes decisions about the processing of the data as principal in his capacity as liquidator (or administrator) rather than as agent of the company.[28]

Thus, central to the knowledge and understanding of data protection laws in cross-border insolvency or restructuring, is the definition of personal data; the disclosure obligations owed to the data subject; the concept of consent; and whether the appointment of a controller or processor is required under the law. The Court in *Green* also separated out the responsibilities of office holders appointed by the entity to those appointed by regulation. It noted further that office holders are not personally responsible for compliance with the applicable data protection law. Moreover, two key questions arose from the High Court's decision in *Green*:

1 Is it in the interests of the general body of creditors, or a necessary part of the discharge of their statutory duties, to help the data subject pursue his data rights?
2 If they decided not to help, would that have caused unfair harm to the interests of the data subject as a creditor?[29]

The Court highlighted that there is 'no general duty on administrators to investigate "data breaches" occurring before their appointment; and the duty of the administrators is to seek to achieve the objectives of the administration process as quickly and efficiently as reasonably practicable'.[30] Moreover, the joint administrators were bound to examine material available to them to investigate potential breaches of duties owed by the directors of the company, but not in relation to particular third parties. Neither was it their

> investigatory duty to examine breaches of duty by the company to particular third parties if they considered that there was no prospect of a distribution to such third parties; and it would be the duty of administrators as officers of the Court to assist a regulator in such investigations insofar as it did not impede the achievement of the purposes of the administration.[31]

The conclusion of this case is another demonstration of the divergent approach taken towards data protection laws. As highlighted later, some jurisdictions regulate the appointment of a controller or some other position to be responsible for

28 Ibid.
29 Ibid., 61.
30 Ibid., 62.
31 Ibid., 63.

the collection, storage and use of personal data. However, other jurisdictions do not impose such requirements. The distinction between an self-regulated office bearer and a regulated appointee is increasingly complex, but still important. Firstly, administrators are appointed by the parties to an insolvency. Secondly, depending on the state where the data is collected, the entity that is subject to insolvency proceedings might be required by domestic laws to appoint a controller or processor. The ensuing question is to delineate the line of responsibility between the party-appointed officer and the regulator appointed controller relating to data disclosure requirements and data breaches. In partially answering this question, the controller and to a lesser extent, the processor will have responsibility for the collection, storage and use of personal data, although that responsibility will be dependent on the domestic law. Viewed as a whole, the *Green* case reaffirms the impact that data protection law is having upon the regulation of insolvency and restructuring.

Developments of data protection legal decisions in the EU have been distinctive. In 2020, in an opinion by the European Court of Justice in *Land-Nordrhein*,[32] the applicant in the main proceedings was the insolvency administrator of a company located in Germany, J & S Service UG. In that capacity, 'he requested certain information from the tax administration in relation to the tax situation of the insolvent company under his administration, in order to examine the possibility of bringing insolvency avoidance claims against the competent tax office'.[33] The Advocate General was required to provide an opinion on a preliminary ruling from the Bundesverwaltungsgericht (Federal Administrative Court, Germany) and asked the Court to interpret:

> Article 23(1), points (e) and (j), of Regulation (EU) 2016/679 of the European Parliament and of the Council of 27 April 2016 on the protection of natural persons with regard to the processing of personal data and on the free movement of such data, and repealing Directive 95/46/EC (General Data Protection Regulation), even though that provision is not directly applicable to the situation at issue in the main proceedings. Indeed, that situation falls, for a number of reasons, outside the scope of Regulation 2016/679. Article 23(1) thereof has been made applicable to the situation before the referring court solely by virtue of a *renvoi* contained in the applicable national legislation.[34]

The applicant in the main proceedings was an insolvency administrator of J & S Service UG.[35] In that capacity, the tax administration requested certain information in relation to the tax situation of the insolvent company under the applicant's administration, in order to examine the possibility of insolvency avoidance claims

32 Case C-620/19, *Land Nordrhein-Westfalen v. J & S Service*, Opinion of the Court of Justice, September 2020.

33 Ibid., 18.

34 Ibid., 4.

35 Ibid., 18.

being brought against the competent tax office.[36] The Court, in comparing the German Tax Code to the GDPR, reasoned that Article 23(1) is a provision of the General Data Protection Regulation encompassing: 'a corpus of rules governing the processing of personal data in the single market'.[37] The Court elaborated that:

> recitals 2 and 4 and Article 1 of GDPR Regulation 2016/679 provide that the regulation lays down limits to the use of data processing in order to protect the fundamental rights of data subjects. On the other hand, paragraph 32c (1)(2) of the German Tax Code was a very different legal instrument altogether. The provisions included in that instrument, including those on data processing, were geared towards ensuring uniform and lawful taxation and the safeguarding of tax revenue.[38]

The insolvency administrators were able to demand that the tax authorities provide tax information relating to the insolvency debtor. That enabled the administrators to decide, with full knowledge of the facts, whether to bring insolvency avoidance claims against those authorities. However, that possibility did not exist with respect to private creditors of the insolvency debtor, given that those creditors were not subject to laws limiting the freedom to provide personal information under the GDPR.[39]

Accordingly, the European Court examined the differences between the objectives of the two provisions, observing that:

> Article 23 of GDPR Regulation 2016/679 seeks to strike a fair balance between respect for natural persons' fundamental rights affected by data processing (for example, private and family life) and the need to safeguard other legitimate interests in a democratic society (for example, national security).[40]

By contrast, the Court noted that Paragraph 32c(1)(2) of the AO (Tax Code – Abgabenordnung oder) aimed at redressing a perceived 'imbalance' in how tax authorities weigh these when tax avoidance claims brought in the context of insolvency proceedings.[41] That said, the central point in issue was that Regulation 2016/679 sought to strike a balance between the right for a data subject to have personal data materially protected. This included the protection of personal data that involved tax data. However, the tax law enabled and facilitated the transfer of data between organisations, including personal data included within the data protection law, in order to detect and determine breaches of the tax law.

36 Ibid.
37 Ibid.
38 Ibid., 78–79.
39 Ibid., 84.
40 Ibid., 84–85.
41 Ibid., 86.

The European Court elaborated that the German Government had explained that, under national law, the insolvency administrator is a 'third party' under Article 4, point (10) Regulation 2016/679,[42] for the purposes of access to data of the insolvent debtor. Therefore, the Court determined that the insolvency administrator could not be regarded as having acted on the basis of rights which the data subject (the company under administration) had transferred to him. Yet, the Court expounded further, Article '23(1) of Regulation 2016/679 is concerned with rights of data subjects and obligations of data controllers'.[43] While the European Court of Justice declared that it lacked jurisdiction to answer the questions referred for a preliminary ruling by the Bundesverwaltungsgericht (Federal Administrative Court, Germany), it concluded:

> [I]n essence, whether a national provision, such as Paragraph 32c(1)(2) of the AO, that limits the right of access to data held by the tax authorities, when that data may be used to bring insolvency avoidance claims against those authorities, is compatible with Article 23(1)(e) of Regulation 2016/679. The Commission argues, however, that establishing equal treatment between the tax administration and private-law creditors in actions such as that in the main proceedings does not constitute a general public interest, but an interest proper to the State which cannot be weighed against the fundamental right of the data subject to have access to the data collected concerning him or her. Therefore, the Commission considers that Article 23(1)(e) of Regulation 2016/679 must be interpreted as precluding a national provision such as Paragraph 32c(1)(2) of the AO. The rationale behind the distinction between 'general public interests' and 'interests proper to the State', and the precise contours of the two concepts, frankly escape me. Failing an explanation from the Commission on this point, and finding no trace of it in the text of Regulation 2016/679, I find the Commission's arguments unpersuasive. In the light of the above, it was concluded that a national provision, such as Paragraph 32c(1)(2) of the AO, that limits the right of access to information held by the tax authorities, when that information may then be used to bring insolvency avoidance claims against those authorities, cannot be said to be incompatible with Article 23(1)(e) of Regulation 2016/679, but in practical terms primarily because the latter provision has nothing to say on that specific issue.[44]

This case highlights the fundamental elements of data protection law(s), such as the responsibility of a data controller. Concurrently, to understand the role and responsibility of that controller, an administrator or tax regulator must also have a thorough

42 Ibid., 10, 'third party' means a natural or legal person, public authority, agency or body other than the data subject, controller, processor and persons who, under the direct authority of the controller or processor, are authorised to process personal data.

43 Ibid., 89.

44 Ibid., 136–139.

understanding of what personal data constitutes. The administrator or regulator must also know how the concept of consent operates.[45] Moreover, the Court reinforced the matter raised earlier in this chapter, that data protection is a fundamental human right across the EU, and with that in mind, that the controller has a higher threshold of responsibility than their counterparts in other nation states.

Notwithstanding the above, a central element that administrators and liquidators will need to carefully consider under EU Law is an entity's exposure to the data protection laws in the relevant jurisdiction. Even though it is generally accepted that insolvency practitioners are not controllers, processors or some other regulatory appointee under data protection law, the applicable law is likely to require them to assume some responsibility for personal data management.

The European Court's construction and application of EU data protection law in this case provides a prospective direction for its protection in the future in and, arguably, beyond the EU. That is well justified across such global sectors as trans-border finance and critically, in insolvency and reconstruction cases. The challenges in achieving greater global uniformity lies in the fragmentary nature of domestic data protection laws directed at resolving cross-border insolvency and restructuring uncertainties. The EU's data protection regulations, arguably, provide a viable pathway for other states to replicate, in whole or part, in protecting personal data in insolvency and reconstructing proceedings. Administrators, known by that or another name, in insolvency and restructuring proceedings will need to understand differences in the definition of personal data across the jurisdictions that are connected to the main proceedings. They will also need to appreciate the nature and degree of consent that entities under administration need to have provided data subjects in order to collect, process, store or otherwise use their data. Unless the entity under administration has kept and maintained comprehensive records of consent requested and received from data subjects, its use of their personal data will be subject to prospective legal challenge. The administrator will also need to determine what, if any, data protection laws in the applicable jurisdiction mandate the appointment of a controller, processor, officer. That understanding will encompass different domestic data protection laws in relation to corporate entities and more specifically, legal divergence over the roles of officers who are appointed, or otherwise responsible, to protect that data.

8.3 Personal Data – What Does It Constitute?

A starting point for data protection law and the management of personal data, is to determine its legal meaning. What does this mean for insolvency practitioners? In responding to this question, there will be a continued shaping and evolving area of the law. It is far from settled, and as stated earlier, the current jurisdictional legal regimes are profoundly divergent.

45 Robert Walters, Insolvency and Data Protection, *Business Law Review* 11, 42 (2020), 8–14.

Nonetheless, components in definition of personal data that states share can provide a roadmap for the parties, liquidators and/or administrators in determining what constitutes personal data in a particular jurisdiction.

It will stress the importance of regulators, and parties to insolvency and restructuring schemes, appreciating the legal significance of data protection. That knowledge is especially significant in relation to the sale or other use of personal data of the employees, officers, creditors, and customers of an entity that is subject to insolvency or winding up proceedings. Drawing from the earlier work of Walters and Trakman, this section will highlight the key components in the definition of personal data in the jurisdictions selected for study.[46] It must be noted that at the time of concluding this book in 2021, China had released their new Personal Information Protection laws, which are similar to the EU. However, this chapter does not compare the PIPL.

Australia

The definition of personal information in Australia encompasses information or the opinion about an identified individual,[47] or an individual who is reasonably identifiable; whether that information or opinion is true or not; and whether it is recorded in a material form or not.[48] Australia's Privacy Act 1988 does not define commercial data. However, Section 6 defines the information that can identify a person that includes, a person's full name, alias or previous name, date of birth, sex, current or last known address and driver's license. Important personal identifying information also includes the person's current and last employer. Comparable to the GDPR, a person is definition as a natural person in accordance with Section 6(1) of the Privacy Act. Rather than have a national identification card similar to other nation states such as Singapore, Australian law determines that further identifying information resides in a person's Tax File Number (TFN). However, this last identifying information is only relevant for a person who has acquired a TFN. Moreover, Section 6 defines the data in a person's TFN as 'sensitive information'. The classification of certain personal data being more sensitive than other personal data places a higher threshold on the personal nature of sensitive personal data, and accordingly, a higher standard of protection from the misuse or abuse of that data, such as relates to a person's level of debt.

Sensitive personal information encompasses:

> Racial or ethnic origin; Political opinions; Membership of a political association; Religious beliefs or affiliations; Philosophical beliefs; Membership of a professional or trade association; Membership of a trade union; Sexual orientation or practices; Criminal record; Health information about an individual; Genetic information (that is not otherwise health information); Biometric

46 Robert Walters, Leon Trakman, Bruno Zeller, *Data Protection Law: A Comparative Analysis of Asia-Pacific and European Approaches*, Springer, 2019. This section draws upon earlier work of the authors in the area of data protection and data flows.

47 Robert Walters, Insolvency and Data Protection, *Business Law Review* 11, 42 (2020), 4–10.

48 Privacy Act 1988, Section 6, in Robert Walters, Leon Trakman, Bruno Zeller, *Data Protection Law: A Comparative Analysis of Asia-Pacific and European Approaches*, Springer, 2019, 115–146.

information that is to be used for the purpose of automated biometric verification or biometric identification; or Biometric templates.[49]

Importantly, Australian Law provides that the collection of sensitive data cannot be undertaken without the individual's consent.[50] The problem, however, is in establishing functional means of protecting sensitive personal data. Biometric technology is an exemplar of how sensitive personal data is widely shared and is difficult to protect from seemingly unavoidable data sharing. As an illustration, every time persons enter or exit international airports, they unavoidably provide some biometric information. Such information is also becoming more accessible through new and emerging areas of personal identifiers, such as facial recognition or fingerprints that are used as identifiers as a person passes through a customs check. The scope of access to personal information across Australia is also expanding. Section 5B(3)(c) of the Privacy Amendment Act provides for its collection from an individual who is physically present in Australia or in an external Territory, regardless of where the collecting entity is located or incorporated.[51] Australia's definition of personal data is therefore broad in scope. It has also captured unique and emerging areas in which a person's identity can be accessed and used. It has also opened the door to the abuse of personal identify in that data being used without that data subject's consent or used otherwise contrary to law.

As in other jurisdictions, the use of technology is playing an ever-greater role in Australia, in identifying and storing personal data that identifies a person in significant detail. Advancing identification and storage technology is also likely to expand access to personal data even further in coming decades. In issue, among other advancing technologies, is the enhancement of surveillance mechanisms by which to detect misuse in the storage and illegal transfer of personal data. A further issue is the prospect of civil and criminal penalties arising from such illegal acts that are commensurate to the violation of personal data.

These issues are germane to cross-border insolvencies when the surveillance of personal data is used. This will apply to the sale of personal data for profit, but to gain advantage by disclosing, or threatening to disclose, such personal information in relation to insolvency proceedings.

China

The framework for Cybersecurity Law in China is based largely on preserving China's cyberspace sovereignty and protecting its national security.[52] At the time of finalising this book in September 2021, China had released their long-awaited

49 Ibid., 115–135.

50 Australian Privacy Principle 3.

51 Explanatory Memorandum, Privacy Amendment (Enhancing Privacy Protection) Bill 2012, 218.

52 Translation: Cybersecurity Law of the People's Republic of China, 1 June 2017, https://www.newamerica.org/cybersecurity-initiative/digichina/blog/translation-cybersecurity-law-peoples-republic-china/. See also an earlier published article: Robert Walters, Current Status of China's Cybersecurity – Data Protection Laws, *Privacy Law Bulletin* 17, 4 (4 August 2020), 60–64.

Personal Information Protection Law.[53] However, it is out of scope of this chapter to compare the PIPL with the Cyber Laws or the other jurisdictions discussed. China's laws and those in countries with comparable governance-institutional frameworks, are structured differently to the laws in the other countries studied in this book. Chinese Cybersecurity Law extends to regulating the construction, operation, maintenance and use of networks, as well as cybersecurity supervision and management within the mainland territory of the People's Republic of China.[54] The Cybersecurity Law in the People's Republic of China does not define personal data or personal information or sensitive personal data.[55] The only reference to personal information is contained in Article 22 of China's Cybersecurity Law. It states that 'where network products and services have the function of collecting users' information, their providers shall explicitly notify their users and obtain their consent'.[56] If any user's personal information is so used, the provider is required to comply with this law and provisions in relevant laws and administrative regulations on the protection of personal information, such as information relating to a person's debts or prospective bankruptcy.[57]

However, a more comprehensive definition of both 'personal information' and 'sensitive personal information' is contained in China's Information Security Technology-Personal Information Security Specification (ISTPISS).[58] Firstly, 'personal information' constitutes all information, whether it is recorded by electronic or other means and whether that information is used alone or in combination with other information, that can identify a natural person. Secondly, personal information extends to the information that reflects the activities of a natural person. Being able to identify a person from their activities is a unique feature of China's cybersecurity framework and is not explicitly stated in the laws of other countries studied in this book. Nonetheless, the definition of personal information in China is generally consistent with other states, including the EU that is discussed in the next sub-section. In China, personal information includes the 'names, date of birth, identity card numbers, biometrics, addresses, telecommunication contact methods, communication records and content, account passwords, property, credit, location data, accommodation, health, physiological and transaction information'.[59]

53 Personal Information Protection Law of the Mainland, https://www.pcpd.org.hk/english/data_privacy_law/mainland_law/mainland_law.html. The Personal Information Protection Law, the first piece of legislation in the Mainland dedicated to the protection of personal information, was passed by the Standing Committee of the National People's Congress on 20 August 2021 and will be effective from 1 November 2021.

54 Cybersecurity Law of the People's Republic of China, Order No. 53 of the President, http://en.pkulaw.cn/display.aspx?cgid=4dce14765f4265f1bdfb&lib=law.

55 Ibid., Article 2.

56 Ibid.

57 Ibid., Article 22.

58 TC260 Chinese, (English version) Information Security Technology-Personal Information Security Specification, https://www.newamerica.org/cybersecurity-initiative/digichina/blog/translation-chinas-personal-information-security-specification/ Chinese version, https://www.tc260.org.cn/upload/2018-01-24/1516799764389090333.pdf.

59 Ibid.

Chinese law also recognises sensitive personal information. Not unlike general personal information, sensitive information includes identity card numbers, biometrics, addresses, telecommunication contact methods, communication records and content, account passwords, property, credit, location data, accommodation, health, physiological and transaction information. Such personal information would inevitably include information about a person's level of debt and liability to an entity facing bankruptcy. It also includes all personal information pertaining to children under the age of 14, who were provided with extended legal protection in 2019.[60]

Chinese law reflects a slightly distinctive approach in determining the scope and effect of the use of sensitive personal information. It stipulates that, once it is leaked, provided, or used illegally, it can threaten the personal property and property security of an individual. The Law also identifies the consequences arising from the illegal use of such data, in causing reputational, physical or mental health damage, or in discriminating against an individual. Such consequences might vary from discrimination based on ethnicity or sex, or socio-economic standing including level of debt.

The protection of personal data in China is likely to have material significance to cross-border insolvency not limited to cases in China is the place of "main" or secondary proceedings, or simply connected to a party to such proceedings. The scope of such protection is reflected, in part, in the definition of personal data adopted there, the legal boundaries of sensitive performance information, and in the consequences of abusing such data. These issues are not widely tested to date in cross-border insolvency proceedings in China. However, they are particularly germane to China, given the massive involvement of Chinese entities in global trade and investment, in the collection, processing and use of personal data. That involvement extends further to Chinese parties providing access to such data prior to, or during the course of insolvency proceedings. This may become more complicated when dealing with private entities in and from China, as opposed to state owned enterpises.

The European Union

Article 4 of the GDPR defines personal data to mean any information relating to an identified or identifiable natural person (data subject).[61] An identifiable natural person is one who can be identified, directly or indirectly, particularly by reference

60 Ibid., Section 3.1, 3.2. S. Xia, *China's New Child Privacy Protection Rules*, 2019, https://www.chinalawblog.com/2019/09/chinas-new-child-privacy-protection-rules.html. Huton Andrews Kurth LLP, China Issues Provisions on Cyber Protection of Children's Personal Information, https://www.lexology.com/library/detail.aspx?g=625d3bb3-ec70-4626-b37d-ae0b9092c307&utm_source=lexology+daily+newsfeed&utm_medium=html+email+-+body+-+general+section&utm_campaign=australian+ihl+subscriber+daily+feed&utm_content=lexology+daily+newsfeed+2019-10-09&utm_term.

61 Regulation 2016/679 of the European Parliament and the European Council, on the protection of natural persons with regard to the processing of personal data and on the free movement of such data and repealing Directive 95/46/EC (General Data Protection Regulation), Official Journal of the European Union L 119/1. See also, Robert Walters, Insolvency and Data Protection, *Business Law Review* 11, 42 (2020), 3–12.

to an identifier such as a name, an identification number, location data, an online identifier, or to one or more factors specific to the physical, physiological, genetic, mental, economic, cultural or social identity of that natural person. The GDPR does not specifically define sensitive data. Rather, Article 9 deals with 'processing special categories of personal data'. It prohibits the processing of personal data based on racial or ethnic origin, political opinions, religious or philosophical beliefs, or trade union membership, and the processing of genetic data, biometric data for the purpose of uniquely identifying a natural person. It also prohibits the processing of data on a person's health or a natural person's sex life or sexual orientation. However, there are exemptions to this prohibition. Article 9 (2) of the GDPR recognises that sensitive data can be processed where consent has been obtained. Furthermore, it provides for the processing of sensitive data for employment, social security and social protection law.[62] Exemptions from protection extend further to areas in the public interest, such as those related to health and national security. Article 9 entitles EU Member States to introduce additional conditions regarding the processing of genetic data, biometric data or data concerning health.

The exemptions from data protection, introduced by Article 9(2) of the GDPR, are considered far reaching and extend to genetic data used in research. Kärt Pormeister considers whether specific or broad consent is required to support such exemptions under EU or the national laws of Member States.[63] Pormeister argues that the research exemption creates a situation in which, once genetic data has been obtained from the data subject, it can be further processed for any research purposes, and stored for an unspecified time to enable such processing.[64] Therefore, the right of an individual to object to the processing of sensitive data for research purposes could be excluded by a Member State under Article 89(2) or Article 21(6) of the GDPR. Pormeister argues that an individual purporting to invoke the 'right to be forgotten' to the processing of personal data, is likely to be unsuccessful, as the GDPR shifts determining the balance of interest in that data from the data subject to the data processor or controller.[65] This leaves the data subject with little control over sensitive personal information in relation to scientific research. The broad approach that Pormeister imputes to Article 9 of the GDPR could lead to regulatory shifts. Regulators could require the consent of data subjects to use their personal information in other EU Member States and national laws outside the EU. It is beyond the scope of this book to examine those EU laws and national laws that exempt data processing and control from the consent of the individual, other than to note that it is subject to judicial scrutiny in the EU as courts assert the right of data subject to consent to the use of their personal information. The nature and scope of that judicial scrutiny is considered next.

62 Regulation 2016/679, Recital 10, 34–35, 51.

63 Kärt Pormeister, Genetic Data and the Research Exemption: Is the GDPR Going too Far?, *International Data Privacy Law* 7, 2 (2017), 137–146.

64 Ibid., for example, the exemption is not subject to purpose or storage limitation.

65 Ibid.

An EU Court has restrictively construed the exemptions to the requirement that data subjects consent to the use of their personal data. It states that the:

> characterization of personal data cannot be excluded: a) by the fact that the information is provided as a part of the professional activity and b) by the circumstance that the identity of the experts and the comments were previously made public on the EFSA website and c) by the circumstance that the persons concerned do or do not object.[66]

The case is an example of a court balancing three elements: (1) data privacy, (2) the data market and (3) the concept of personal data. This balance is not easy to achieve. It is likely to be further complicated by the third country laws that require different issues to be addressed from the data protection laws. That is, protection of personal data as a fundamental right in a third country may depend on a combination of its data protection laws, economic situation and acceptance of privacy over the Internet. That assessment will also entail balancing, these priorities differently. In some nation states, the economy will come first before any protection of data or privacy. In others, where data protection law is underdeveloped, there may be only limited opportunity for courts to engage in such balancing. The US is one jurisdiction in which such balancing is challenging for the courts.

United States

The Federal Trade Commission Act (15 U.S.C. §§41–58)[67] (FTC Act) does not define personal data or sensitive personal data. However, rather than defining personal (general or sensitive) data or information, the Health Insurance Portability and Accountability Act[68] (HIPPA) Privacy Rules define 'health information', 'protected health information', 'individual identifiable health information' and 'genetic information'.[69] Firstly, 'health information' means any information, including genetic information, whether oral or recorded in any form or medium, that is created or received by a health care provider, health plan, public health authority, employer, life insurer, school or university, or health care clearinghouse. Walters and Novak elaborate on the expanse of health information in the US.[70] It encompasses information relating to the past, present or future physical or mental health or condition of an individual; the provision of health care to an individual; or the past, present or future payment

66 Case C-615/13, *ClientEarth and Pesticide Action Network Europe (PAN Europe) v. European Food Safety Authority*, 16 July 2015, para. 29–30.

67 Federal Trade Commission Act (15 U.S.C. §§41–58), https://uscode.house.gov/view.xhtml?req=granuleid%3AUSC-prelim-title15-chapter2-subchapter1&edition=prelim.

68 §160.103. In Data Protection Law: An Overview Congressional Research Service, 25 March 2019, https://fas.org/sgp/crs/misc/R45631.pdf.

69 HIPPA Privacy Rules, §160.103, Definitions, https://www.hhs.gov/hipaa/for-professionals/privacy/laws-regulations/combined-regulation-text/index.html.

70 Robert Walters, Marko Novak, *Artificial Intelligence, Cyber Security and Data Protection Law*, Springer, 2021, 14.

for the provision of health care to an individual.[71] Secondly, protected health information encompasses individually identifiable health information that is transmitted by electronic media, maintained in electronic media or transmitted or maintained in any other form or medium. However, protected health information excludes individually identifiable health information.[72] Thirdly, individually identifiable health information is information that is a subset of health information, including demographic information collected from an individual, and is created or received by a health care provider, health plan, employer or health care clearinghouse.[73] This information can relate to the past, present or future physical or mental health or condition of an individual. Furthermore, identifiable health information includes the provision of health care to an individual; or the past, present or future payment for the provision of health care to an individual; and identifies the individual, or believes the information can be used to identify the individual.[74] Fourth, genetic information means information with respect to an individual, information about genetic tests, the genetic tests of family members of the individual, and the manifestation of a disease or disorder in family members of such individual.[75] Centrally, genetic information constitutes any request for, or receipt of, genetic services, or participation in clinical research which includes genetic services, by the individual or any family member of the individual.

Comparative Differences

There are significant differences in how the laws in Australia, China, the EU and the US protect personal data. However, a direct comparison is misleading as their respective laws use different terms to satisfy essentially the same requirements. The law in some of these countries refers to 'personal data', while the law in others refer to 'personal information', although those terms are applied generally to the communication of personal information in cyberspace. In addition, what is termed 'sensitive information' is determined not only by legislation, but by whether that information is treated as sensitive in fact, and hence is accorded greater protection.

Generally, the laws studied identify both 'personal information' and 'personal data' as encompassing the name, date of birth, residential address of the person. The EU's GDPR has responded to rapid technological development more specifically, by seeking to protect the personal data of 'natural' persons processed by 'automated means', including online identifiers such as Internet Protocol (IP) addresses and cookie identifiers that create profiles on individuals and identify them.[76]

Walters, Trakman and Zeller make the point that these basic concepts were employed long before the development of the Internet and are commonly found in

71 HIPPA Privacy Rules, §160.103, Definitions, https://www.hhs.gov/hipaa/for-professionals/privacy/laws-regulations/combined-regulation-text/index.html.

72 Ibid., §160.103.

73 Ibid.

74 Ibid.

75 Ibid.

76 Ibid.

passports.[77] Australia's Privacy Act[78] specifically states what and how personal data and information is defined. The Act defines general personal data and information to be a person's full name, alias or previous name, date of birth, sex, current or last known address, and driver's license. Interestingly, important identifying information also includes that person's current and last employer.[79] However, once a person begins working or undertaking business, no matter what his/her age may be, that person has a Tax File Number. The authors highlight that the EU does not specify a person's alias or previous name as general data or information.[80] They stress that, on the one hand, not identifying persons by their previous name protects their privacy. On the other hand, this could sometimes have negative effects when a person wants to maintain anonymity about a previous life such as sex crimes but that information remains material in protecting public safety. Not identifying a person's prior identify may well be justified, in contrast, when a person has assumed another name, to avoid being identified, such as after being a public witness to a mass crime. There may also be a public safety interest in protecting that identity to ensure the willingness and confidence of witnesses to testify to alleged crimes in the future. Regarding the mass transmission of personal data, the use of the term 'personal data' in the EU is significant because new technologies initiated in the 1970s resulted in easily accessible datasets that were the catalyst for the EU establishing a data protection framework.[81] However, the GDPR does not apply to non-automated processing of personal data which is not intended to be part of a filing system.[82]

Viewed comparatively, some jurisdictions have begun to identify personal data as being 'sensitive'. For example, Australia has identified sensitive personal information as encompassing a person's racial or ethnic origin; political opinions; membership of a political association; religious beliefs or affiliations; philosophical beliefs; membership of a professional or trade association; membership of a trade union; sexual orientation or practices, or criminal record; health information about an individual; and genetic information (that is not otherwise health information). Under Australia's Privacy Act, biometric information that is used for the purpose of automated biometric verification or biometric identification, is also treated as sensitive data.[83]

While Australian law defines 'sensitive information' specifically, the EU has adopted a broad approach in determining the scope of personal data, grouping general personal and sensitive personal data under a single definition.[84] Unlike Australia,

77 Robert Walters, Leon Trakman, Bruno Zeller, *Data Protection Law: A Comparative Analysis of Asia-Pacific and European Approaches*, Springer, 2019, 265–290.
78 Privacy Act 1988.
79 Robert Walters, Leon Trakman, Bruno Zeller, *Data Protection Law: A Comparative Analysis of Asia-Pacific and European Approaches*, Springer, 2019, 265–290.
80 Ibid.
81 Article 29 Data Protection Working Party, Opinion 4/2007 on the Concept of Personal Data, European Commission, 20 June 2007, http://ec.europa.eu/justice/data-protection/article-29/documentation/opinion-recommendation/files/2007/wp136_en.pdf.
82 General Data Protection Regulation, Official Journal of the European Union 2016/679. Article 2.
83 Ibid., Article 2.
84 Robert Walters, Leon Trakman, Bruno Zeller, *Data Protection Law: A Comparative Analysis of Asia-Pacific and European Approaches*, Springer, 2019, 265–290.

the GDPR encompasses sensitive data as general personal data that reveals a person's racial or ethnic origin, political opinions, religious or philosophical beliefs, or trade union membership, and the processing of genetic or biometric data.[85]

8.4 Data Localisation

One of the critically emerging areas of data protection law is data localisation. A focal point of data protection law, data localisation involves a nation state exerting its sovereignty by ensuring their citizens' most important personal data is stored in the country and not in a third country. From approximately 2015 onwards, there has been a steady global trend towards 'data localisation' in which data, including personal data, is required to be maintained and processed within the geographic boundaries of its state of origin.[86] This development has raised concerns about its possible adverse impact on emerging data-intensive technologies such as cloud services/e-commerce, big data, artificial intelligence and the Internet of Things. However, the question arises over what such data localisation has to do with cross-border insolvency, While not fully settled, data that is part of contractual arrangements between companies located in different states, and due to financial stress or for some other reason, the entity becomes insolvency or undertakes a restructure, thenthis data will form a part of that insolvency or restructuring process. Therefore, where the local national laws require all or part of the data subject to the contractual arrangements to be stored in a jurisdiction, that data needs to be carefully managed there. Included in that stored data is the personal data of individuals who are associated in various capacities with the impacted entity.

Importantly, the inability to reach an international agreement on rules for cross-border data flows has potentially significant adverse consequences for all future users of the Internet. That adversity is likely to be exacerbated by the strict application of localisation requirements relating to data storage. Moreover, the lack of consistent rules on cross-border data flows is likely to have a corresponding impact on cross-border insolvency and restructuring activities. Richard Taylor makes the point that the basis of:

> Data Localization is grounded in two distinct but inter-related policy models: Data Sovereignty and Trans-Border Data Flows. These two concepts have different origins. 'Data Sovereignty' is derived from the historic power of a state of absolute and exclusive control within its geographic borders.[87]

Such assertions of absolute sovereignty create yet another potential layer of complexity in cross-border restructuring and insolvency. The largely unknown factor at this time is the nature in and extent to which data localisation laws will impact on restructuring and insolvency proceedings and outcomes. Thus, this section will identify whether Australia, the EU, the US and China have specific data localisation

85 Regulation (EU) 2016/679 Article 9.

86 Richard Taylor, 'Data localization': The Internet in the Balance, *Telecommunications Policy* 44, 8 (2020), https://doi.org/10.1016/j.telpol.2020.102003.

87 Ibid.

laws and the prospective impact of those laws upon the obstacles to data sharing and the significance of data protection that are raised earlier.

Among the jurisdictions compared, Australia[88] and China[89] both have levels of data localisation laws. Australia, on the one hand, allows for health records to be transferred between health organisations. On the other hand, China Cybersecurity Law requires entities responsible for critical infrastructure to store personal and business information in the territory of the country. This extension by nation states of domestic control over personal data – through data localisation – is a manifestation of the evolving nature of data protection laws. Even a close to minimalist approach to restrict the localisation of health data storage, such as by requiring storage in Australia, is arguably counter to the universalist approach that cross-border insolvency and restructuring law has aimed to achieved over decades. Attempts to break down insulated regulatory frameworks from the cross-border transmission of data, is especially difficult, not only due to assertions of sovereignty in the national interest, but also to offset fragmentation in data protection from one state to the next.

Yet, in our view, data localisation is not the enemy of globalisation, nor an incontrovertible threat to shifts towards universalism in cross-border and restructuring laws. The dichotomy between localisation and globalisation here is a result of the competing issues that are unavoidably dealt with disparately across nation states. Data protection laws, broadly construed, have more general functions than is associated with data usage in cross-border insolvency. On the one hand, the trans-border business community strives for legal certainty through the international harmonisation of rules, notably in regulating insolvency and restructuring proceedings. On the other hand, nation states compete and develop laws governing the collection, storage and use of personal data as an exercise of state sovereignty. On the other hand, the case for protecting or not protecting cross-border data flows of personal data in diffusely regulated but critical sectors like insolvency, is more contentious. In part, such contention is difficult to resolve because not only nation states, but entities in some countries, along with data subject who are associated with them, often expect a high level of protection of their personal data. However, such protection may be overstated, not only when the sharing of data is neither materially intrusive, nor a pervasive threat to personal autonomy. Rather, the importance of protecting personal data may be less justified than the need to maintain the stable, transparent and efficient regulation of insolvency proceedings for which the disclosure of personal data is well justified.

8.5 Consent

The concept of consent has become one of the most important legal concepts underpinning the very notion, collection, use and storage of personal data.[90] How will this personal data be managed within a restructure or insolvency? Arguably, there should be

88 *My Health Records Act 2012*, Section 77.

89 2017 Cybersecurity Law China, https://www.newamerica.org/cybersecurity-initiative/digichina/blog/translation-cybersecurity-law-peoples-republic-china/.

90 Robert Walters, Insolvency and Data Protection, *Business Law Review* 11, 42 (2020), 4–10.

very few issues arising where the entity has obtained consent from the data subject to use the data. It will come down to the consent obtained. Generally, the practice today is that, when a data subject provides consent, they are not necessarily providing consent for their data to be managed through an insolvency disclosed in a reorganisation. This can become problematic and therefore an understanding of what data subjects consent to at the point of collecting their data should be undertaken and understood. Nonetheless, consent allows for and provides data subjects with a further layer of control, by ensuring that their consent is obtained prior to using their personal data.

In Australia, consent can be expressly or impliedly, written, verbal or by silence.[91] The definition of consent requires that an individual is adequately informed of the issues and obligations before giving consent expressly or by implication.[92] That consent must be current and specific, and voluntary. Importantly, the person alleged to have consented must have the capacity to understand and communicate that consent. This formulation, of consent, in our view, ensures that people who require assistance or suitably informed advice before providing their consent, should be preserved.

To date, there is no court decision in the EU that demonstrates authoritatively how far the requirement to secure consent to use personal data extends, nor how to so determine that a person has the capacity to provide consent. However, there are exceptions when personal data can be used without having to satisfy all the requirements for consent identified above.

Australia

The Australian Privacy Principles (PP 7.2, 7.3, 7.4) allow an organisation to use or disclose personal data in direct marketing when that organisation has collected that information for which express consent is given explicitly, either orally or in writing. Applied in other jurisdictions, a data subject can provide such express consent either in writing or orally, depending on the jurisdiction. This consent could be in the form of a handwritten signature, oral statement or the use of an electronic or voice signature.

Generally, it cannot be assumed that a person has provided consent on the basis that they did not object in the first place to allow their data to be processed or transferred to a third party. In practice, too, it will be difficult for an APP entity to establish that an individual's silence can be taken as consent. A on an opt-out mechanism, in which consent is assumed unless the person "opts out", fraught unless the opt-out mechanism presented to a person is articulated clearly and succinctly, so that the person understands the implications of opting out in the discrete circumstances.[93] Importantly, consent does not exist where it is deemed to have been provided under duress, coercion or some other kind of pressure. An individual must be aware of the implications of providing or withholding consent, for example, whether access to a service will be denied if consent is not given for

91 *Giller v. Procopets* (2008) 24 VR 1.

92 Privacy Act 1988, Section 6.

93 Robert Walters, Leon Trakman, Bruno Zeller, *Data Protection Law: A Comparative Analysis of Asia-Pacific and European Approaches*, Springer, 2019, 128.

the collection of a specific item of personal information. Such consent, arguably, would be effective and equitable when the individual has been fully informed of the risks and implications arising from the use of that information. In Australia, it is sufficient that the individual is advised and consents in broad terms to that use.[94]

Consent to use personal information for use in insolvency and restructuring proceedings, including in relation to publicity about such proceedings, would also need to be clearly provided to ensure that data subjects is fully informed about the consequences arising from the use of that data. A qualification is that such data might be required to be disclosed to the public on public interest grounds, to ensure that adequate information is provided for the transparent and stable management of insolvency and restructuring proceedings. The nature of consent to the disclosure of personal data might depend on whether the administrator deems such a disclosure necessary for transparency and information gathering purposes. It might also depend on the publication complying with the applicable regulations. Publicity about personal information from unofficial sources, such as published by online media sources, would more likely justify a higher level of consent, as when the data subject be fully informed about, understands and consents to the proposed public disclosure. It is one thing for an administrator to use personal information of the CEO or directors of a company that is materially related to the insolvency proceedings. It is another thing to encourage news outlets to publish information about data subjects who are involved in such proceedings in order to maximise on sensationalism and public voyeurism.

Subject to contextual qualifications, such as stated earlier in relation to the use of personal data in insolvency proceedings, our view is that informed consent of data subjects is a pressing requirement at a time in which access to personal data is extensive and capable of mass communication, including for sensationalism and/or profit. In our view, too, the GDPR can well serve as a benchmark for nation states to replicate, in whole or part, to protect personal data. If the GDPR is adopted as a template, its six requirements related to consent could be adopted. These include: consent itself, the performance of the contract, compliance with a legal obligation, protection of vital interest, public interest, and the legitimate interest pursued by the controller.[95]

The European Union

The EU requires that consent constitute more than an informal conversation. It must be freely given, specific, informed and unambiguous.[96] In other words, the persons providing consent must be able to understand the purpose(s) for which they are providing consent. This requirement removes some ambiguity in a person's understanding of the implications arising from granting consent. Securing such informed consent from data subjects to collect or use their personal information can also require disclosure of the legal implications that arise from transferring information,

94 *Rogers v. Whitaker* (1992) 175 CLR 479, 490.
95 Regulation (EU) 2016/679, Article 6(1)(a).
96 Ibid., Article 4.11.

such as to store it, or convey it to down-stream users and/or viewers. Requiring that adequate information is provided to the data subject to make informed choices is reinforced by Recital 32 of the EU Regulation. The Recital requires that consent should be given through a clear affirmative act which demonstrates that it was freely given, specific, informed and provided with an unambiguous indication of the data subject's agreement to the processing of personal data. These requirements are ordinarily satisfied by data subjects ticking a box indicating that they have visited the Internet website. Such action is sufficient to constitute their consent to use personal information, so long as the website provides data subjects with clear information on the nature and extent of the consent to which they are agreeing.

Walters, Trakman and Zeller maintain that the processes surrounding consent have enabled monitoring systems to be developed that track consent provided by data subjects.[97] This imposes a responsibility on the organisation seeking consent to use personal information through a data retrieval, storage and transmission on, or linked by a portal to, their website. The system would require a tick box of some description to confirm that users, for example, accept all cookies, or accept specific ones. In addressing these issues, the GDPR requires the data controller to collect data only for a specified, explicit and legitimate purpose. Once that data is collected, it must not be processed further in a manner that is incompatible with the original purpose.[98] However, the GDPR provides an exemption. Personal data that is collected as part of scientific, historical or statistical purposes will be exempt from the requirements of consent. A related purpose is to ensure that the organisation collecting personal data carefully considers the actual purpose to which the data is going to be used. Interestingly, the GDPR does not separately provide for the use limitation principle; it is encompassed instead within the purpose specification principle.

The 'use limitation' principle ensures that personal data is used specifically for the purpose to which it is supposed to be used.[99] Many nation states laws, including the EU, have incorporated this principle into their data protection laws. The GDPR has a list of purposes on how personal data is to be used; it calls for active consent; and provision for consent must align within the organisation's privacy policy. The purpose is to enable data subjects to better understand how their data is being managed, used and processed.

The proposed EU Regulation on Privacy and Electronic Communications provides an exception for personal data that is used in web analytics,[100] At the time of writing this book, the proposed Regulation on Privacy and Electronic Communications had not been updated.

97 Robert Walters, Leon Trakman, Bruno Zeller, *Data Protection Law: A Comparative Analysis of Asia-Pacific and European Approaches*, Springer, 2019, 265–290.

98 Article 29 Data Protection Working Party, Opinion 06/2014 on the notion of legitimate interests of the data controller under Article 7 of Directive 95/46/EC, European Commission, http://ec.europa.eu/justice/data-protection/article-29/documentation/opinion-recommendation/files/2014/wp217_en.pdf.

99 Organization for Economic Cooperation and Development, Privacy Principles, http://oecdprivacy.org/#use.

100 European Commission, https://ec.europa.eu/digital-single-market/en/news/proposal-regulation-privacy-and-electronic-communications.

China

In the case of China, where network products and services have the function of collecting users' information, providers are required explicitly to notify their users and obtain their *consent*. If any user's personal information is involved, the provider is also required to comply with this law in regard to that use.[101] The term consent is only used once in the law. Consent is neither defined nor described in terms of how and what it might constitute.[102] Arguably, the fluid nature of the term has been developed to meet China's needs as a sovereign state with a huge population, when compared to the needs of significantly smaller populations in most other countries.

Nevertheless, it is arguable that a minimal level of consent is required from data subjects, including them being notified by a network or other service that collects both personal and non-personal information. Even so, China's Information Security Technology-Personal Information Security Specification (ISTPISS) might well provide this minimal level of consent. The ISTPISS describes how the concept of consent operates in relation to personal information,[103] in requiring that the controller receive consent prior to the collection of personal information.[104] While this requirement does not clarify the meaning of authorised consent, it does apply to the purpose, manner and frequency of its collection, along with the storage location and period for which the information will be stored. Such storage requirements, in turn, encompass the controller's data security capabilities, and further information related to the sharing, transfer and public disclosure of that data. On the other hand, when personal information is collected indirectly, there is a requirement that the provider of that information inform the recipient of the information source and ensure that its legitimacy has been confirmed by the relevant authority. Again, the processor of personal information that has been collected indirectly is required understand the nature and purpose of the authorised consent to share, transfer and make public disclosure of that information.

However, where an organisation needs to process the personal information for its own business needs, which extends beyond the scope of the initial authorised consent, the organisation will need to obtain explicit consent from the data subject. Nevertheless, there are exceptions to this, and the controller responsible for handling personal data is not required to obtain authorised consent for the collection and use of that information when it directly relates to national security, national defence,

101 Ibid.

102 Robert Walters, Marko Novak, *Cyber Security, Artificial Intelligence, and Data Protection Law*, Springer, 2021.

103 TC260 Chinese, (English version) Information Security Technology-Personal Information Security Specification, https://www.newamerica.org/cybersecurity-initiative/digichina/blog/translation-chinas-personal-information-security-specification/. Chinese version, https://www.tc260.org.cn/upload/2018-01-24/1516799764389090333.pdf.

104 Cybersecurity Law of the People's Republic of China, Order No. 53, Article 5.3–5.4. Note further exemptions also apply where the controller who is acting as a news agency to make legal news reports, or as an academic research institute to conduct statistical or academic research that is in the public interest, which has also de-identified the personal information before providing to these institutions (academic research), or specified by any other law.

public safety, public health and interest.[105] That exemption also applies to criminal investigations, prosecution, trial and a judgement of enforcement. Further exemptions apply when there is a need to safeguard major lawful rights and interests pertaining to the property of the data subject or other persons, and when it is difficult to obtain the consent from the data subject. The exemptions also extend to when the data subject voluntarily allowed the collection and transmission of their personal information to the general public. This would likely arise when individuals upload their personal information to apps and websites that are generally available to the broader public. When the personal information has been made public for example, through news reports and open government information, authorised consent is also not required. That exemption also pertains to circumstances in which it is necessary to sign and perform a contract that has been agreed to and approved by a data subject and directed at maintaining the safe and stable operation of products and services.

On the backdrop of this exemption(s), the requirement for a controller to obtain explicit consent for the collection of sensitive personal data, such as relates to debts, extends to when a data subject has provided the information freely, specifically, clearly and unequivocally.[106] Additionally, there are further requirements whereby a controller collects personal sensitive information. Prior to the collection of this information, whether voluntarily or automatically, the controller is required to inform the data subject of the core function of the products or services provided and the sensitive information that will be collected. The controller is also required to disclose the impact which may occur if the data subject refuses to provide consent. What this means is that the controller is required to disclose to data subjects the likely impact on them of the release of their data. This could entail a number of impacts of data disclosure on employment, health, marital status and potentially financial and residence data. These requirements for consent differs in relation to children who are 14 years old or younger.[107]

China's Cybersecurity Law also encourages controllers to provide choices to the data subject, to choose whether the automatic collection of their sensitive data should be allowed. In practice, the data subject would need to be fully informed as to why that information is being collected, including its function or purpose of that collection. Importantly, where the data subject rejects the collection of that sensitive data, the function of collection is to cease.[108] Yet, any request to cease the collection of data should not impede the business operations of a hospital to collect important sensitive personal information. However, a local garage that services one's car is unlikely to require, or be authorised to require, that sensitive personal information be collected and used. Similarly, a request from an administrator to receive the financial records of debtors and creditors of an entity facing insolvency would conceivably be treated as material to insolvency and restructuring proceedings. That request would ordinarily be subject to a far greater level of consent, when it is made by a newspaper specialising in gossip, scandal and intrigue.

105 Ibid.
106 Cybersecurity Law of the People's Republic of China, Order No. 53, Article 5.5.
107 Ibid., Article 5.4, 5.5, 5.6.
108 Ibid.

The United States

Consent to the use of personal data is not required in most other leading jurisdictions. Notably in the US, the FTC Act does not specifically address consent.[109] Under Section 57 b2, consent only applies to a person who produces the material, thing or transcript. The application of consent under that sub-section is fluid at best. It provides that, while in the possession of the custodian, no documentary material, tangible things, reports or answers to questions, and transcripts of oral testimony shall be available for examination by any individual, other than a duly authorised officer or employee of the Commission, without the consent of the person who produced the material, things or transcripts.[110] It provides further that, nothing in this Section is intended to:

> prevent disclosure to either House of Congress, or to any committee or subcommittee of the Congress, except that the Commission immediately shall notify the owner or provider of any such information of a request for information designated as confidential by the owner or provider.[111]

However, the FTC's Behavioural Advertising Principles suggest that website operators should obtain express consent before using sensitive consumer data, but stops short of providing further information or guidance as to its functionality and application of this guidance. For example, there is likely to be uncertainty over the responsibility of website operators to obtain consent from the CEO of a public company that is being financially probed for illicit debts, to disclose historical theft charges brought against that CEO prior to the prospective insolvency of that company.

The US HIPAA Privacy Rules,[112] on the other hand, are less certain. They generally require covered entities to obtain consent in writing from a data subject before disclosing that data. This requirement is subject to certain exceptions such as in providing information to medical service providers for the purpose of providing data on past medical treatment. Consent must generally be in writing and contain the signature of the data subject and the date.

The HIPAA Privacy Rules also provide specific statements that must be included in the consent. These include the consent of minors.[113] The HIPAA Privacy Rules elaborate by requiring that:

> the minor consents to such health care service; no other consent to such health care service is required by law, regardless of whether the consent of

109 Robert Walters, Marko Novak, *Artificial Intelligence, Cyber Security and Data Protection Law*, Springer, forthcoming.

110 Federal Trade Commission Act (15 U.S.C. §§41–58). In Robert Walters, Insolvency and Data Protection, *Business Law Review* 11, 42 (2020), 4–10.

111 Ibid.

112 United States Health Information Privacy, https://www.hhs.gov/hipaa/for-professionals/privacy/laws-regulations/combined-regulation-text/index.html.

113 Ibid., Section 3.

> another person has also been obtained; and the minor has not requested that such person be treated as the personal representative.[114]

Furthermore, on that basis:

> [t]he minor may lawfully obtain such health care service without the consent of a parent, guardian, or other person acting *in loco parentis*, and the minor, a court, or another person authorized by law can consent to such health care service;

or that a 'parent, guardian, or other person acting *in loco parentis* can assent to an agreement of confidentiality between a covered health care provider and the minor with respect to such health care service'.[115] Moreover, §164.506 provides for the uses and disclosures required to carry out treatment, payment or health care operations, and stipulates for standard permitted uses and disclosures. Except with respect to uses or disclosures that require an

> authorization under §164.508(a)(2) through (4) or that are prohibited under §164.502(a)(5)(i), a covered entity may use or disclose protected health information for treatment, payment, or health care operations as set forth in paragraph (c) of this Section, provided that such use or disclosure is consistent with other applicable requirements of this subpart.[116]

Moreover, the standard of consent for use and disclosure of that information specifies when a covered entity may obtain consent of the individual to use or disclose protected health information to carry out treatment, payment or health care. Additionally, consent shall not be effective to permit a use or disclosure of protected health information when, under §164.508, that authorisation is for the use or disclosure of protected health information for a research study.[117] Nonetheless, informed consent of the individual is to be obtained for the individual to participate in the research. However, there is no clear direction as to what informed consent constitutes. Due to the sectorial approach taken by the US, there appears to be no clear direction of how and when consent will apply.

Overview

In our view, consent, along with disclosure and the definition of personal data, is one of the most contentious concepts under the law. It is argued that while the legal frameworks of the jurisdictions compared earlier and many other countries provide for the concept of consent, it is quickly becoming unclear as to whether

114 Ibid.
115 Ibid.
116 Ibid.
117 This also extends to another authorisation for the same research study, with an authorisation for the creation or maintenance of a research database or repository, or with a consent to participate in research.

data subjects fully understand what they are consenting to. Some argue that there is consent fatigue that has crept into people's daily lives,[118] whereby we are generally consenting to our data being used without contemplating who is using it, and for what purpose. This is problematic, whether related to general data protection law in general or to cross-border insolvency particularly. This problem is accentuated in relation to insolvency and restructuring proceedings in which personal data can be used for multiple illegal purposes. These purposes vary from the abuse of the personal data of multiple parties, varying from customers to the officers of debtor and creditor entities. Their misuse includes their divergent use such as to expedite or delay insolvency, and to influence the conduct of arbitration or judicial proceedings. Importantly, if the information of data subjects is subject to such abuse or misuse, their consent to use is arguably, inadequate, misleading and at worse, deceptive.

8.6 Controller – Processor

Responsibility for the collection, storage and use of personal data in some jurisdictions,[119] but not all, has been extended to a specific group of persons. Of the jurisdictions compared, the EU has arguably the most comprehensive structure for those who are responsible within an organisation for handling personal data. The multi-layered approach taken by the EU identifies four core appointees: (1) data controller, (2) joint controllers, (3) processor and (4) data protection officer.[120] The roles of these prospective appointees vary, depending on where they are located within an organisation. The controller has the most responsibility and is accountable for organisational data protection policies and procedures. Joint Controllers can exist within an organisation; however, their roles and responsibilities must be separated. This can pose issues where there is not a clear demarcation of roles and responsibilities. Therefore, in cases of insolvency or restructuring, it would need to be clarified who is responsible for what function(s) by the administrator or liquidator. This will assist in clarifying the storage requirements under data localisation laws, and the governance of consent.

The structure of the EU requires that a data processor be appointed. This is a restricted role in which data processors can only act on the instruction of the controller.[121] The limitations in their duties include imposing confidentiality obligations on personnel who process data. They are required to provide the controller with information on request to demonstrate compliance with the GDPR. Sub-processors may be appointed by the processor; however, their powers are limited to what the processor prescribes. Nonetheless, the processor must keep records of its processing activities performed on behalf of the controller.

118 Simon Chesterman, Privacy and Our Digital Lives, https://simonchesterman.com/blog/2017/09/02/our-digital-selves/. See also Leon The Boundaries of Contract Law in Cyberspace', *Revue de Droit des Affaires Internationales* 2 (2009) 159, 198.

119 Robert Walters, Insolvency and Data Protection, *Business Law Review* 11, 42 (2020), 4–10.

120 Robert Walters, Leon Trakman, Bruno Zeller, *Data Protection Law: A Comparative Analysis of Asia-Pacific and European Approaches*, Springer, 2019, 45–81.

121 Ibid.

The GDPR requires the data controller and processor to assess the risks and implement security measures to mitigate those risks. Among those risks is the threat of data being inadequately or incorrectly processed; in enabling data users to subvert insolvency or restructuring initiatives and/or proceedings; and in causing harm to classes of data subjects, or individuals. Responsibility for non-or insufficient compliance is significant, as it allows a data subject to make a claim directly against the processor. The data controller is responsible for demonstrating compliance with principles relating to the processing of personal data, such as the purpose limitation, data accuracy and storage limitation principles.[122] Data controllers must also review and update such technical and organisational measures whenever necessary.

Australia makes an organisation in general accountable to protect personal data, rather than by appointing a particular person such as a controller or processor to assume such responsibilities. Australia also does not distinguish between a data controller and data processor. However, it does require credit rating bodies to undertake regular audits. These audits are to be carried out by an independent person to ensure that credit providers comply with certain agreements including those that relate to data protection.[123] Australian Privacy Principles (APPs) mandate open and transparent management of personal data and information. An APP entity must take reasonable steps to ensure the implementation of privacy practices and systems within the entity, to ensure compliance with the privacy law. In addition, an APP entity must take reasonable steps to protect such information from misuse, interference, loss, unauthorised access, modification or disclosure. An APP entity must also destroy or de-identify personal information which is no longer required by an entity for any purpose. APP Section 8 provides that these entities must take reasonable steps to ensure that cross-border transfers do not breach any of the obligations set out under the Privacy Act and the APPs. A breach of a privacy principle is said to occur when any activity of an entity is contrary to or inconsistent with the provisions set out under any of the APPs.[124] The requirements could apply to the data protection of sensitive information about persons who are associated with an entity's pending insolvency or reconstruction, such as in determining whether to appoint an administrator to manage that entity.

Both the HIPAA[125] and the FTC[126] in the US do not require the appointment-specific controllers or processors. However, under the HIPAA there is a requirement for an individual within an organisation to be responsible for data security. The HIPAA also requires that Business Associate Agreements[127] be established in rela-

122 Regulation 2016/679, Article 5(2).
123 Privacy Act 1988, Sections 20N (3)(b) and 20Q(2)(b).
124 Privacy Act 1988, Sections 6A, APP 1, 8, 11. Also see the Office of Australian Information Commissioner, Guidelines to securing personal information.
125 Health Insurance Portability and Accountability Act of 1996.
126 Federal Trade Commission Act 1914.
127 A covered entity's contract or other written arrangement with its business associate must contain the elements specified at 45 CFR 164.504(e).

tion to the transfer of health information.[128] In addition to the HIPAA, the HIPAA Privacy Rules apply only to covered entities' health plans, health care clearinghouses and certain health care providers. However, most health care providers and health plans do not carry out all of their health care activities and functions by themselves. Instead, they often use the services of a variety of other persons or businesses.[129] The HIPAA Privacy Rules[130] allow covered providers and health plans to disclose protected health information to these business associates. This only allows such disclosures if the providers or the health plans provide for satisfactory assurances that the business associate will use the information only for the purposes for which it was engaged by the covered entity; will safeguard the information from misuse; and will help the covered entity comply with some of the covered entity's duties under the HIPPA Privacy Rules.[131] This process under the HIPAA Rules establishes and strengthens the broad data risk management approach that is applied across the sectorial legal framework in the US. In other words, the fragmented approach has resulted in different processes to assess the risk of misuse of personal data including prior to or in the conduct of insolvency proceedings.

In a similar manner to other states, the Cyber Law of China imposes obligations on specific agencies to ensure measures are established to protect individuals, businesses and the state from cyberattacks. This is a clear demonstration that cybersecurity and data protection are continuing to move closer together in China. Thus, Article 8 imposes responsibilities on the State Council Department for telecommunications to ensure the public security[132] and other relevant organs are responsible for cybersecurity protection, supervision and management within the scope of their responsibilities, in accordance with the provisions of the Cyber Law and relevant laws and administrative regulations. The Chinese legal framework, embodied in the China's Information Security Technology-Personal Information Security Specification (ISTPISS), places an additional layer of responsibility upon organisations or departments for the appointment of controllers to manage the governance and security of personal information.[133]

Article 10 of China's ISTPISS requires a personal information controller to assume full responsibility for the security of personal information. Additionally,

128 Business Associates, 45 CFR 164.502(e), 164.504(e), 164.532(d) and (e), https://www.hhs.gov/hipaa/for-professionals/privacy/guidance/business-associates/index.html.

129 Ibid.

130 The HIPAA Privacy Rule, https://www.hhs.gov/hipaa/for-professionals/privacy/index.html.

131 Business Associates, 45 CFR 164.502(e), 164.504(e), 164.532(d) and (e), https://www.hhs.gov/hipaa/for-professionals/privacy/guidance/business-associates/index.html.

132 Ibid., Article 8, cybersecurity protection, supervision and management duties for relevant departments in people's governments at the county level or above will be determined by relevant national regulations.

133 TC260 Chinese, (English version) Information Security Technology-Personal Information Security Specification, https://www.newamerica.org/cybersecurity-initiative/digichina/blog/translation-chinas-personal-information-security-specification/. Chinese version, https://www.tc260.org.cn/upload/2018-01-24/1516799764389090333.pdf.

that controller is required to appoint a person who will be responsible for the protection of that information, where appropriate. That is, where the organisation is large enough and requires more than one person to manage and protect the governance arrangements surrounding personal information, another person can be appointed to assist. An organisation where the main business has more than 200 employees is required to establish a multi-layered approach to protect personal information through the in-house personal information officer and the department in charge of the security of that personal information. This requirement resembles the multi-layered approach adopted by the EU that requires the appointment of a controller and/or processor.[134]

Nonetheless, where an organisation processes the information of 500,000 people,[135] or expects to exceed that number as part of the processing requirements within a 12-month period, that entity is required to appoint both a controller and a processor. Apart from overseeing the security of this information/data, the minimum protection extends to, but not limited to, coordinating personal information security work. The controller and processor are also required to formulate, issue and implement regular updates to internal privacy policies and relevant procedures.

Reliance on such multi-layered controls exercised by controllers provide important undertakings, not only by entities facing financial stress, but in averting control violations before then. As such, the adoption of these multi-layered controls increases the protective shield around the entity. It provides more transparent safeguards for itself, as well as for officers, employees, creditors, debtors and customers. It also demonstrates, not limited to insolvency and restructuring, how an entity protects personal and commercial data in the conduct of its business operations and in compliance with data protection laws and regulations.

This requirement for self- and co-regulation under Chinese Law is reflected in comparable data protection models, including across industries such as primary industries, and noticeably in the motor vehicle and airline sectors. As part of China's regulatory approach, the controller or processor is encouraged to undertake impact assessments, training, and examine the extent of security over personal information before a product is launched and implement audits to ensure continuing protection. The security of cyber networks is also of paramount importance to states globally, as for China.[136] Article 14 reflects this focus on the security of cyber systems. It provides that any individual or entity has the right to report conduct that endangers security, through cybersecurity and informatisation systems, telecommunications and public security. Additionally, departments receiving these reports shall promptly process them in accordance with law; where matters do not fall within the responsibilities of that department, that department shall promptly transfer them to the department that is empowered to handle them.

134 Ibid.

135 Ibid., 10. Requirements for Organizational Management, and 10.1 Designating Responsible Departments and Personnel. China's Personal Information Security Specification.

136 Robert Walters, Marko Novak, *Artificial Intelligence, Cyber Security and Data Protection Law*, Springer, forthcoming.

8.7 Data Portability

Data portability is not new, with individuals long being able to take and use their telephones whether landlines or mobiles, in multiple locations.[137] Such data portability is germane to insolvency and reconstruction proceedings because of the multiple jurisdictions in which cross-border proceedings are often conducted and/or in which parties to such proceedings are located. Data portability has functional benefits in data transmission beyond face-to-face and oral communications. It enables data subjects to request their personal data from a data controller within an organisation to transfer that personal data to another organisation. It allows both them and controllers to receive and transmit that data between themselves, but also to multiple third parties, such as data consumers.[138] However, it must be noted that data portability is a concept that benefits data subjects, rather than organisations collecting that data. Yet, it is not widely accepted in all national legal systems. For example, at the point of sale and purchase of a good or product, or some time after, a data subject can request that their personal data be transferred to another entity. It is one way of optimising the consolidation of data into a single organisation, while making it more readily available, while reducing the potential monopolisation of the data. Problematic though is the legal obligation of a controller not to engage in data portability, without the approval of the data subject.[139] In effect, data portability extends beyond the technical ability to transmit/transfer personal data. The right to data portability empowers data subjects to exercise control and have greater choice over how their data is managed. It also establishes a process through which data subjects are better informed about their data usage.[140] Similar to the concepts discussed already, consideration will be required as to whether the local laws of data portability have an impact or otherwise on a cross-border insolvency or restructure. If so, it will need to be understood as to what data has been collected and at the request of the data subject, has been deposited by the collecting entity to another entity. In issue is the security of personal data, including the safety of persons engaged in trans-border dealings in states beyond the state of disclosure in which access to such personal information can have a massive impact. The following sub-sections will illustrate how data portability is managed within Australia, EU, China and United States.

Australia

Australia's Privacy Act (1988) does not provide directly for data portability. However, in July 2020, an amendment to the Competition and Consumer Act 2010

137 A. Erkmen, M. N. Aydın, *A Comparison Between Right to Data Portability and United Kingdom's Midata Initiative*, proceedings of the 5th International Management Information Systems Conference, Ankara, 17–19 October 2019.

138 Lachlan Urquart, Neelima Sailaja, Derek McAuley, Realising the Right to Data Portability for the Domestic Internet of Things, *Personal and Ubiquitous Computing* 22 (2018), 317–322.

139 Ibid.

140 Ibid.

introduced a sharing facility across the banking sector.[141] At this stage, the limited and narrow scope has been concentrated in the banking sector, with other sectors such as telecommunications and energy soon to follow. This limited scope of data portability in Australia will not affect general cross-border insolvency or restructuring. On the other hand, the scope of data portability relates to personal information provided by a consumer and relates directly to a product. It enables the data subject to change suppliers with ease, and/or switch products that assists the consumer by reducing costs in choosing to change providers. The socialised economic benefits, beyond the individual consumer, is in facilitating efficiencies in the market. Those efficiencies extend to efficient markets in cross-border trade and investment, and to resolving debt through insolvency and restructuring proceedings within those markets.

European Union

The right to data portability (RtDP) was introduced into the EU through Article 20 of the GDPR.[142] This innovative concept of data portability has a much wider application in the EU than that of its Australian counterpart.[143] Article 20 of the GDPR provides that the:

> data subject shall have the right to receive the personal data concerning him or her, which he or she has provided to a controller, in a structured, commonly used and machine-readable format and have the right to transmit those data to another controller without hindrance from the controller to which the personal data have been provided, where the processing is based on consent pursuant to point (a) of Article 6(1) or point (a) of Article 9(2) or on a contract pursuant to point (b) of Article 6(1); and the processing is carried out by automated means. In exercising his or her right to data portability pursuant to paragraph 1, the data subject shall have the right to have the personal data transmitted directly from one controller to another, where technically feasible.[144]

Of the states compared in this chapter, the EU arguably has adopted the most comprehensive approach to data portability. Article 20 of the GDPR provides data subjects with the ability to transfer personal data among data controllers. However, that ability has an impact beyond data protection. It encourages competition and innovation in data markets. It also facilitates the reuse of personal data that private companies hold

141 Office of the Australian Chief Information Officer, https://www.oaic.gov.au/consumer-data-right/cdr-privacy-safeguard-guidelines/.

142 Regulation (EU) 2016/679 of the European Parliament and of the Council of 27 April 2016 on the protection of natural persons with regard to the processing of personal data and on the free movement of such data, and repealing Directive 95/46/EC (General Data Protection Regulation) (Text with EEA relevance) Official Journal of the European Union, 119.

143 Inge Graef, Martin Husovec, Nazdhda Purtova, Data Portability and Data Control: Lessons for an Emerging Concept in EU Law, *German Law Journal* 19, 6 (2018), 1359–1398.

144 Regulation (EU) 2016/679, Article 20.

by establishing a 'general-purpose control mechanism of horizontal application'.[145] That is, the horizontal application of data portability enables data subjects to transfer their personal data sideways to other organisations. Graef et al. express the view that Article 20 is agnostic about the type of use that follows from the ported data and its further diffusion. Their opinion is that, rather than data portability fitting well within the current EU legal framework, it fails to accommodate data protection laws generally. They do agree, however, that as a legal tool, data portability does stimulate competition and innovation in an ever-more innovative digital economy. Illustratively, Article 20 of the GPDR is heralded as a new regulatory tool in EU law that aims to stimulate competition and innovation in data-driven markets.

A significant challenge identified by Graef et al., is how the EU's data portability right clashes with other rights such as intellectual property, copyright, trade secrets and database rights. The authors argue that the right to data portability may conflict with other rights , and therefore, there is a level of uncertainty of how to deal with personal data that has been ported by a data subject from one entity to another that is subject to insolvency or restructuring. Such a challenge is particularly prevalent prior to or during insolvency proceedings, when data subjects invoke personal data rights to inhibit the porting of personal data by a financially stressed entity or its creditors. Despite these uncertainties, the right to data portability itself is already being replicated in other nation states, such as Australia, for instance through consumer protection law.[146] It is uncertain how the EU model will affect cross-border insolvency and restructuring. However, despite the uncertainty not being fully resolved, Member States will need to identify what personal data has been transferred, the destination of that data and whether its portability has future implications for insolvency or restructuring proceedings.

China

Under China's current laws, there is no specific right to data portability. The result is that, in cross-border insolvency or restructure proceedings, personal data is treated very differently in China compared to other nation states including the EU. This is due in part to the fact that China construes individual human rights protections somewhat differently to their treatment historically in Western liberal states. In particular, China's Cybersecurity Laws largely regulate data systems and infrastructures operated by data providers to protect business entities, rather than to directly protect the individual rights of data subjects. This diverges from Western liberal states that champion, albeit inconsistently, the personal rights of the individual, the data subject. The consequence is that protecting the interests of an entity engaged in insolvency or restructuring is treated as paramount in China. The consequences in protecting the rights of the individual right-holder from data abuse is a central, but not exclusive, preoccupation of regulators in Western liberal states.

145 Inge Graef, Martin Husovec, Nazdhda Purtova, Data Portability and Data Control: Lessons for an Emerging Concept in EU Law, *German Law Journal* 19, 6 (2018), 1359–1398.

146 Ibid., 1359–1398.

United States

The US's legal regime for data protection is sectorial and does not provide for data portability. On the one hand, the State of California introduced the Consumer Privacy Act (CCPA) in 2018 in which it recognised data portability. On the other hand, the recognition of data portability in particular states, such as California, does not resolve the predicament of having to deal with personal data under the right of data portability. Therefore, the legal regulation of cross-border insolvency and restructuring in regard to data portability is not well developed in the US to date.

Overview

The fragmented approach taken by different states towards data portability, as highlighted earlier, is very evident when comparing the rights and controls that are afforded to data subjects. Some jurisdictions, in which the EU is the most significant, have provided for an extensive data portability right. As highlighted, data subjects can sometimes exercise rights to data portability, such as by requesting a debtor company that has collected their personal data transfer, to transfer it to another entity. This is expressly provided for in Article 20 of the GDPR.[147]

However, the right to data portability raises several interrelated problems. Firstly, not all states, even those with data protection laws, recognise the concept of data portability. Secondly, it is arguable that, after data subjects have exercised the right to transfer their data, they can demand that the entity to which they transferred their data, completely delete it. This is inferred from their request or demand for 'data erasure'. Thirdly, given that the right to data portability varies across jurisdictions, uncertainty arises over the enforceability of that right, given that state laws construe it differently.

In our view, this divergence in laws regulating (and not regulating) data portability is especially problematic, given that personal data that is portable can be transmitted globally. Problems also arise in delimiting the right to data portability in relation to insolvency. Specifically, in what respect is the transfer of personal data arising from corporate insolvency likely to be exacerbated? This concern relates not only to differences in domestic laws that govern consent to the sale of data. It also encompasses protecting the right of data subjects to request transfer of their data in anticipation of impending or actual insolvency. The question and its sequela are likely to grow in significance as corporate insolvencies expand in an era of global instability. They are also likely to expand as uniformity in data protection law becomes ever more pressing in insolvency and restructuring sectors that transcend national boundaries.

This question and the concerns arising in attempting to answer it, is attenuated by the fact that many nation states have opted not to provide for a right to data portability. The implications of laws opting out of regulating data portability for cross-border insolvency and restructuring cannot be fully known or understood at

147 Ronny Hauck, Personal Data in Insolvency Proceedings: The Interface Between the New General Data Protection Regulation and (German) Insolvency Law, *European Company and Financial Law Review* (2019), 724–745.

this precipitous time. Wider research on divergence, not only over data portability laws, but also over the reasons for those differences, how they are construed in fact, and whether they can be reconciled, is urgently needed. What is demonstrable at this stage is that, where the right to data portability exists and a company has branches and offices in third countries, the cycle of data movement, use and storage will need to be considered, at a minimum, within an insolvency or restructure proceeding. The practitioner relying on data portability will need to confirm what, if any, data portability laws exist. Failing to do so could lead to escalating breaches of data protection laws, with devastating impact upon the formation and sustenance of new entities that are attempting to take over the existing data usage and storage. These new entities include, in particular, restructured companies that were subject to mergers and acquisitions rather than outright insolvency.

8.8 Conclusion

The commercial value of personal data has grown beyond all expectations over the last decade. That value is likely to rise exponentially in an ever more vibrant digital economy that extends the boundaries of innovation in technology. The expansion of personal data impacts upon both the organisation and reorganisation of multiple entities within and across nation states, varying from health, education, transport, infrastructure, technology, automated vehicles, health, education, to national security and defense.

The challenges faced in managing personal data are both formidable and complex. There is as yet a lack of international law norms or principles governing the management of personal data in commercial activities, including cross-border insolvency. States and regions like the EU that manage personal data have diverged significantly from one another in doing so, as is demonstrated by the lack of comprehensive and consistent data protection laws, not only internationally, but often not nationally either. These deficiencies include states that have not enacted any data protection laws, either because they do not intend to do so, or the need has not yet grown sufficiently formidable for them engage in such regulation. Other states have engaged in such regulation, but only partially and often incrementally. Yet other states have engaged in large-scale data protection initiatives, the EU being the clearest example, but without adequate evidence that other states have, or will, follow suit.

These differences in regulating, or not regulating, personal data across states and regions are often culturally informed, such as in divergent cultural responses to data privacy over the Internet. They are economically informed, too, such as according to the stage of economic and social development of the discrete state, along with the stratified class-based systems, religious divergence and disparate economic sustainability. It is the level of privacy afforded by different jurisdictions that determines what, if any, data protection laws exist, how they have eventuated and evolved, and how they are likely to evolve in the immediate, intermediate and long-term future. These multiple socio-economic, religious and cultural disparities across and within nation states also account, to some degree, for the reluctance of some states to provide for data protection on grounds of privacy. In issue, therefore, are the reasons for states adopting disparate conceptions of, and approaches to data protection.

The EU views the protection of personal data (sometimes conceived as privacy) over the Internet as a fundamental human and social right. This view is demonstrated by the GDPR placing privacy protection at the forefront of the EU's policy framework. Conversely, other states have highlighted the need to protect a countervailing right to trade in data, as in other tradable commodities. They have treated it as an economic right that, for some like the US, is constitutionally enshrined, or otherwise legally protected, but prioritised over data protection in both cases. In issue, therefore, is not only the socio-economic and cultural reasons for states to regulate the protection of personal data differently. In issue, too, is the degree to which they are willing to entertain data protection in relation to the trade in data in general and in specific contexts, such as in particular sectors of trade and investment. Australia has adopted a middle course. It has promoted the idea of balancing the need for trade in personal data, while providing a level of protection to the subjects of that data. The US and China have each adopted their own distinctive approach. While the US has taken a largely sectorial approach, China has focused on regulating the infrastructure that includes personal data, rather than the users of personal data itself. This divergence between the two largest trading nations in the world, in and of itself, poses challenges to the management of personal data during an insolvency or restructure. That challenge is more complex than states face in managing personal data domestically, as distinct from in cross-border dealings of their otherwise domestic entities.

More problematic though, is how the laws of states studied adopt different concepts and principles in defining personal data, consent and in regulating the appointment of persons to control the use of that data. This chapter has demonstrated how the laws in the states studied define personal data differently. While they concur generally that personal data includes a person's name, residential address and age, they diverge over the identity and rights of that person. Some jurisdictions define personal data according to physical attributes, such as DNA and biometrics notably through eye and facial recognition technologies. They include health data in personal data, which is generally accorded a high level of protection in the jurisdictions studied, notably the EU, while less specifically so in China. States also diverge in their identification of sensitive personal data, such as according to the vulnerability of persons, such as minors and conditions of health such as are associated with COVID-19.

That said, the general data used in cross-border trade and investment is unlikely to include health data or sensitive data. It is also likely to be consumer driven when individuals make transactions either online or in person such as at a retail shop. Vigilance in the protection of personal data will be an important pathway in the transmission and use of personal data commercially, not least of all in entities that publish personal data to maintain their solvency, or by opponents who seek to expose deficiencies, irregularities or abuses in entity management. Such vigilance in protection is likely to grow as insolvency and restructuring of entities in financial difficulties becomes an indelible part of the global vista. In the immediate past, vigilance in protecting personal data was subject to the crucible of health care, such as when a private health provider faced the risk of insolvency or the need to restructure its business. That is likely to be a point of commencement into the regulation of personal data in cross-border insolvency and restructuring more pervasively.

What is central to the collection and use of personal data, now and in the future, is the level of consent that corporate entities are required to secure from data subjects. That requirement is necessarily coupled with establishing a sustainable contractual and legal framework for the exercise of such collection and usages practices. That framework is likely to be tested according to the performance of those who control access to it, and who authorise and manage the processing of personal data. What is currently lacking is the imperfect symmetry across states engaged in cross-border data regulation, including in relation to insolvency and restructuring frameworks. What is missing are deliberate and sustained attempts to establish a uniform legal structure in which the consent of data subjects is secured, and unavoidable differences across nation states are reconciled. The fact that the EU requires a high level of consent for personal data to be collected and transferred between organisations is a worthy benchmark. Yet it is one to which many other states do not, and will not, aspire. On the one hand, it focuses on protecting the social rights of subjects in the public interest, which is likely to be a continuing concern for US lawmakers who focus on protecting user rights in data. On the other hand, EU law is unlikely to satisfy the requirements of China in its policy orientation around the continuing regulation of entities, rather than protecting individuals whose personal data is impacted by the conduct of such entities. The position of each mega-power is explicable. The US is long preoccupied with its Constitutional protection of individual rights operating in free markets, including the alleged right to market data freely. China is preoccupied with establishing manageable regulations in recognition of the difficulty of regulating its massive population or those entities that might infract upon the rights of individuals within that population.

Less than ideal are these inconsistent developments in data protection, and the virtual lack of developed protections in jurisdictions that have not addressed the nature and extent of consent required use the personal information of data subjects. This hiatus in law is especially evident in attempts to protect personal data in cases of insolvency. Still, the EU has, through the Insolvency Recast Regulation,[148] demonstrated that data protection is a fundamental component of insolvency.[149] It arguably has established a functional framework for greater cooperation and

148 Regulation (EU) 2015/848 of the European Parliament and of the Council of 20 May 2015 on insolvency proceedings (recast), Official Journal of the European Union L 141/19, Preamble 83, Article 78–83. In Robert Walters, Insolvency and Data Protection, *Business Law Review* 11, 42 (2020).

149 Ibid., 83. This Regulation respects the fundamental rights and observes the principles recognised in the Charter of Fundamental Rights of the European Union. In particular, this Regulation seeks to promote the application of Articles 8, 17 and 47 concerning, respectively, the protection of personal data, the right to property and the right to an effective remedy and to a fair trial. (84) Directive 95/46/EC of the European Parliament and of the Council (2) and Regulation (EC) No 45/2001 of the European Parliament and of the Council (3) apply to the processing of personal data within the framework of this Regulation. See also Bob Wessels, *Data protection under the Insolvency Regulation (Recast)*, 2018, https://leidenlawblog.nl/articles/data-protection-under-the-insolvency-regulation.

communication in cross-border insolvency proceedings. Arguably, its framework reinforces the UNCITRAL Model Law on Insolvency and Restructuring. The EU's approach towards data protection also supports a more global approach to data protection that focuses on securing cooperation among states in developing uniform cross-border insolvency laws. The EU's Member States have demonstrated such cooperation, in adopting and implementing GDPR data protection laws. This includes their implementation of technical compliance measures, such as to ensure the security of personal data processed in national insolvency registers under Article 24 of the GDPR.[150] In addition, the EU grants powers to the EU Commission to regulate the use of personal data, not unlike data controller who are appointed within commercial entities to control the collection, processing, storage and sale of personal data. Moreover, Article 81 requires the EU Commission to assume responsibilities for such information, so long as it does not prejudice the information to be given to data subjects in accordance with Articles 11 and 12 of Regulation (EC) No 45/2001.[151]

Notwithstanding its advances as a prototype platform for regulating the protection of personal data, the GDPR does not provide an adequately comprehensive framework for identifying the consent of data subjects to the use of their personal data. What remains unclear, not limited to the EU's GDPR, is how consent to the sale or other use of personal data is expressed within the regulations of discrete states.[152] It is unclear whether consent provided by a data subject automatically allows a company to trade multiple times in that data; whether the second purchasing company has approval to sell that data to a third party; and when personal data can be down-streamed to particular Internet users or users in general. It is also unclear as to how to regulate both cross-streamed and down-streamed personal data for purposes other than sale. Pertinently, the misuse of personal data can have a massive impact upon corporate insolvency and restructuring laws, given the number of persons whose data can be abused, the disparate functions these persons play in relation to that entity, and the devastating impact that such disclosures can have upon the continuing operations of or termination of that entity. The personal harm, first and last, is to the individual data subject. The collateral harm is to those with whom that individual is associated, such as the entity as the employer, and the supplier, buyer or in some other related individual or entity. Data protection law should never lose sight of its first target, the individuals who are subject to harm arising from the abuse of their personal data. However, the commercial context in which their personal data is at risk is also material. It resides in the nature and effect

150 Ibid., Article 78.

151 Regulation (EC) No 45/2001 of the European Parliament and of the Council of 18 December 2000 on the protection of individuals with regard to the processing of personal data by the Community institutions and bodies and on the free movement of such data, Official Journal of the European Union, 8, 12 January 2001.

152 Robert Walters, Leon Trakman, Bruno Zeller, *Data Protection Law: A Comparative Analysis of Asia-Pacific and European Approaches*, Springer, 2019, 265–290.

of harm of data disclosure upon them and to the commercial activities and persons with which they are associated.

In requiring that corporate entities secure informed consent to use personal data in order to cross-stream or down-stream that data, it will be important to demonstrate how the first corporate entity informed the data subject of the nature and extent of the consent sought. It will be similarly significant to demonstrate the contractual and legal consequences arising from that entity using that data in both commercial and consumer transactions.[153] For the insolvency practitioner dealing with corporate clients specifically, it will be necessary to ensure that corporate records are maintained over what and how such consent was acquired within the regulatory framework surrounding that corporate entity. It will also sometimes entail securing records of other entities that are associated with it, such as a subsidiary or holding company.

The varied approach adopted by states in the localisation and portability of personal data will also need to be reconciled in cross-border insolvency or restructuring proceedings. That will require careful consideration of what and where personal data has been transferred, and the nature and extent to which the data subject consented or limited consent to that transfer. Typically, when data subjects have requested their personal data to be transferred from entity A to entity B, and unknown to them, entity B is a subsidiary of entity A and that entity A is in financial stress, the insolvency and/or restructuring practitioner will need to be fully informed about the nature of that intended transfer.

Comparably and at a macro-level, how nation states design their data localisation laws in response to domestic sovereigntist policies will impact on cross-border insolvency and restructuring. As highlighted in this chapter, states will do so, not wholly in response to policies focused on sovereignty by disassociation with other states, but by policies directed at competition with each, or one another. Finally, the divergent and rapidly changing legal landscape of data protection laws, and the lack of cross-border data flow and data adequacy regulation will pose challenges in cross-border insolvency and restructuring. The brief comparison demonstrated the fragmented approach will require insolvency and restructuring practitioners to understand and consider multiple jurisdictions data laws.

153 Ibid.

9

ARTIFICIAL INTELLIGENCE AND INSOLVENCY

Technology will change the way the law is developed, administered and applied. This chapter will explore some of the developments in artificial intelligence (AI) technology that are assisting the law in stabilising the economy and financial system. The chapter will identify how technology is being used by the financial sector to predict a company's level of financial stress. Technology increasingly enables creditors to undertake a risk assessment to predict, with an ever-higher level of accuracy, whether an entity is likely to become insolvent. It has significantly progressed, such as in enabling contracts to be developed and administered online.

Viewed positively, technological innovation can dilute subjective factors that influence the administration, application and practice of the law, albeit without eliminating subjectivity in devising and applying technology to law. Viewed negatively, obstacles arise in reconciling the application of technology to law with the diffuse attributes and functions of law, such as the diffuse attributes and functions of judicial decision-making. Those obstacles are exacerbated in legal systems in which regulatory responses to the development and use of AI are deficient or absent. This chapter highlights this lack of regulation, and the need for an urgent and coherent response to it, both nationally and internationally and in cross-border financial regulation.

9.1 Introduction

Technology is changing every aspect of our daily lives, including the functioning of the legal profession. Put another way, the insolvency profession, and the 'legal profession more broadly is currently experiencing digital disruption because of a growing reliance upon technologies such as smartphones, cloud computing, data

DOI: 10.4324/9781003312024-3

analytics and social media'.[1] Various areas across the legal profession have been experimenting with a range of technology to undertake traditional legal tasks, such as the burgeoning eDiscovery[2] software that has emerged over the past five years. This technology alone is able to undertake specific word searches of large quantities of documents in a very short period of time. The ability of such technologies to cross professional boundaries means that professionals are no longer considered to be the sole custodians of specialist, complex knowledge and training in law and finance. Today, the insolvency profession's stranglehold on specialist knowledge has been diluted and will continue to be so, as new technologies, such as machine learning, defined generally as artificial intelligence (AI), persist in their growth.[3]

AI has also begun to transform the legal profession, with experts from around the world now working to improve greater access to justice and legal services.[4] It is beginning to resolve legal disputes, through AI-powered judges and AI robots expected to be used in day-to-day legal decision-making.[5] In the contemporary world and up until three decades ago, individuals rarely thought about using word processing software and printers to produce high-quality documentation. 'These facilities were rare as recently as the 1980s and only came into widespread use in the 1990s'.[6] Most people today, at work and at home, have immediate access to technologies that can support the production of high-quality printed material. A succession of technological innovations, such as 'large-volume photocopiers, transferable word processing files, high-capacity printers, and Internet-based file transfer, have changed the way we produce and distribute documents'.[7] This chapter will extend discussion in this book to the onset of modern technology and its potential impact on the insolvency and restructuring profession and upon professionals within it.

Critical to these changes is an Internet that has grown through 'websites, social networks, and online publishing [that] have generated more source material than before, most of which, once again, is impenetrable to the non-specialist'.[8] This alone renders cross-border insolvency and restructuring legal issues more visible through an Internet that is publicly accessible. Notwithstanding its complexity, national laws on cross-border insolvency and restructuring can ordinarily be found

1 Jennifer Dickfos, AI and the Insolvency Profession: The State of Play, *Insolvency Law Journal* 26, 172 (2018), 1.
2 eDiscovery solutions in Microsoft 365, https://docs.microsoft.com/en-us/microsoft-365/compliance/ediscovery?view=o365-worldwide.
3 Jennifer Dickfos, AI and the Insolvency Profession: The State of Play, *Insolvency Law Journal* 26, 172 (2018), 1.
4 Marco Kauffman, Marcelo Soares, AI in Legal Services: New Trends in AI-Enabled Legal Services, *Society of Clinical Anatomists* 14 (2020), 223.
5 Ibid.
6 Jennifer Dickfos, AI and the Insolvency Profession: The State of Play, *Insolvency Law Journal* 26, 172 (2018), 1.
7 Ibid., 1.
8 Ibid., 148–151.

online. However, such legal information is often fragmented and difficult to navigate. Its online articulation, emanating from disparate legal sources and structures and expressed in different languages, complicates its understanding and interpretation. As Jennifer Dickfos opines:

> even though lay users can undertake basic searches online – in medicine, law, architecture, accounting, and elsewhere – the fruits of this work tend to be collections of potentially relevant but technically complex documents or web pages rather than answers to problems or distilled advice.[9]

Today, what has emerged is how AI is performing a number of functions in and across the legal profession. Daniel Fagella highlights how AI is being used to perform due diligence, predictions, analytics, document automation, intellectual property and billing.[10] There are a number of technology and software systems that support these postulations. However, it is out of scope to discuss these technologies.

Central to the study of the technological developments in AI and its influence on legal practice and financial management has been a series of studies conducted by Daniel Katz. Katz found that the challenges posed by predictive tools are due to the complexity of legal systems and how they these tools can be adopted to be applied to law.[11] Katz notes that the precise level of complexity varies between AI systems and infrastructure,[12] or as he puts it, across sub-domains. As a result, shifts in the ongoing accuracy of predictive tools is likely to be questioned by the judiciary. Nonetheless, AI that provides only approximate estimates of the financial position of an entity will go some way to determine how to proceed with an insolvency or restructure of that entity. More recently in 2012, Katz, Bommarito and Blackman concluded a study of AI and machine learning for predicting decisions of the Supreme Court of the United States.[13] The authors identified the predictions over

9 Ibid.

10 Daniel Fagella, *AI in Law and Legal Practice – A Comprehensive View of 35 Current Applications*, The AI Research and Advisory Company, 2020, https://emerj.com/ai-sector-overviews/ai-in-law-legal-practice-current-applications/. Fagella stresses the manner in and extent to which AI informs and influences commercial and legal decision-making and lead to greater degrees of predicative accuracy. His illustrations include the recognition and assessment of these factors:

> Due diligence – Litigators perform due diligence with the help of AI tools to uncover background information. We've decided to include contract review, legal research and electronic discovery in this Section. Prediction technology – An AI software generates results that forecast litigation outcome. Legal analytics – Lawyers can use data points from past case law, win/loss rates and a judge's history to be used for trends and patterns. Document automation – Law firms use software templates to create filled out documents based on data input. Intellectual property – AI tools guide lawyers in analyzing large IP portfolios and drawing insights from the content. Electronic billing – Lawyers' billable hours are computed automatically.

11 Daniel Katz, Quantitative Legal Prediction-or-How I Learned to Stop Worrying and Start Preparing for the Data-Driven Future of the Legal Services Industry, *Emory Law Journal* 62 (2013), 962.

12 Ibid.

13 Daniel Katz, Michael Bommarito, Josh Blackman, A General Approach for Predicting the Behaviour of the Supreme Court of the United States, *PLoS One* (2017), 14, https://doi.org/10.1371/journal.pone.0174698.

nearly two centuries, and achieved a 70.2% accuracy at the case outcome level and 71.9% accuracy of decisions by specific judges.[14] Among other things, the authors believe that such improvements in modelling should be of interest to court observers, litigants, citizens and markets.[15] Arguably, it is the ongoing advancements in AI technology in capturing and interpreting data where the accuracy will improve over time. That said, to obtain 100% accuracy is some way off, if attainable at all.

Nonetheless, and on the backdrop of this, Dickfos proposes three ways in which to predict the nature impact of technology in the future. First, even if there are no advances in technology in the next decade as fundamental as the personal computer, the web and social media, if the 'community follows existing and emerging technologies to their probable and much greater exploitation, this alone takes us into a very different world'.[16] The mistake, Dickfos maintains, is to presume that, because we cannot foresee any revolutionary changes, we should not extrapolate from what we already have changed. If we work within our current frame of reference and in the context of technologies that seem steadily to be taking hold, then we are more likely to have a sense of where we are going, than if we choose to ignore the future altogether. Dickfos is of the view that we may well miss the next revolution, but at least we will keep pace with the evolution in current technologies.[17] Should that be the case, the challenges facing the legal profession and the broader commercial community may become even more complex. On the one side, there will be the opportunity for those companies that respond rapidly to new technology to embrace and adopt whatever the new systems might be that will build greater efficiencies into their operations. On the other side, new developments will go unnoticed and there will be a failure of entities to recognise and adopt a new technology. The resulting effect is that the technology, when rolled out by a few, will gain a monopoly in the market. This will possibly be unavoidable, but any monopoly will only inhibit the benefits of technology use in cross-border insolvency-restructuring.

Secondly, 'people think that it is important to seek to identify overall direction and general trends in technology'.[18] Dickfos points out further that, beyond this search for trends in AI, we can expect that many Internet-based systems that have not yet been invented, will change our lives over, say, the next 20 years. However, it is a mistake to assume that predictive technology is limited to certain sectors. For example, it is 'increasingly being used in policing as a tool of early warning and intervention'[19] in crime. The least likely 'future for technology is that our systems

14 Ibid.

15 Ibid., 14–15.

16 Jennifer Dickfos, AI and the Insolvency Profession: The State of Play, *Insolvency Law Journal* 26, 172 (2018), 154–155.

17 Ibid.

18 Ibid.

19 Andrew Ferguson, *The Rise of Big Data Policing, Surveillance, Race and the Future of Law Enforcement*, New York University Press, 2017, 149. See also Tero Karppi, 'The Computer Said So': On the Ethics, Effectiveness, and Cultural Techniques of Predictive Policing, *Social, Media, Society, Sage Journals* (2018), 1–3.

will stay as they are today'.[20] Yet, those who dismiss attempts to predict the future often fall into the trap of assuming there will be no change. Making qualified predictions of the kind we have in mind is like having the headlights on. Dickfos responds that most people accept that there is much that we still cannot see.[21]

Thirdly, predictive technology can, and has begun to be used by the financial sector to determine what companies are experiencing financial stress and the possibility of falling into insolvency. More specifically, predicting bankruptcy of companies has been a hot subject of focus for many economists. It now pervades the legal landscape over which states are beginning to use predictive technology for use in regulating insolvency matters.

On the other hand, Daniel Ogachi et al. make the point that 'bankruptcy prediction is a technique of forecasting and projecting on company financial distress of both public and firms'.[22] The purpose of predicting bankruptcy is fundamental in assessing the financial condition of a company and the prospects in its continuing operation. It has wider commercial and economic benefits to nation states. That is, having these predictive tools enables governments, regulators and financial institutions to advise entities on their financial positions. It further enables governments and regulators to develop and respond rapidly to changes in the economy through law reform and regulatory policy change. Corporate bankruptcy prediction is also salient economically, as the financial soundness of a company is vital to the various actors and participants in the relevant business cycle.[23] Arguably, enabling the prediction of corporate bankruptcy also has a political dimension by enabling governments and regulators to manage, where they can, economic fallout through financial or regulatory intervention. Such regulatory intervention was evident in many states as the pandemic took hold and governments responded by providing financial stimuli and legislative reforms to stabilise the broader economy.

Dickfos further points out, however, that the third category of prediction allows technologies to be incorporated into regulatory systems, including in the insolvency's profession's endorsement of its use in insolvency proceedings. An example highlighted by Dickfos has been AI innovations providing for the participation of creditors in insolvency proceedings in Australia. This is reflected in the adoption of the Insolvency Law Reform Act 2016 (Cth) and the related Insolvency Practice Rules (Corporations) 2016 (Cth) and Insolvency Practice Rules (Bankruptcy) 2016 (Cth) (the Rules).[24] Section 75–75 of the Insolvency Practice Rules provide for participation in creditors' meetings by electronic means, contrasted with

20 Jennifer Dickfos, AI and the Insolvency Profession: The State of Play, *Insolvency Law Journal* 26, 172 (2018), 173.

21 Ibid.

22 Daniel Ogachi, Richard Ndege, Peter Gaturu, Zeman Zoltan, Corporate Bankruptcy Prediction Model, a Special Focus on Listed Companies in Kenya, *Journal of Risk Management and Financial Management* (2020), 1.

23 Ibid.

24 Ibid.

Sections 5–35 that require notice of electronic facilities for meetings to be held. Today, the insolvency profession in Australia has legal backing to use predictive technology for collating information to provide creditors, for managing an insolvency. In this way, predictive technology in being used to manage uncertainty,[25] play a fundamental role in social and economic coordination by providing a more, or less, coherent anticipation of the future.[26]

In anticipating such systems and in proposing a technologically innovative method of operating, Daniel Ogachi et al. note that technology systems have been adopted in some professions but not others, and argue for their wider adoption.[27] In support of their wider use, technologies are evolving in ways never before imagined, such as to forecast and predict how companies are tracking financially. The authors make the point that bankruptcy prediction is of great importance to all participants in proceedings including the insurance market, financial markets, governments, regulators, policyholders, agents and business community.[28] Assessing or predicting the solvency of a company will enable these groups to develop risk management strategies to minimise the impact of insolvency or restructuring on the broader economy.

Therefore, a key question is what can this new technology predict? More specifically, how would such technology impact on cross-border insolvency? There is no doubt, in our view, that being able to have technology predict financially stressed entities comes with many benefits. It could prevent significant economic shocks, nationally and internationally. However, to achieve such predictive ends, AI predictive systems need to be internationalised. Achieving that end, in and of itself, will be challenging when jurisdictions operate at different levels of technology. Some are more sophisticated and willing to accept that technology significantly drives their economies. Other jurisdictions take a more cautious approach.

9.2 Predicting Financial Stress – Insolvency

Predicting financial stress, whether in and across banks and financial institutions, or, in other trade and investment sectors is not new. Put another way, financial distress forecasting is basically a dichotomous decision, either being financially distressed or not.[29] Most statistical and artificial intelligence methods estimate the probability of financial distress, and if this probability is greater than the cut-off value, then

25 Jens Beckert, Richard Bronk, *Uncertain Futures: Imaginaries, Narratives, and Calculation in the Economy*, Oxford University Press, 2018, 85.

26 Ibid.

27 Daniel Ogachi, Richard Ndege, Peter Gaturu, Zeman Zoltan, Corporate Bankruptcy Prediction Model, a Special Focus on Listed Companies in Kenya, *Journal of Risk Management and Financial Management* (2020), 1.

28 Ibid.

29 Jae Kwon Bae, Predicting Financial Distress of the South Korean Manufacturing Industries, *Expert Systems with Applications* 39, 10 (2021), 9159–9165.

the prediction is financial distress.[30] However, and similar to legal developments to standardise transnational commercial laws, predictive tools are not new. They have been developed and used, albeit in different forms, since the early 1900s.

Since the development of the first predictive models in the 1930s, hundreds of bankruptcy prediction models have been introduced worldwide.[31] Single country studies tend to play a significant role in the research of bankruptcy prediction. However, the results of many research studies confirm that the reliability and predictive accuracy of the models decreases when they are used in different national environments and time horizons than those in which they were originally formulated. As a result, a starting point is the vital importance for the development of prediction models in unique national conditions in order for financial risks to be estimated correctly.[32] William Beaver developed a 'parametric statistical model to predict financial distress of a company by using the information in the financial statements by applying the techniques of data analysis of one variable (univariate technique)'.[33] Beaver determined that using financial ratios can be useful in predicting business success or failure, solvency or insolvency and bankruptcy of a distressed company. Two years later, Edward Altman made a significant contribution to the development of predictive models to detect insolvency.[34] Altman focused on the development of a statistical model for predicting the insolvency of a company through the technique of multiple discriminant analysis (MDA). Altman maintained that the:

> prediction of the probability of bankruptcy of the company, in addition to the use of the individual (partial) financial ratios, such as, ratios based on financial information of great significance, can be done by synthetic (aggregate) financial ratios which are the weighted sum of several financial ratios, including the well-known Z-Score ratio. These models take the microeconomic approach to predict the financial distress of the company.[35]

However, these predictive models were developed in a time where technology was not as advanced as today.

30 Ibid.

31 Elena Gregova, Katarina Valaskova, Peter Adamko, Milos Tumpach, Jaroslav Jaros, *Predicting Financial Distress of Slovak Enterprises: Comparison of Selected Traditional and Learning Algorithms Methods*, Sustainability, MDPI, 2020, 3954.

32 Ibid.

33 William Beaver, Financial Ratios as Predictors of Failure, *Journal of Accounting Research* 4, (1966), 71–111. In Dragana Bešlić Obradović, Dejan Jakšić, Ivana Bešlić Rupić, Mirko Andrić, Insolvency Prediction Model of the Company: The Case of the Republic of Serbia, *Economic Research-Ekonomska Istraživanja* 31, 1 (2018), 139–157.

34 Edward Altman, Financial Ratios, Discriminant Analysis and the Prediction of Corporate Bankruptcy, *Journal of Finance* 23, 4 (1968), 589–609. In Dragana Bešlić Obradović, Dejan Jakšić, Ivana Bešlić Rupić, Mirko Andrić, Insolvency Prediction Model of the Company: The Case of the Republic of Serbia, *Economic Research-Ekonomska Istraživanja* 31, 1 (2018), 139–157.

35 Ibid.

Dragana Bešlić et al. note that this early approach by Altman did not lead to accurate predictions. That deficiency is understandable, given significant advances in technology since 1968. Today in 2020–2021 the advancement in technology has resulted in more accurate predictions. The new digital economy will demand even greater accuracy as commercial data becomes increasingly important to banks, finance organisation, governments, regulators and the business community. According to Bešlić et al., the most common conventional models that have been adopted are discriminant analysis,[36] logistic regression (LR)[37] and neural network.[38] These authors assert that they are '1) available in most software packages; 2); [are] relatively easy to understand and 3) fairly robust (strong, powerful) and reliable tool for predicting the financial problems of the company'.[39] More recently, Chris Charalambous et al.[40] have predicted bankruptcy by measuring the financial healthiness of firms that have coupon-paying debts. The approach is based on a framework created by Leland and Toft; and is embodied in optimal capital structure, endogenous bankruptcy and the term structure of credit spreads.[41] Significantly, the model developed by Leland and Toft incorporates the effects of taxes and bankruptcy costs when evaluating corporate debt and maturity. In other words, under this model it takes into consideration debt that pays coupons, as opposed the firm issuing a zero-coupon debt.

Even as a preventative measure, financial institutions have used technologies for decades to assess an individual's credit worthiness. Credit scoring (CS) is widely utilised by financial institutions to determine the default probability of applicants, and subsequently classify them into good applicants (the 'goods', for simplicity) or bad applicants.[42] Applicants may then be rejected or accepted as customers based on that classification. CS adopts a binary classification in which the binary response variable represents a default in payment by the customer, or potential default in payment for order requests that have been declined. To evaluate the credit risk of loan applications, CS is targeted at isolating the effects of the applicants' financial characteristics on their default probability. The default probability is mapped to a

36 Radu Stroe, Nicoleta Barbuta-Misu, Predicting the Financial Performance of the Building Sector Enterprises – Case Study of Galati County (Romania), *The Review of Finance and Banking* 2 (2010), 29–39, http://www.rfb.ase.ro/articole/A3-Stroe.pdf.

37 Petr Jakubík, Petr Teplý, *The Prediction of Corporate Bankruptcy and Czech Economy's Financial Stability Through Logit Analysis*, IIES Working Paper Series 19, IIES, 2008, 1–19.

38 Fatih Ecer, Comparing the Bank Failure Prediction Performance of Neural Networks and Support Vector Machines: The Turkish Case, *Economic Research-Ekonomska Istraživanja* 26, 3 (2013), 81–98.

39 Ibid.

40 Chris Charalambous, Spiros H. Martzoukos, Zenon Taoushianis, Predicting Corporate Bankruptcy Using the Framework of Leland-Toft: Evidence from U.S., *Quantitative Finance* 20, 2 (2020), 329–346.

41 Ibid. See also Hayne Leland, Klaus oft, Optimal Capital Structure, Endogenous Bankruptcy and the Term Structure of Credit Spreads, *Journal of Finance* 51 (1996), 987–1019.

42 Leonardo Vanneschi, David Micha Horn, Mauro Castelli, Aleš Popovicˇ, An Artificial Intelligence System for Predicting Customer Default in E-Commerce, *Expert Systems with Applications* 104 (2018), 2.

numerical expression, usually called *score*, which indicates the applicants' creditworthiness and enables the creditor to rank the applicants.[43] These types of preventative predictive tools are important to determining whether a person is likely to fall into financial stress leading to bankruptcy.

The importance of these bankruptcy tools extends beyond specific applicants. They impact on overall market value by assessing equity, debt and total firm value. Charalambous et al., in supporting the 'Leland-Toft model, analysed 5460 US public firms from which 333 filed for bankruptcy in a specific year between the 20-year period 1995–2014'.[44] Bankruptcy filings were identified from Bankruptcy Data and included firms that filed for bankruptcy under Chapter 7 or Chapter 11 of the US Bankruptcy Act.[45] However, to avoid 'problems related to sample selection bias and increase efficiency of regression estimates, the authors collected all available observations in the selected period for each bankrupt and healthy firm. As a result, the sample increased to 39830 firm-year observations'.[46] The study concluded that the Leland-Toft model expanded on the aforementioned Altman model, and out-performed other approaches to predicting insolvent entities. Charalambous et al. further pointed out that augmenting Altman's model with the Leland-Toft model, further improves performance. On the other hand, they stopped short of concluding that the resulting model is conclusive, and instead proposed further work to apply the model to individual firms and to their specific circumstances. We agree with this conclusion, because as technology evolves and becomes more sophisticated, technologies such as AI will be able to predict with greater accuracy whether entities under financial stress are likely to become insolvent. Thus, the question arises, apart from the aforementioned predictive model(s), what will the current and future impact of AI have on and to the law? The next section briefly samples some of the emerging areas of AI and their impact upon the law, and upon finance and insolvency law in particular.

9.3 Artificial Intelligence – Restructuring

Not only has AI emerged to predict and manage insolvent entities, it has for some time also been used to analyse and predict financial stress and assist in managing a restructure. Ordinarily, a company taking a restructuring charge will record an expense, generally an estimate, and will set up a reserve for a like amount. An example provided by Owen Hall et al. highlights the technique used by a firm

43 Ibid.

44 Chris Charalambous, Spiros Martzoukos, Zenon Taoushianis, Predicting Corporate Bankruptcy Using the Framework of Leland-Toft: Evidence from U.S., *Quantitative Finance* 20, 2 (2020), 329–346. Leland and Toft belongs to a class of models that extends Merton, to incorporate the effects of taxes and bankruptcy costs to the valuation of equity and a corporate coupon-paying debt with finite maturity. Other significant features of their framework are that bankruptcy can occur prior to the maturity of the debt but also, they consider the case when the bankruptcy point is determined endogenously.

45 Ibid.

46 Ibid.

when it sells an operating unit.[47] It is very likely that the sale will result in a one-time gain that could cause a spike in earnings. To avoid this, the firm will record a restructuring charge in an amount that approximates the gain. The charge will be an estimate of future expenses that could result from the restructuring action.[48] The importance of understanding current and future expenses of an entity provide the very basis for the restructure. This data goes some way to influencing and directing the overall outcome of a restructure. However, and similar to insolvency predictive modelling, restructuring technology and elements of AI have been used dating back to the 1940s. That is, Artificial Neural Networks (ANNs) are a branch of artificial intelligence that addresses the problem of analysing and forecasting data by simulating the biological neural network found in the human brain.[49] First proposed in 1947, ANNs use complex network relationships to mimic the connections between sets of data. Among other things, ANNs have the advantage of not requiring prior assumptions about possible relations, as is the case with traditional analysis methods, such as regression.[50] Hall et al. note that the architecture of an ANN consists, at a minimum, of two layers: an input neuron or neuron layer and an output neuron.[51] There may also be one or more intermediate or 'hidden' layers of neurons. It is these hidden layers of neurons and the complexity of the interconnections that increase the computational power of ANNs.[52] Yet, it must be noted that this technology, while still relevant today, has evolved into more sophisticated technologies.

Doubts about the predictive value of new technologies also appear to be dissipating. A 2019 study was undertaken by INSOL International, consisting of a world-wide federation of national associations for accountants and lawyers who specialise in turnaround and insolvency. INSOL found that only around 14% of respondents surveyed disagreed that the use of technology was either already a key part, or was likely soon to become an integral part of their service offering in the future.[53] It therefore does not appear to be the case that operators of Internet Protocols (IPs) are in any way lacking in awareness of the issues presented by the increasing adoption of business-orientated technology and their growing role and likely importance to their own practices. Christian Toms and Jane Colston observe that, with all the technological progress being made across the business community, IPs now find themselves in an era of so-called 'big data'.[54] This means an increasing amount of electronic data is being produced and stored every day, the current

47 Owen Hall, Owen, Charles McPeak, Using Neural Net Technology to Analyze Corporate Restructuring Announcements, *Journal of International Information Management* 12, 2 (2003), 1–2.

48 Ibid., 329–346.

49 Ibid.

50 Ibid

51 Ibid

52 Ibid.

53 Christian Toms, Jane Colston, *The Role of Artificial Intelligence (AI) and Technology in Global Bankruptcy and Restructuring Practices*, 2019, http://www.brownrudnick.com/wp-content/uploads/2019/07/Role-of-Artificial-Intelligence-AI-FINAL-1-July-2019-3.pdf.

54 Ibid., 6–9.

statistic is that around 2.5 quintillion bytes of data come into existence per day during 2019 alone; therefore, this is only set to increase.[55] Over the next decade this quantity of data will only become even greater and more sophisticated. As stated earlier, it will become more accurate and be used to predict issues in the economy that quite possibly have not even been thought of in 2020.

As a consequence, Toms and Colston further note some of the challenges faced when investigating large and complex insolvencies. They argue that one must take the time to understand the inner workings of a business in order to:

> determine the most appropriate next steps; in a turnaround scenario where analysis and data analytics can be applied to raw, system-generated information to speed up the identification of issues and assist in identifying key drivers of performance to inform the most effective strategies to impact business performance; when tracing assets; and when considering potential litigation and scans are conducted of key data sets in order to identify trends, anomalies and potential individuals and time periods of specific interest.[56]

Toms and Colston go onto say that the utilisation of some form of technology-aided review (TAR) is employed in order to enhance the conduct of any review of the books and records of the company being assessed. The technology is able from the outset to cluster documents by concepts so that humans can more quickly and easily begin reviewing key subject areas and concepts, hopefully finding what they need before time or money runs out.[57] The authors further state that:

> As a secondary stage, some TAR systems can be made actively to learn from the human reviewers as to what is relevant and what is not. This learning can then intermittently be applied by the system to the remainder of the data still to be considered, through a process of 'predictive coding', to serve up more relevant material for review at an earlier stage than a more linear human review process otherwise might have enabled. However, it would appear that the use of such technology is far from widespread amongst IPs. Only around 35% of responders to the INSOL survey confirmed they had made use of any such tools in the past year or so and of that sub-group only around 28% of them had made use of the more sophisticated predictive coding capabilities of their TAR system.[58]

The rapid growth in technology systems, applications and infrastructures are changing the landscape of business and the ability for insolvency and restructuring to not only be predicted, but also prevented and managed. The dynamically

55 Ibid., 7–8.
56 Ibid., 9.
57 Ibid.
58 Ibid.

expanded capacity of technologies will provide many benefits to the economy. However, it can also pose challenges to the security and management of commercial and personal data that is used to predict financial stress. This caution notwithstanding, the evolution of technology, viewed through the lens of economic management and developed, can have significant benefits for the global economy. This positive outcome is subject to the presupposition that governments and regulators will develop and endorse international technology systems that are in the common interest of states, not only in the interests of a few powerful states. The affirmative outcome is also prefaced on the global community of states focusing on maintaining and strengthening economic stability in the collective interest. In our view, while there will be significant challenges in balancing individual rights to the protection of personal data against the economic benefits of trading in their personal data, technology will strengthen both. It will do so through technologies that promote international productivity within a renewing digital economy while also protecting individual rights within that economy.

9.4 Artificial Intelligence (AI) and Law

AI has been studied for decades, but is still one of the most elusive subjects in computer science.[59] The term artificial intelligence was first coined by John McCarthy in 1956 when he held the first academic conference on the subject.[60] AI, today, constitutes machines truly capable of thinking and determining how to search algorithms used to play board games. Renewed technology can effectively replicate human behaviour and thinking across business and social sectors. It has applications in and implications for nearly every way we use computers across society. Alan Turing, in 1950, wrote a paper on the notion of machines being able to simulate human beings and behaviour, and the ability to do intelligent things, such as playing chess.[61] Turing proposed a method for evaluating whether machines can think, known as the Turing test. The test, or 'Imitation Game' as it was called in his paper, was a simple test that could be used to prove that machines could think, for themselves.[62] Nearly 80 years on, Themistoklis Tzimas has asserted that, over time, there will be the emergence of personhood, with an autonomous intellect, through the development of AI systems and infrastructure.[63] Importantly, Tzimas favoured developing and using that autonomous intellect as a response that states

59 Chris Smith, Brian McGuire, Ting Huang, Gary Yang, *The History of Artificial Intelligence*, https://courses.cs.washington.edu/courses/csep590/06au/projects/history-ai.pdf.

60 Ibid.

61 Ibid.; Alan Turing, Computing Machinery and Intelligence, *Mind* 49 (1950), 433–460.

62 Ibid., the Turing test takes a simple pragmatic approach, assuming that a computer that is indistinguishable from an intelligent human actually has shown that machines can think.

63 Themistoklis Tzimas, Artificial Intelligence as Global Commons and the 'International Law Supremacy' Principle, *Advances in Social Science, Education and Humanities Research* 211 (2018); in Robert Walters, Marko Novak, *Cyber Security, Artificial Intelligence, Data Protection and the Law*, Springer, forthcoming, Ch. 2.

can share through the supremacy of international law.[64] The argument put forward, reinforced in this book, is that an additional international response is needed in the shared regulation of cross-border and restructuring in the future. Part of that response lies in a technological contribution to that continuing development.

Viewed this way, and as highlighted by Walters and Novak, 'AI algorithms can provide faster and easier data processing, prediction of legal decisions, and automation of legal decision-making as such'.[65] AI will make a significant contribution to improving information and data analysis, making predictions and reaching decisions more rapidly and reliably than human beings. However, and arguably, this result is some way off, with challenges of AI in the law ahead in predicting and processing insolvency and restructuring initiatives both fully and effective. To date, new technologies can analyse the reasoning that individual judges are likely to use and the outcomes that courts are likely to reach in rendering legal decisions. Furthermore, a project in the UK has produced a programme to foresee processes, reasoning and decisions by the European Court of Human Rights with 75% reliability.[66] It is not a quantum leap to extend predictions of these judicial outcomes to the processes, reasoning and decisions reached in insolvency and restructuring proceedings.

Predictive decision-making tools used generally are capable of extension to be applied in specific contexts, such as to corporate financial stress leading to insolvency. Machine-generated language can be translated into language and importantly, can be used to predict outcomes, such as insolvency itself. Ross Riskin aptly demonstrates that:

> in the area of law there already exist decision-making or consulting tools such as *Lexis Answers* in the frame of *Lexis Answer Card*, where legal questions are asked in the natural language and (machine generated) replies are provided in return in the form of a best legal solution.[67]

On the basis of such technology the *Ross (Intelligence)* project was developed, and based on the then IBM Watson technology.[68]

The significance of these technological developments lies in the ability to find the best possible answer based on searching within natural language. However, the problem of AI in the law is inseparably connected to legal argumentation. It is impossible for natural language to predict legal outcomes without understanding

64 Ibid.

65 Ibid.

66 Nikolas Aletras, Dimitri Tsarapatsanis, Daniel Preoţiuc-Pietro, Vasileios Lampos, Predicting Judicial Decisions of the European Court of Human Rights: A Natural Language Processing Perspective, *PeerJ Computer Science* (2016), 93.

67 G. Riskin, *Ross Intelligence Update: How IBM Watson App Helps U.S. Lawyers with Legal Research*, Law Firm Technology, 2017; in Robert Walters, Marko Novak, *Cyber Security, Artificial Intelligence, Data Protection and the Law*, Springer, forthcoming, Ch. 2.

68 David Ferrucci, Anthongy Levas, Sugato Bagchi, David Gondek, Eric Mueller, Watson: Beyond Jeopardy, *Artificial Intelligence* 199 (2013), 93–105.

legal language.[69] One of the first attempts of natural language to understand legal language arose in the TAXMAN programme that sought to analyse, computationally, the majority and minority opinions in a known legal case.[70] Since then, experts in AI and law have analysed legal arguments from either a formal[71] or an empirical perspective,[72] focusing primarily on formal logical decision-making and the legal justifications in law.[73] The problem in such AI studies is in their capacity to address, through formal logic, the complex nature of legal decisions and the diverse reasons that give rise to them. Typically, AI studies of common law decisions require significant subjective analysis, given the adversarial nature of common law proceedings and the complex nature of binding precedents. Civil law decision-making, arguably, does not require AI to engage in comparable subjective analysis, given the predominantly non-adversarial nature of civil law and the absence of legal precedent.

Advances in AI are attempting to respond to these obstacles in being applied as tools in predicting the nature and application of law. Notably, different AI tools are increasingly being used to analyse legal reasoning and decisions. For example, the Supreme People's Court in China created an AI-based tool FaXin to help judges identify precedents.[74] Another example is Intraspexion that leverages upon AI 'deep learning' to predict and warn users of their litigation risks. Predictive analytical company CourtQuant, in turn, has partnered with two litigation financing companies to help evaluate litigation funding opportunities using AI.[75] Intelligent property lawyers can also use AI-based software from companies like TrademarkNow and Anaqua to perform IP research, brand protection and risk assessment.[76]

The result is that AI tools are being used for different purposes in predicting the nature and application of law. AI learning is also exposing limitations in legal service sectors globally that are shaped by custom and tradition and slow to adapt to advances in information and communication technologies.[77] Brooks et al., in their study, noted that 'the legal industry has missed out on the digitisation and workflow improvement process that most industries went through in the 90s and

69 Robert Walters, Marko Novak, *Cyber Security, Artificial Intelligence, Data Protection and the Law*, Springer, forthcoming, Ch. 2.

70 L. T. McCarty, Reflection on TAXMAN: An Experiment in Artificial Intelligence and Legal Reasoning, *Harvard Law Review* 90 (1976), 837.

71 H. Prakken, G. Sartor, Law and Logic: A Review from an Argumentative Perspective, *Artificial Intelligence* 227 (2015), 214–245.

72 T. Bench-Capon, Hypo's Legacy: Introduction to the Virtual Special Issue, *Artificial Intelligence and Law* 25 (2017), 1–46.

73 Eveline Feteris, *Fundamentals of Legal Argumentation*, Springer, 2017, 33–41.

74 Marco Kauffman, Marcelo Soares, AI in Legal Services: New Trends in AI-Enabled Legal Services, *Society of Clinical Anatomists* 14 (2020), 223.

75 Ibid., 223.

76 Ibid., 223.

77 Chay Brooks, Cristian Gherhes, Tim Vorley, Artificial Intelligence in the Legal Sector: Pressures and Challenges of Transformation, *Cambridge Journal of Regions, Economy and Society* 13, 1 (2020), 135–152.

2000s'.[78] Law generally has stayed reasonably behind the curve in regard to technological innovation.[79] What is problematic is that law is not immune to social change; and contemporary trends in AI learning are placing pressures on legal service sectors to absorb new AI learning. That pressure is also reflected in incumbent law firms seeking more innovative AI responses to solve problems that have traditionally lacked 'deep' analysis undertaken in other sectors, notably in defence. While not all legal sectors will be receptive to AI solutions, it is well arguable that legal services sectors in general are approaching an inflection point where it is likely that law firms that engage with emerging technologies will have an advantage going forward.

That said, AI systems are routinely said to operate autonomously, exposing gaps in industry and commerce operations that assume the centrality of human actors. Simon Chesterman observes that:

> little attention is given to precisely what is meant by autonomy and its relationship to those gaps. A key feature of modern artificial intelligence is the ability to operate without human intervention. It is commonly said that such systems operate autonomously.[80]

However, the problem of:

> autonomy is commonly treated as a single quality of AI systems, this article develops a typology of autonomy that highlights three discrete sets of regulatory challenges, epitomized by three spheres of activity in which those systems display degrees of autonomous behaviour.[81]

The challenges are evident in the 2020 case between Quoine and B2C2, in relation to the use of software programmes that executed trades involving the cryptocurrencies Bitcoin and Ethereum, with prices set according to external market information.[82] The case focused on seven trades that were made when a defect in Quoine's software executed trades worth approximately $12m at 250 times the prevailing exchange rate.[83] The Court noted that:

> Quoine claimed that this was a mistake and attempted to reverse the trades, reclaiming its losses. B2C2 argued that the reversal of the orders was a breach of contract, while Quoine argued that the contract was void or voidable,

78 Ibid.

79 Ibid.

80 Simon Chesterman, Artificial Intelligence and the Problem of Autonomy, *Notre Dame Journal on Emerging Technologies* (2019), 211–248.

81 Ibid.

82 *B2C2 Ltd. v. Quoine Pte. Ltd.* [2019] SGHC(I) 3 (2019).

83 Ibid.

> relying on the doctrine of unilateral mistake. At common law, a unilateral mistake can void a contract if the other party knows of the mistake. If it cannot be proven that the other party actually knew about the mistake, but it can be shown that he or she should have, the contract may be voidable under equity. What became crucial in this case was the judge's finding that the computer programs in question were incapable of knowing anything about the algorithmic programmes in the present case are deterministic, they do and only do what they have been programmed to do. They have no mind of their own. They operate when called upon to do so in the pre-ordained manner. They do not know why they are doing something or what the external events are that cause them to operate in the way that they do. As a result, the question of knowledge rested with the original programmer of B2C2's software, who could not have known about Quoine's subsequent mistake.[84]

The Singapore High Court adopted the view that the software was carrying out actions that could have been carried out by a human being, and that it was necessary to look at the intention and knowledge of the operator or controller of the machine to determine the intention and knowledge of the machine. In this case, the programmer, Mr. Tseung, believed that the computer would only force-close in circumstances that would have led to a margin call if everything was operating properly, and hence that there was no mistake. The decision was upheld on appeal, with the majority emphasising that the deterministic nature of the algorithms was central to its analysis.[85] Importantly, to date, such software is far from reaching the capacity and capability of a human operator. The Court tenaciously maintained that, humans know or, at a minimum, understand what they are doing. Yet, a computer or algorithm does not.

Given these observations, conditions are ensured for recognising the text between legal forms (including applicable case law and commentaries) and the facts in the mentioned forms. This alone is problematic, when there is a lack of coherence in the law surrounding AI, particularly where that technology will make decisions that have in the past otherwise been undertaken by humans.[86] However, this is outside those military and other industries such as the airline industry, where AI technology has been making human-based decisions for some time. What is being advocated here is that AI predictions relating to decision-making in law entails significantly subjective elements. This is, and of itself, very different to AI assessing objective-based decisions, such as in the manufacture and deployment of machinery such as aircraft in the defence industry.

84 Ibid.

85 *Quoine Pte. Ltd. v. B2C2 Ltd.* [2020] SGCA(I) 2 (2020), 97–128.

86 Robert Walters, Marko Novak, *Cyber Security, Artificial Intelligence, Data Protection and the Law*, Springer, forthcoming, Ch. 2.

Arguably, many benefits will derive from the application of AI to law, especially to trans-border insolvency law. At this early-stage AI 'has the potential to improve the accuracy of predicting and resolving insolvencies and provide an enhanced level [early intervention] evidence-based approach to restructures'.[87] Such an approach, directed at accuracy in predicting and managing financial debt will strengthen universalist approaches, such as in predicting and managing insolvency risks. In our view, the economic benefits from early intervention arising from the use of predictive AI tools would have significant benefits in assessing how best to resolve cross-border insolvency stress, even though the accuracy of such predictions will often be difficult to measure. It will enable a solvent party located in a third country to be made aware of the other party's financial stress, and work with that party to negotiate a way to financial viability. While an early interventionist approach is potentially obstructionist, if it orchestrates a loss of control by a financially stressed entity in managing its business. Safeguards would need to be built into both the AI and legal systems to provide a barrier to premature, undue or excessive intervention. For example, once intervention is triggered, the financially troubled entity would need to agree that material financial information be released to other parties such as creditors.

The next section focuses on regulating AI. It examines the value of AI assisting to predict and facilitate financial and legal change in specific sectors, such as trans-border restructuring and insolvency. It also reflects on the legal regulation of AI systems that err, or more accurately, whose operators err, in predicting insolvency risks.

9.5 Regulating Artificial Intelligence

One of the functions of law is to prevent and resolve disputes. These include disputes over intellectual property rights concerning AI algorithms. Among these IP questions are: 'who holds moral rights to their invention', and 'how material rights to invention are to be transferred to another person by means of a contract of license, involving also the law of contracts; and torts if some kind of damage occurred in the exercise of such'.[88] Problematic, too, is the observation that AI currently lacks specific international, regional or national legal authority to regulate the emerging area of technology as it applies to law. More directly in issue is the lack of an agreed international or national definition of AI, outside of a military definition. The next sub-section will briefly examine current definitions of AI that are emerging to lead the legal race in developing law such as is capable of application to insolvency. It will reflect on the difficulties faced by regulators and courts in regulating the use of AI technologies that miscalculate the risks of insolvency, and conceivably, precipitate insolvency.

87 Ibid.
88 Ibid.

9.5.1 Defining Artificial Intelligence

The definition of AI is far from settled. There is no single definition of AI[89] that has been accepted by all technology or legal practitioners. However, Phillip Jackson has defined AI as the ability of machines to do things that people would say require intelligence.[90] The phrase sometimes refers to 'intelligent machines' themselves.[91] Therefore, AI attempts to emulate the mental steps of human beings. Such mental steps include understanding languages, responding to questions, identifying patterns, solving problems, and learning through experience.[92] Among these languages is the language or languages of law. Arguably, the definition of AI traced back to 1985 falls short of what AI is today. At the same time, the challenges faced in both defining AI and applying it across industrial sectors and professions remains largely untested.

Nonetheless, the US has made what appears to be an early move in developing a definition of AI and applying it to defence. During the 115th Congress 2019,[93] 39 bills were introduced that had the phrase 'artificial intelligence' in their text. Four of these bills were enacted into law. Section 238 of the John S. McCain National Defense Authorization Act for Fiscal Year 2019 directed the Department of Defense to undertake several activities regarding AI.[94] Sub-section (b) required the Secretary of Defense to appoint a coordinator who will oversee and direct the activities of the Department

> relating to the development and demonstration of artificial intelligence and machine learning. Subsection (g) provides the following definition of AI:

(1) Any artificial system that performs tasks under varying and unpredictable circumstance without significant human oversight, or that can learn from experience and improve performance when exposed to data sets.
(2) An artificial system developed in computer software, physical hardware, or other context that solves tasks requiring human-like perception, cognition, planning, learning, communication, or physical action.
(3) An artificial system designed to think or act like a human, including cognitive architectures and neural networks.

89 Robert Walters, Matthew Coghlan, Data Protection and Artificial Intelligence Law: Europe Australia Singapore – An Actual or Perceived Dichotomy, *American Journal of Science, Engineering and Technology* 4, 4 (2019), 55–65.

90 Phillip Jackson, *Introduction to Artificial Intelligence*, Dover Publication, Inc., 1974, 2nd ed., 192–338.

91 Ibid.

92 World Intellectual Property Organization Technology Trends, *Artificial Intelligence*, https://www.wipo.int/edocs/pubdocs/en/wipo_pub_1055.pdf.

93 Law library of Congress, Regulation of Artificial Intelligence in Selected Jurisdictions, January, 2019, https://www.loc.gov/law/help/artificial-intelligence/regulation-artificial-intelligence.pdf.

94 Ibid., John S. McCain National Defense Authorization Act for Fiscal Year 2019, Pub. L. 115–232, §238, 132 Stat. 1658, 2018, https://www.congress.gov/115/bills/hr5515/BILLS-115hr5515enr.pdf.

(4) A set of techniques, including machine learning that is designed to approximate a cognitive task.
(5) An artificial system designed to act rationally, including an intelligent software agent or embodied robot that achieves goals using perception, planning, reasoning, learning, communicating, decision making, and acting.[95]

Yet, sub-section (f) instructs the Secretary of Defense to delineate a definition of the term artificial intelligence for use within the Department no later than one year after the law's enactment. While broad, but at the same time specific, the definition does direct the community generally on what AI constitutes. Arguably, as technology continues to evolve, this definition is likely to change. Rather than define AI, another approach by some states has opted to define what an autonomous vehicle constitutes.

It is out of scope of this book to examine other definitions of AI. However, in December 2018, the European Commission (EU) released draft ethical guidelines developed by a High-Level Expert Group on Artificial Intelligence (AI HLEG). Apart from setting out a framework for designing trustworthy AI, the HLEG proposed a broad definition of AI:

> Artificial intelligence refers to systems designed by humans that, given a complex goal, act in the physical or digital world by perceiving their environment, interpreting the collected structured or unstructured data, reasoning on the knowledge derived from this data and deciding the best action(s) to take (according to pre-defined parameters) to achieve the given goal. AI systems can also be designed to learn to adapt their behaviour by analysing how the environment is affected by their previous actions. As a scientific discipline, AI includes several approaches and techniques, such as machine learning (of which deep learning and reinforcement learning are specific examples), machine reasoning (which includes planning, scheduling, knowledge representation and reasoning, search, and optimization), and robotics (which includes control, perception, sensors and actuators, as well as the integration of all other techniques into cyber-physical systems).[96]

In addition, the term artificial intelligence has been coined by the EU:

> Defining the precise object of regulation in dynamic technological domains is a challenge in itself. Given that AI is still an open-ended notion that refers to a very wide range of products and applications, there is no transnational agreement on a commonly accepted working definition, neither

95 Ibid., FAA Reauthorization Act of 2018, Pub. L. 115–254, §548, 132 Stat. 3186, https://www.congress.gov/115/bills/hr302/BILLS-115hr302enr.pdf.
96 AI HLEG, *A Definition of AI: Main Capabilities and Scientific Disciplines*, 18 December 2018, https://ec.europa.eu/newsroom/dae/document.cfm?doc_id=56341.

> at the technical nor the legal/policy level. As there is no legal and political consensus over what AI is, a plurality of definitions has emerged in Europe and worldwide that are either too inclusive or too sector-specific. This fragmented conceptual landscape may prevent the immediate development of a *lex robotica* and possibly undermine all efforts to create a common legal nomenclature, which is particularly instrumental for the drafting, adoption and effective implementation of binding legal norms. Alternatively, a broad and technology-neutral definition that is based on the fulfilment of a variety of structural criteria, including the level of autonomy and the function, may be a more plausible option.[97]

On the backdrop of this, Singapore has, through the Road Traffic Act in 2017, defined the meaning of an automated vehicle. It provides that:

> automated vehicle technology means any particular technology that (a) relates to the design, construction or use of autonomous motor vehicles; or (b) otherwise relates to advances in the design or construction of autonomous motor vehicles; autonomous motor vehicle means a motor vehicle equipped wholly or substantially with an autonomous system (also commonly known as a driverless vehicle), and includes a trailer drawn by such a motor vehicle; autonomous system, for a motor vehicle, means a system that enables the operation of the motor vehicle without the active physical control of, or monitoring by, a human operator.[98]

Defining the scope and application of AI poses significant legal challenges. These challenges arise from different AI definitions in general, divergence in how AI is regulated in specific sectors, and how AI is regulated in national and transnational law. The challenges are exacerbated when definitions of AI are unsettled in national and across supranational law, when regulators and courts fail to regulate AI or do so disparately. The threats arising from IA processes are damaging when they wrongly predict financial threats to solvency and in so doing, conceivably precipitate

97 Mihalis Kritikos, *European Parliamentary Research Service Scientific Foresight Unit* (STOA) PE 634.427, March 2019, https://www.europarl.europa.eu/at-your-service/files/be-heard/religious-and-non-confessional-dialogue/events/en-20190319-artificial-intelligence-ante-portas.pdf. See also, Council of Europe, *Artificial Intelligence and Data Protection: Challenges and Possible Remedies*, https://rm.coe.int/artificial-intelligence-and-data-protection-challenges-and-possible-re/168091f8a6.

98 Road Traffic Act (Cap. 276) (Ordinance 26 of 1961, revised 31 December 2004, version in force, 31 August 2018, https://sso.agc.gov.sg/Act/RTA1961?ValidDate=20180831&ViewType=Pdf&_=20181012232618. Max Ng and Amira Nabila Budiyano, New Regulations to Address Automated Vehicle Technology, *Lexology*, 10 April 2017, https://www.lexology.com/library/detail.aspx?g=64a38d35-6b97-48a5-91ff-9a59817ac955, archived at https://perma.cc/E8HG-4536. Road Traffic Act (Cap. 276) s 2(1). Also see Robert Walters, Matthew Coghlan, Data Protection and Artificial Intelligence Law: Europe Australia Singapore – An Actual or Perceived Dichotomy, *American Journal of Science, Engineering and Technology* 4, 4 (2019), 55–65.

insolvency. They are illustrated, too, when AI threatens the security of personal information of those who are involved in insolvency or restructuring proceedings.

9.6 Applying Artificial Intelligence in Law

There are broad areas of law that are capable of regulating AI, such as the law of torts (delicts in civil law) and contracts. Such regulation occurs, for example, in determining whether and how the law of negligence in torts regulates AI technologies that cause harm to entities and individuals related to them, such as through the negligent processing of personal data. Comparable regulation arises in the use of AI in cross-border contracting, such as in regulating the use of AI to formulate and process online contracts that potentially undermines the financial security of cross-border entities or their executives and directors. The following section evaluates these threats arising from the use of AI specifically in relation to cross-border insolvency. It will argue the use of AI in predicting financial and personal information relating to entities engaged in cross-border dealings that are subject to liability for misrepresenting data or negligence in calculations based on that data. So too, liability could arise where an AI programme represents a significantly higher level of predictive capacity than is reasonably attained.

A further issue arises when AI is subject to regulation for failing to protect personal and/or commercial data. Significant legal issues are emerging when the use of AI is evaluated in relation to cybersecurity. On the one side, AI is an excellent instrument for processing big data for which it would take days or years for humans to be equally efficient, and where errors in human scrutiny could seriously undermine the collection, processing and use of that data.[99] On the other side, data collection and processing is traditionally regulated by specific laws. This observation would support the rationale that, while AI can be used negligently, in breach of contract or otherwise contrary to law, it is arguably often far more reliable than reliance on calculations made with the benefit of AI.

Moreover, data (including sensitive data) has been collected and processed well before the advance of AI. This is subject to the qualification that AI that is engineered before being applied in specific cases, is generally more reliable than data collection and processing prior to the development of AI. The question then arises whether AI that is faster and more reliable than pre-AI data analysis carries further risks and jeopardies that are peculiar to it. Arguably the development and role of AI is multi-layered. On the positive side, notwithstanding its complex nature and operation, AI is considered as providing more accurate normative assessments based on quantifiable data than prevailed in the past. Furthermore, AI is viewed as becoming increasingly reliable as it evolves further.[100] At the same time, AI is

99 Ibid.

100 Robert Walters, Marko Novak, *Cyber Security, Artificial Intelligence, Data Protection and the Law*, Springer, 2021, Ch. 2.

viewed as an instrument that is effectively used to extract data from sources that were previously deemed impervious to cybertheft, hacking or related threats.[101] Ryan Goosen et al., in referring to a 2018 *New York Times* report on the replication of dial phone technology through the use of AI, noted that researchers in the US and China had successfully commanded AI systems developed by Amazon, Apple and Google to access phones and open websites, without the knowledge of the AI systems' users. It is a short step to more nefarious commands, such as unlocking doors and transferring money.[102] Goosen et al. contend that:

> It's not hard to imagine cyber-thieves targeting a financial institution's AI-controlled customer recognition software or a shady competitor attacking another company's AI pricing algorithm. In fact, more than 90% of cybersecurity professionals in the US and Japan expect attackers to use AI against the companies they work for, according to a survey by cybersecurity firm Webroot.[103]

Viewed this way, AI in the law and for the law has both advantages and disadvantages. The technology is an important advance over human capabilities in prediction, such as in predicting business outcomes than were realistically attainable prior to the development of AI. The advances in AI, however, are portents of significant current and future risks of two distinct kinds.[104] The first risk is that criminals, bad state actors, unscrupulous competitors and inside threats will manipulate their companies' fledgling AI programmes. The second risk is that attackers will use AI in a variety of ways to exploit vulnerabilities in their victims' defences. The commercial reality is that cross-border entities engage in, or are the victims of, an arms race between enhancing AI to address cybersecurity risks, while conversely accentuating those risks.[105] Goosen et al. adopt a negative perspective. They warn that 'AI systems are generally empowered to make deductions and decisions in an automated way without day-to-day human involvement'.[106] They can be detected but the detectors cannot substantiate the source of that vulnerability or reliably attribute it to defects in, or the abuse of AI. AI can also compromise cybersecurity without being detected for lengthy time periods.

Deficiencies in reliably detecting and acting upon cyberthreats attributable to AI, arguably, are often difficult to address. Machine-based learning associated with

101 Ibid.

102 R. Goosen, A. Rontojannis, S. Deutscher, J. Rogg, W. Bohmayr, D. Mkrtchain, *Artificial Intelligence Is a Threat to Cybersecurity: It's Also a Solution*, 2018, https://www.bcg.com/publications/2018/artificial-intelligence-threat-cybersecurity-solution.aspx; in Robert Walters, Marko Novak, *Cyber Security, Artificial Intelligence, Data Protection and the Law*, Springer, forthcoming, Ch. 2.

103 Ibid.

104 Ibid.

105 Ibid.

106 Ibid.

AI programmes often make deductions and reach decisions that are not readily apparent to their overseers. The underlying decision-making models and data are not necessarily transparent or quickly interpretable, even though there is significant effort currently underway to improve the transparency of such tools. This means that, even if a violation is detected, its purpose can remain opaque. As more machine learning or 'AI systems are connected to, or placed in control over physical systems, the risk of serious consequences – including injury and death – from malevolent interference rises'.[107] Goosen et al. identify the tension addressed earlier in this sub-section. On the one hand, AI enhances existing detection and response capabilities. On the other hand, it also enables new means of, and the capacity to, impede or prevent detection. Goosen et al. add that AI can also facilitate intelligent responses to attacks, either outside or inside the perimeter, based on shared knowledge and learning. That knowledge can be employed, comparably, to impede shared learning.

Managing Financial Risks through AI

The authors are of the view that AI can have a major role in detecting, governing and processing insolvency risks, as well as exploring how to, effectively, avoid those risks, limit damage arising from their materialisation and mitigate any ensuing or consequential losses. Specifically, AI has the capacity to assist in rendering insolvency procedures efficient and to streamline future restructuring processes. Conversely, AI can be used to deploy semiautonomous, 'intelligent lures or "traps" that create a duplicate of the environment to be infiltrated to make attackers believe they are on the intended path and then use the deceit to identify the culprit'.[108] This being the case, AI is likely to resolve one risk, while creating another. Apart from being likely to predict financial stress more reliably than human agency in the absence of AI, it can be used to conceal the very data that is needed to engage, reliably, safely and effectively, in an insolvency or restructure.

An earlier study proposed the importance of addressing three key issues in developing a financial solvency model: the characteristics of the model, dimensionality reduction and feature selection.[109] The primary models used in bankruptcy research are based on classification, on statistical inference and machine learning methods. However, models are not applicable in all cases because each model has different information requirements with differing degrees of transparency and comprehension.[110] For instance, different bankruptcy models are applicable to stressed and non-stressed firms and included a financial verification feature – the auditor's decision. Standard statistical models work best when statistical assumptions for the

107 Ibid.
108 Ibid.
109 Sergio Davalos, Richard D. Gritta, Bahram Adrangi, Deriving Rules for Forecasting Air Carrier Financial Stress and Insolvency: A Genetic Algorithm Approach, *Journal of the Transportation Research Forum* 46, 2 (2007), 63–81.
110 Ibid.

predictor variables are met: (1) the values are normally distributed; (2) the variables are linearly separable and are independent from other predictor variables and (3) there is a function that relates the predictor variables to the dependent variable; and (4) that the variance-covariance matrix is homogeneous.[111] Arguably, based on this, further work in AI technology and the algorithms that support it, is needed to reconcile cross-border financial stress that arises in environments in which functional financial systems vary. The essential question, then, is what these factors infer in managing discrete cross-border insolvency and restructuring cases. The first proposition is that, if AI technology is truly fit for purpose, it can significantly reduce the risk of entities becoming financially stressed, and if they do become stressed, than in impeding insolvency. The second proposition is that advanced AI technology can assist financially stressed entities to avoid insolvency, and to engage in a cost-effective and timely restructuring programme. The third proposition, that countervails against the first two propositions, is that the merging of complex technologies in complicated market environments can lead to significant harm. That is most likely where technologies are combined, whether they lack uniform or adaptive effectiveness in the markets in which they are applied, or when they fail to recognise the import of market disparities.

Arguably, these issues require careful further and ongoing consideration. In part response to these obstacles, Remesh Tamachandran advocates for a positive outcome. He contends that 'current day technology has come a long way and highlighted that by December 2019 end-point security is taken to the next level as AI can quickly detect, block and analyse attacks and perform extensive behavioural analysis'.[112] In support of his contention, the use of AI in endpoint data protection can provide multiple benefits that include, but are not limited to, providing immediate notification on its detection of any form of unauthorised behaviour from applications running in an applicable information systems or network service.[113] AI can also automatically block suspicious websites and actions even before they are executed; AI can also automatically stop all kinds of unauthorised data transactions. Tamachandran illustrates how AI-driven data privacy and protection can materially assist enterprises to identify an array of sensitive data, and track and control data movement within and outside the enterprise.[114]

Arguably, then, AI can play an enormous role in analysing and monitoring risks involved in exposing or otherwise misusing sensitive data within a cross-border entity. AI-driven technology can help in the protection and monitoring of personal data to make sure that the organisation is always in compliance and control with all privacy

111 Ibid.

112 Remesh Tamachandran, *How Artificial Intelligence Is Countering Data Protection Challenges Facing Organizations: AI Technology Can Help Enterprises in Endpoint Security, Data Privacy and Against Phishing, Malware and Ransomware Attacks*, https://www.entrepreneur.com/article/343267; in Robert Walters, Marko Novak, *Cyber Security, Artificial Intelligence, Data Protection and the Law*, Springer, 2021, Ch. 2.

113 Ibid.

114 Ibid.

standards and guidelines.[115] In achieving these goals, AI can reconcile foregoing obstacles to the protection of personal data that have not been adequately resolved through reliance upon a single piece of technology, platform or system. No system, even if used in tandem with other complementary systems, can provide 100% safeguards against illegal intrusions and the collection of personal data in the future. What they can do, through technological advances that both meet current needs and respond to past data violations, is create roadblocks to security breaches of systems, infrastructure and platforms that were previously, seemingly, impregnable to subjugation. AI can therefore redress threats to corporate entities in order to avoid and redress financial declines, just as the abusive use of AI can exacerbate such risks.

The implications for advancement in AI's protection of data is nevertheless offset by concerns that its effectiveness constitutes a threat to the freedom to access and use data on grounds of freedom of speech and association. In contention is a clash between the privacy rights of individuals, such as the privacy of those who direct the operations of financially stressed entities, and the right of others, including competitor entities, to have access to that data. Redressing this tension between data privacy and access to data is difficult to accomplish, given the ideological conflict that inhere between privacy and free-market aspirations. Adding to the difficulty in reconciling that tension is the significant divergence across states and regions over the protection of privacy or personal data on the one hand, and protecting freedom of expression on the other. For example, countries such as Singapore and China view privacy over the Internet very differently to that of the EU.

Beyond governmental action, cross-border enterprises both inside and outside the technology sector are integrating advances in AI technologies into the production, marketing and sale of their products and services.[116] Many of these new technologies rely on large databases of personal information that is increasingly controlled by entities outside government.[117] The challenge in assigning accountability, liability and responsibility for violations of data privacy and protection are growing more pressing in redressing both personal and corporate abuse. Both public interest and mainstream entities are seeking human and social rights protections from perceived breaches of personal data and privacy of stakeholders in companies engaged in cross-border trade and investment. Proponents of human rights reforms have lobbied state regulators to adopt coordinated AI technologies that are designed to protect entities and individuals associated with them. Some of these protections sought are focused on planning, organising and sustaining the transparent management of personal data. Regulators, notably in the EU, have responded by requiring the appointment of inhouse administrators or liquidators to managing insolvent party. Foremost among their administrative responsibilities is their ability to identify and respond to risks of violations of personal privacy and the risk of denying confidentiality to the transmission of commercial data. Part of the responsibility

115 Ibid.
116 Ibid.
117 Ibid.

of regulators, such as GPDR regulators, is to oversee corporate administrators in detecting and remediating violations of personal data and corporate security.

The implications for administrators being appointed to manage entities in financial stress will inevitably change. One such change is the likelihood of them facing an ever more complex combination of AI technologies that assist in sustaining entities at risk. The alternative risk is that administrators who fail to anticipate the effect of such combined technologies upon corporate survival may have the exact opposite effect: they may shorten the life of an otherwise sustainable entity.

On the backdrop of this chapter, one means of establishing greater unifying and consistency in regulating the administration of entities at risk is to draw upon an international business framework that is directed at the protection of human rights.[118] This is the position that Australia and other jurisdictions are considering in attempting to reconcile the gap between the use of advanced technologies in relation to law. However, adopting this gap-filling role in regulating personal data is subject to filling other gaps in the order of economic priorities that, arguably, might supersede data protection. Notable among these is the perception that parties with an interest in a financially stressed entity, varying from its competitors to the public at large, ought to have access to personal data that throws light on the source of its financial difficulty and the capacity to be resuscitated in an economic downturn.

Difficult too is the rationale that the use of innovative technologies to enhance a threatened entity's economic sustainability outweighs any right protections that need to be sacrificed in attaining that economic goal. Nevertheless, there is a growing body of evidence of significance spill-over harm to society when AI compromises personal data to protect enterprises that are at risk. This is readily evident when debtors, their suppliers and employees are rendered into collateral damage in seeking to resuscitate a financially besieged entity, at all costs.

AI Going Forward

At this stage, further studies are needed to fully understand the nature and scope of advances in AI technology: when they are likely to become available and operative; to whom will they be available; how they will be used in practice, and the likely result that will arise from their use. The GDPR is an example of a regulation that still falls short of closing the gap between AI to protect personal data, such as in relation to an insolvency, and AI that is used to further exploit that data for adverse economic gain. Roberts and Novak respond to this tension thus:

> The EU GDPR provisions that do take into consideration both AI and personal data, gaps still remain. It will be important to see how the application of the EU's GDPR will impact profiling practices, including with the use of AI, and on automated decision-making that impacts individuals. According

118 Ibid.

> to article 22 of the GDPR, '[t]he data subject shall have the right not to be subject to a decision based solely on automated processing, including profiling, which produces legal effects concerning him or her or similarly significantly affects him or her.' Moreover, according to article 29 Data Protection Working Party, 'to qualify as human intervention, the controller must ensure that any oversight of the decision is meaningful, rather than just a token gesture.' Importantly they note that Article 22 will not apply when the decision is (a) provided by the law, such as in the case of fraud prevention or money laundering checks; (b) necessary for the performance of or entering into a contract; or (3) based on the individual's prior consent. Nevertheless, even in these cases, the data controller needs to inform the data subject about the existence of automated decision-making, providing meaningful information about the logic involved, as well as the significance and the envisaged consequences of such processing for the data subject.[119]

Those authors go further, in questioning whether the current concept of consent would address these issues:

> As regards the principle of consent, a GDPR-compliant privacy information notice cannot adopt the form of a blank cheque covering any type of machine learning or AI technology. The information notice to the data subject needs to explain the main elements considered in reaching the decision, the source of the information obtained and their relevance. In other words, these principles underscore the autonomy of and respect for the data subject by requiring, for example, explicit consent and clear proof of significant interference of the right.[120]

Viewed this way, current data protection laws focus on primarily core principles, such as consent, fairness, purpose limitation and data minimisation. These principles are important as operational safeguards in the exercise and enjoyment of the right to privacy. However, these principles also need to be adopted, even fine-tuned, to accommodate AI technologies that have multiple capabilities, but are also able to be used for different purposes and to achieve competing results.[121] The nature of consent, in our view, is problematic on a number of fronts. While out of scope of this chapter, its woeful limitations as an instrument of consent in online transactions is readily displayed when users are invited to click 'accept' on online forms, as an alternative to access an often highly complex set of contract conditions in a related document that are virtually indecipherable for many. These risks are likely obstacles in attempts to avoid insolvency or reduce its harsh impact upon creditors, and other dependent groups, not least of all its employees, but also its

119 Ibid.
120 Ibid.
121 Ibid.

customers. As Trakman et al. propose, a comprehensive study is required in applying a narrowly framed concept of consent to commercial contexts in which the attributes of consent are multifaceted and operate multidimensionally.[122] Regulatory policy relating to cross-border insolvency is only sustainable, contractually, if it takes account of the technologically complex environment in which consent is expected to function. A party cannot be expected to consent, knowingly, to a full spectrum of issues on corporate resurrection, insolvency and restructuring based on technologies that are incomprehensible to most human beings. Taking technology on faith as an instrument of regulation in modern society is one thing. Taking technology on faith as a justification for consent is duplicitous if the consenting party believes that the purpose of AI is to provide a predictable pathway to preserving the threatened entity, when the purpose of the AI is the exact opposite. The fact is that the use of AI can be used to threaten the survival of an entity as much as to protect it. It can be duplicitous, or at least misleading, to maintain otherwise.

Researchers at the Diplo Foundation highlight that, when talking about the human rights implications of AI, we are implicitly referring to the unprecedented need for data to build AI.[123] They elaborate that, generally speaking, data in all its forms (big data, open data, personal data and sensitive data) is at a critical juncture in understanding human rights with regard to AI.[124] Importantly they highlight that:

> The autonomy of AI, the quality of the training data it uses, and the opaque nature of the algorithms employed can lead to inadvertent interferences with human rights, most notably the prohibition of discrimination linked with the right to privacy, the right to employment, the right to liberty and security, the right to a fair trial, and the right to freedom of expression and information. There is concern that AI can result in unintended consequences for human rights and even has the propensity to harm. Therefore, the quality of data used by AI models is crucial.[125]

Nevertheless, when coupled with the current regulatory approach to AI, there is a lack of a coherent definition of AI, particularly relating to legal systems, infrastructure and decision-making. Centrally, there are many variables related to the accuracy of data and prediction of whether an entity is experiencing financial stress. Generally, today, it is widely accepted that data generated by AI is sufficiently accurate to confirm the conclusion that an entity's financial position is unfavourable. Whether this conclusion is warranted in a particular case, it is a quantum leap to presuppose that the conclusion is warranted generally. The assumption that, when AI is applied to law, those who make law, practice and apply it, understand how

122 Leon Trakman, Robert Walters, Bruno Zeller, Digital Consent and Data Protection Law – Europe and Asia-Pacific Experience, *Information and Communications Technology Law* 29 (2020), 218–249.

123 Mapping the challenges and opportunities of artificial intelligence for the conduct of diplomacy, DiploFoundation Ministry of Foreign Affairs Finland, https://www.diplomacy.edu/AI-diplo-report.

124 Ibid.

125 Ibid.

it complements the law. The assumption is exaggerated. Problematic is the lack of training and use of AI in the legal profession. This is further compounded by difficulties in appreciating the virtue of upgrading AI, the manner of doing so, and the legal impact of that upgrading. For larger law firms that have the resources to adopt and use modified technologies, this concern is generally not an issue. For practitioners within medium to smaller firms who lack the capital to engage in technological upgrading, these obstacles remain.

9.7 Conclusion

There are considerable challenges facing the use and application of AI technology in insolvency and restructuring.[126] This chapter has highlighted the human rights challenges, where one state views personal data protection as a fundamental human right, as opposed to others that subject it to the right to free expression. It has also been argued that the use of AI will become increasingly complex when personal data form part of the overall commercial operations of an entity that is either restructuring or entering insolvency. Opposing conceptions of the value and use of AI will be further heightened because of the fragmented approach which states and corporate entities have taken to regulate AI.

It could be argued that the current legal framework that supports commercial activities goes across many different sectors of the economy. An example is the law of negligence, which could be used to determine fault when an individual or entity has been compromised and incurred a loss. In addition, as technology evolves, contracts will be adopted increasingly online and could in the future displace lawyers in overseeing their development or approval for legal use. However, this supposition that AI advances will displace the need for lawyers is arguable. Equally suspect is the view that AI machines will supplant lawyers in having predictive capabilities that lawyers lack. Somewhat overstated, too, is that, because AI analysis is more comprehensive than legal analysis, AI is more reliable and trustworthy. The benefit of AI is to supplement not displace human initiative. AI provides a more detailed basis to assist lawyers – and judges – in reaching decisions. It does not displace their ability to reach decisions with the aid of AI. However, as the reliability and accuracy of AI develops, it will become a more dependable reason to and means of supporting a legal decision. The same reasoning applies to the use of AI in regulating trans-border insolvencies and restructuring. As AI becomes more reliable in predicting financial stress, it becomes more sustainable as a tool in redressing that stress. As lawyers – and judges – become more familiar in using AI, they will be better able to rely on it in arriving at reliable legal outcomes. Whether AI is sufficiently advanced to rely upon steadfastly in predicting legal risks and means of

126 Robert Walters, Marko Novak, *Cyber Security, Artificial Intelligence, Data Protection and the Law*, Springer, 2021, Ch. 1.

redressing them, can only truly be answered contextually. In issue is how it is used; the confidence it provides to lawyers in their assessment of the risks, outcomes and means of avoiding those risks and outcomes in specific cases. Applied to insolvency and restructuring proceedings, AI can affirm a lawyer's confidence in whether, how and when to proceed to insolvency or restructuring, including the justification or reason for so deciding.

Such legal use of AI faces impediments from the outset. Importantly, as highlighted in this chapter, the definition of AI is far from agreed or settled nationally or internationally. This is problematic and in need of resolution, particularly where technology is used to assist in processing and resolving disputes between two or more parties.

The advantaged use of advanced technologies in insolvency and restructuring in the future is potentially immense. These instruments of prediction have the capacity to produce reliable results providing greater certainty and predictability in managing finances of fragile entities facing insolvency. Greater certainty in using algorithms as tools of prediction, while never providing perfect insight, can also provide greater economic stability in proceeding with an insolvency, and sometimes preferentially, with a restructure. If AI is integrated more consistently into national systems of law, it is likely to receive greater international recognition as well. The benefit in greater homogeneity in applying AI instruments to trans-border insolvency and restructuring disputes is to have greater faith in the reliability of the outcomes reached.

AI cannot ever reach the euphoric state of perfect accuracy. Still, it can be invoked to develop a high level of evidence-based early intervention to assist in managing restructuring of companies that are located. If and when it is adopted internationally, its economic and social benefits are potentially enormous, such as in flagging when an entity is likely to sustain financial stress and how to address that stress.

At the other extreme, the premature, and indeed comprehensive, reliance on AI as a predictive tool in redressing financial stress in cross-border trade would be to ignite uncertainty, indeed anxiety, in the commercial sector over its accuracy as an analytical tool. The use of AI in law could also unravel in the face of long-standing faith in human judgement in assessing the materiality of discrete economic risks in each specific case. Applied to insolvency, overzealous faith in AI could result in parties racing to dismantle an entity in financial stress because of AI prediction of an accelerating rate of financial decline due to market instability. If this AI determination is false, the economic and social harm is likely to be the insolvency of an entity that might otherwise have survived without insolvency, or alternatively have benefitted from a restructuring. The further harmful consequence of overreliance on AI is the potential flight of capital from financial sectors that are predicted to be in retreat and the race of capital to sectors that are deemed to be in growth phases. The implications of such capital shifts upon cross-business solvencies could be to significantly increase the risk of insolvency of entities in sectors from which capital has fled. The shift of capital to sectors in which AI has predicted growth, if erroneous, could lead to significant capital depletion should the AI predicted growth not materialise.

The comments here are unavoidably speculative, especially given wide divergence over the reliability of AI, in general and in specific sectors of the global economy. A more comprehensive and continuing investigation into the viability of AI in general and in select industrial contexts, could provide greater confidence in the use of AI in law.

10

INTERNATIONALISATION OF COMMERCIAL LAW AND PATHWAY FORWARD

This final chapter recommends that states, as well as corporate entities engaged in cross-border initiatives, give greater attention to establishing policies and principles in pursuit of greater harmonisation across national legal systems. The chapter also calls for the further globalisation of cross-border insolvency law. These comments are reinforced by commentary on prior chapters, and by examining legal developments in Australia, European Union, India, Indonesia, China, Singapore, United Kingdom and United States, as well as internationally. It demonstrates that these jurisdictions have a level of legal convergence across the areas of law compared. However, significant progress to achieve greater convergence is needed. The benefit of greater harmonisation in law, including cross-border insolvency law, is greater consistency, certainty and predictability in the multistate adoption of uniform legal principles to resolve trans-border disputes, not limited to insolvency and restructuring. The message to states that resist such harmonisation is that their failure to adjust their laws on insolvency and restructuring in response to the internationalisation of cross-border insolvency, can lead to their loss of transnational business. At risk is, not only competition to many business-oriented laws in other national jurisdictions that are connected to a cross-border proceedings, but also to non-state institutions. Harmonisation can also lead to more institutionalised rules and guidelines that guide parties in reaching agreements, such as through close-out netting provisions, schemes of arrangement and letters of comfort. There is already encouraging evidence of harmonisation, such as the UNCITRAL Model Law on Cross-Border Insolvency. Ideally, further harmonisation is achievable through the enhancement of principles of insolvency and restructuring law that states share; with international organisations like the UNCITRAL and UNIDROIT unifying divergent national laws on insolvency. The book's assertion is not for idealism in its search for homogeneity in cross-border trade and investment law. Its rationale is rather that the harmonization of law is a means towards economic stability across

DOI: 10.4324/9781003312024-4

trans-border financial markets. Harmony in finance law is instrumental in progressing economic development, and in raising productive benchmarks in the playing fields of multilateral trade and investment. Effective harmonization is informed by commercial practice and in legal responses to it. It is reactive, in responding to failing self-regulation in local, regional and global financial sectors, and in legal systems that contribute to those failures. The purpose of the book is reactive, in seeking pathways to redress such deficiencies. It is proactive in proposing best practice in harmonization efforts. It does not purport to be a magic wand, nor a cure for multiple commercial ills in the often diffuse, confusing and contradictory legal regulation of cross-border insolvency or restructuring.

10.1 Introduction

The globalisation of the law has been shaped variously: by language and culture, trade and commerce, statehood and nationalism and legal traditions across nation states. The interdependence of states in trade and investment embodies multicultural and multinational values at work and is embodied in the internationalisation of commercial law. The result is reflected in the movement of goods, services, investment and capital across national and regional borders and between nation states and their subjects. Intended beneficiaries of these movements are developed and developing states, as well as their respective subjects.

An important observation that has been commonly identified is that the transnationalisation of trade and investment law dates back centuries to medieval times.

Trakman's book on the Medieval Law Merchant elucidates on the growth of transnational merchant law.[1] The product of merchant trade across Western Europe and North Africa, the Law Merchant sought to transcend local boundaries. With the support of local kinds and principles, it included measures directed at redressing financial stress among transnational merchants. It used functional legal instruments suited to disparate trades and industries and adapted to suit local merchant markets. The transnationalism underlying trade and investment in its more modern genesis in the 17th century is attributable to the Westphalian System that evolved from the instruments of peace adopted at Munster and Osnabruck that ended the Thirty Years' War.[2] The notion of sovereignty was a central conception of an absolutist Westphalian System. Determinative was absolutism which was vested as a natural right in the local prince or other potentate. The result was a system of law between

1 Leon Trakman, The Evolution of the Law Merchant: Our Forgotten Heritage (Fred B. Rothman, 1983) 1.

2 Stephan Hobe, The Era of Globalisation as a Challenge to International Law, *Duquesne Law Review* (2002), 657. See also Martin Shapiro, The Globalization of Law, *Indiana Journal of Global Legal Studies* 1, 1 (1993), 38–39; Terence Haliday, Pavel Osinsky, Globalization of Law, *Annual Review of Sociology* 32 (2006), 447–470; Brian Mccormack, A Historical Case for the Globalisation of International Law: The Chaco War and the Principle of *Ex Aequo et Bono*, *Global Society* 13, 3 (1999), 287–312; Pierrick Le Golf, Global Law: A Legal Phenomenon Emerging from the Process of Globalization, *Indiana Journal of Global Legal Studies* 14, 1, Article 7, (2007), 121–124.

independent kings and princes within the then known world, predominantly in modern-day Europe and northern Africa. The scope of trans-regional law was limited to the conduct of ruling monarchs in their mutual dealings, and in regulating commerce through laws governing maritime shipping and trade at local markets and fairs. Trans-regional law embraced the rights of kings and princes to engage in warfare, the rules of international maritime law (freedom of the High Seas) and rules of international diplomatic law.[3] This framework of law, however, was grounded in affirming the absolute power of states and framing laws by which they asserted their powers both *inter se* and in relation to third parties, such as merchants that traded in goods and services at maritime towns including in the provision of financing.

Local laws, dominated by power-based rights of rulers of principalities and local kingdoms, were gradually transformed into greater uniformity of trans-regional trade across 16th-century nation states. This development was expressed variously, through the formal unification of principalities into modern-day states, such as the gradual amalgamation of hundreds of principalities into the German state, and by revolutions against the absolute powers of kings identified with the French Revolution. The powers of the people gradually emerged, such as to operate and engage in markets to which they could sell and buy goods and services. Still, newly formed states asserted their sovereignty both in sovereign relations between and among states, but also in their regulations of those so-called free markets. The type of law that started to develop in the mid-19th century and grew at an increasing pace in the 20th century nevertheless preserved the powers of states. However, these powers were often exercised collectively, notably in the sovereign state, as distinct from the king, to abrogate that sovereignty to the joint actions of states, notably provided for by treaty.[4] That continued into the 20th century. In 1927, the Permanent Court of International Justice described international law in the famous Lotus Case as follows:

> International law governs relations between independent states. The rules of law binding upon states therefore emanate from their own free will as expressed in conventions or by usages generally accepted as expressing principles of law and established in order to regulate the relations between these co-existing independent communities or with a view to the achievement of common aims. Restrictions upon the independence of states cannot therefore be presumed.[5]

Yet the advancing 20th century did not see harmony evolving either uniformly or stably between and among states, contrary to the modernist depiction of the development of laws of 'civilised' nations. The 20th century has borne witness to the fall and dilution of dynasties, empires, monarchs, kingdoms. It has experienced two world wars, and more recently, the rise of conflict through terrorism. It has borne witness to the evolving manifestations of socialism and communism, along the investiture of democracy and its periodic sublimation. The economic, social

3 Ibid.

4 Ibid.

5 *The Lotus Case (Fr. v. Turk.)* 1927 P.C.I.J. (ser. A) No. 10, at 18.

and human health implications of these instabilities and achievements upon international commercial activities in the modern era, stretching into the 21st century, have been profound.

Exploring the significance of modernisation warrants reflection on the dynamic installation of multilateralism in the 20th century, a key moment following WWII. Largely initiated under the Bretton Woods system was the foundation of the emerging internationalisation of commercial laws as a unifying tool to unify states rather than drive them apart. Conversely, this multilateralism did favour the elites, in protecting wealthy classes primarily from wealthier states. This resulted in the partial departure from treaties of friendship, commerce and navigation, as euphemisms for treaties of domination by powerful Western liberal states and developing ones. The democratisation of treaties, at least between states, continued. However, international codes and conventions sought to empower developing states to protect their national policies, including in promoting domestic economic growth and allaying domination by inbound international and multinational corporations supported by their powerful states of origin.

While it is out of scope to discuss the evolution of transnational commercial law based on these historical watersheds, it is fitting to recognise the continuing tension between nationalism and internationalism. It is equally important to appreciate the unresolved tension between absolute and indivisible sovereignty in the conduct of trade on the one hand and sovereignty by association between and among states in collaborating on the rules of trans-border trade on the other hand.

Material, too, is to appreciate the extent to which sovereignty by association has led to the growth of regionalism. In effect, states establish rules of association by which they share their sovereignty with other states and differentiate themselves from state and non-state actors beyond their regional association. The EU is the prototype illustration of sovereignty by association. Embedded within it is a common market framework that has, by and large, regionalised commercial laws. The creation of regional economic zones, arguably, creates a pathway towards consolidating international commercial law beyond the region, such as the influence the EU's GDPR increasingly has beyond the region. EU regionalism is also a template for the growth of an international market framework that displays greater inclusivity and equality of treatment among EU Member States and their subjects. So too, regional regulation does not supplicate national law norms as much as it borrows from them, such as in the EU's adoption of domestic regulatory norms in responding to anti-competitive conduct in commercial markets, and raises insolvency threats.

Importantly, the advances of the globalisation of commercial law, including insolvency law does not infer the subordination of national law regulation. Rather, it infers the dilution of overly rigorous boundaries between domestic and international commercial law, and the development of a transformative process of implementation, construction and application of domestic norms internationally.[6] Transnational commercial law including insolvency law constitutes the selective

6 Marcelo Dias Varella, *Internationalization of Law Globalization, International Law and Complexity*, Springer, 2014, 1.

internationalisation of domestic law norms. Transnational commercial law also amalgamates otherwise disparate domestic laws under the rubric of shared regulatory norms, such as in governing transparency in financial transactions. At the same time, international commercial laws lead to distinctive regulatory norms to guide the interface between state and multistate, state and non-state norms of conduct such as at international insolvency hubs in Europe, North America and Asia. The result of that interface is the intermeshing of 'public' and 'private' frameworks for regulatory action, such as through the participation of financial and banking institutions in the evolution of cross-border insolvency law. What is emerging, too, is an imperfect shift from regionalization to globalization in trade in goods and services including financial services.[7]

Internationalising the regulation of commercial laws nevertheless does not represent a seamless transition from localism to globalism. Delocalisation does entail the sacrifice of localised attributes for the purpose of emboldening transnational laws. However, the means of doing so are not necessarily, nor desirably exclusionary of domestic norms. Gainful internationalisation is armed by regulatory norms adopted from states. It is also affirmed by regulatory norms which states can share, such as through treaties governing financial transparency and trans-border insolvency. These multiple domestic sources of international commercial law cannot be mechanically reconstituted into international commercial law, although AI attempts to do so. Those domestic sources can serve as both functional sources of international law and outlets for the adoption and application of that law. The result is that transnational commercial law often has localised origins directed at preserving financial security and stability in delocalised settings. Those localised norms continue to influence norms underlying international law, such as those relating to efficiency and transparency underlying trans-border insolvency and restructuring law. But the dictation of these norms by singular state action is ideally and practically supplanted by international law norms that are determined multilaterally not unilaterally.

The internationalisation of localised law includes the supplication of domestic law norms, such as freedom of parties to contract, and the binding force of their promises (pacta sunt servanda). These are applied through choice of forum and law clauses in party agreements, and through letters of comfort and close-out netting provisions, as demonstrated earlier in this book. These preferences of the parties are reflected often in their choice of domestic laws in states with established commercial law traditions. They also adopt clauses that refer disputes to financial hubs where both the law and judicial proceedings are tailored, institutionally and functionally, to meet their perceived needs for expeditious, cost effective and transparent proceedings. As illustrated throughout this book, cross-border insolvency proceedings often devolve from localised into delocalised law, albeit inconsistently and sometimes insufficiently tailored to the requirements of cross-border disputes.

7 Leon Trakman and Nicholas Ranieri (ed.) *Regionalism in International Investment Law*, Oxford, 2013.

The internationalisation of law is therefore a process that is operationalised through the actions of diverse actors, including national legislatures and courts that operate across multiple jurisdictions. That process of internationalisation is disparately impacted by local norms, such when civil law traditions are intermeshed with common or customary law traditions, and by their interdependent evolution. Functional internationalisation therefore does not infer unbridled delocalisation. Legal divergence in the restructuring of localised insolvency laws and procedures reorder them to embody their multi-directional use and application.[8] Dias Varella identifies three important traditional theoretical concepts of international law that recognise disparate sources of international law, that encourage their divergent conceptualisation and, ultimately, actualisation. First is the 'possibility of or the limits of conceptualizing law as a system organized in pyramid-shaped, hierarchical, tree-like form, compared with the notion of constructing legal phenomena in networks. sources of international law'.[9] Second is a vision of 'international law as a fragmented, conflicting, and ineffective collection versus international law as a theory of greater complexity, density, and effectiveness, with new lines of reasoning that give cohesion to and explain international law as a system'.[10] Third is the:

> propriety of revisiting old ideas, considered outdated, such as a global republic (civitas maxima) of *jus gentium*, based on the universalization of values related to core themes (human rights, environmental, humanitarian, economic, penal, financial, and so on), or perhaps only serving as an imperialist expansion of developed-country values throughout the rest of the world.[11]

Arguably, whether the current international rules-based system is upheld or changed, it will be influenced by the aforementioned factors, along with different legal cultures. It will be, incongruently, hierarchical, fragmented, complex, conflicting and universalising. However, mutually exclusive and incompatible these incongruencies might be, it is in attempting to reconcile them that congruency can be achieved, even if only incompletely and temporarily.

The transposition of domestic commercial into delocalised law is also reflected in cross-border legal practice. Cross-border commercial law is evidenced when both 'business activities and dispute resolution has been accompanied by the internationalisation of lawyers who now regularly advise clients with regard to international business transactions and the resolution of related disputes'.[12] That is, as Nedim Peter Vogt identifies, major law firms headquartered in London and New York have become worldwide networking enterprises, with partners in major offices around the globe, and English law firms, and to a lesser extent American

8 Ibid.
9 Ibid.
10 Ibid.
11 Ibid.
12 Nedim Peter Vogt, Anglo-Internationalisation of Law and Language: English as the Language of Law, *The International Legal Practice* 29 (2004), 112.

firms, have emerged as the early leaders in this area. Today, Singapore and Member States of the EU along with Australia have emerged as central international legal hubs, with most of the top international law firms present. Yet, these legal and commercial hubs are being challenged, and the rise of third countries such as India, Indonesia and China are emerging as leaders in the commercial and digital economy of the present. Purportedly uniform legal regimes are being recast into incongruent regulatory systems, reinforced by variations in cultural and legal traditions. Disparities in client needs and legal services have led to discrete commercial, accounting, and legal services being offered at distinct financial hubs. These hubs have also institutionalised trans-border insolvency laws. These have inculcated these into their financial offerings. They are depicted as representing a coalescence between law in theory and practice, such as in offering transparency and security to debtors and creditors in insolvency and restructuring proceedings.

10.2 Culture, Legal Culture, Legal Tradition

A further important influence on the development of transnational legal frameworks is the correlation between culture, national and cross-national legal traditions. Culture, in our view, is emerging as an even stronger influence in the development of national laws that, over time, will modify the cultural and legal pathway followed by international commercial law. Cultural influence is readily evinced in tensions between divergence and convergence between common and civil law systems as primary sources of trans-border law, illustrated by tensions across pre-Brexit European law. National cultures will also impact upon the evolution of transnational culture, notably as dominant nation states mould new transnational legal developments to suit their sovereign needs, somewhat at the expense of the international community more generally. Should this progression of state hierarchies direct the globalisation of commercial law, it is likely to undermine transparency in regulatory practice; and raise barriers to a sustainable future for cross-border insolvency and restructuring.

The communality, and distinction, between legal culture and legal tradition can materially influence the outcome of regional and international legal instruments and mechanisms. As Trakman argues, culture combines social, political and economic traditions.[13] Legal cultures are reflected in codes of law, statutes and judicial decisions, and embodied in principles, standards and rules of law that govern, *inter alia*, international commercial arbitration.[14] These traditions are also expressed in the opinions of jurists through which law is extolled, interpreted and applied.[15] Legal traditions also serve as the source and foundation of a legal system. Such sourcing is exemplified by legal traditions that served as primary sources of Roman law institutions, such as Justinian's 6th-century codification of Roman law. A legal tradition also follows both a directional and a directing evolution,

13 Leon Trakman, Legal Traditions and International Commercial Arbitration, *American Review of International Arbitration* (2007), 3–6.

14 Ibid.

15 Ibid., 4–8.

illustrated by the evolution of Roman law into civil law, its reception into 'modern' European law and its particularisation in different national legal systems with the advent of the modern nation state in the 16th century.[16]

The source of shared legal traditions, however, devolve differently. The legal traditions underlying Roman law evolved into divergent common and civil law traditions. The traditions of the common law of England extended across the then British Empire. It continues to materially influence the evolving law in Commonwealth legal systems, such as Australia, Singapore and India and also, the US. Traditions of the common law also vary to accommodate local cultures that reflect both cultural and through it legal interdependence; but are the subordination of cultures such as in developing countries in colonial eras. This interface among legal cultures traces back many centuries, such as to the early Romans, with their inculcation being conceived as 'civilising'. The content of a:

> legal culture may lead to so-called cultural determinism, as when one legal culture is perceived as determining the nature and content of other cultures, as was imputed to the 'Civilizing' culture of Rome over the customary legal cultures of pre-medieval Europe, or more controversially, the 'Americanization' of commercial law in the Twentieth Century.[17]

Cultural determination is also repeated over time, albeit subject to contextual diversity. Some commentators analogise the prominence of the US over the globalisation of law to the history heralded by European colonialism.[18] Arguably, throughout the 20th and 21st centuries the legal cultures and traditions of Europe, and later the US, have significantly dominated the ascent of globalisation predominantly in the West, in which ascent is depicted as legal convergence, harmonisation of law, or more directly, as embedding cultural implantations. The evolution of international commercial law is an illustration of the transposition of legal cultures. In genesis, it is the product of cultural dictation but also cultural coalescence, with both being embodied in the evolution of Roman civil law and later, the common law, in Africa, Asia and the Americas.

States that supplant their legal cultures and traditions upon others, whether through the exercise of despotism or socio-economic functionalism, can undermine inclusivity grounded in dialogue and consensus among states. Conceived affirmatively, the result of despotically imposed norms of globalisation can undermine a rules-based system of international commercial law. Conversely, internationalisation can embody an institutional legal framework that is capable of functional application and adaption, albeit differently and adaptably and never wholly flawlessly. Applied to international commercial law, notably to the law of insolvency, is the adaption of borrowed legal cultures, such as rules directed at transparency and

16 Ibid.

17 Ibid.

18 Bryant Garth, *The Globalisation of the Law, the Oxford Handbook of law and Politics*, edited by Gregory Caldeira, Daniel Kelmen, Keith Whittington, Oxford University Press, 2008.

fairness in the conduct of insolvency proceedings. Among these borrowings is the transplantation of norms of fairness, known in the common law as the rule of law.

10.3 The Rule of Law

Dominance in the transposition of legal cultures and traditions is not invariably the source of regulatory instability or partiality in the treatment of parties, such as debtors and creditors in cross-border insolvency proceedings. Nor is such dominance a typical prelude to substantive and procedural injustice. Norms of fair and equal treatment in insolvency and restructuring proceedings are transitional instruments originating in domestic law that are absorbed into transnational law. The English rule of law is a potentially adaptive medium by which to dispense justice between the subjects of states that are engaged in cross-border financial and banking transactions. A localised rule of law is also the source of legal convergence and harmonisation in which a multiplicity of states embraces it as a fundamental medium by which to ingrain regulatory equality between and among parties to insolvency disputes. This is not to suggest that an overarching rule of law jurisprudence is inexorably equal handed in managing traffic through a trans-border gate of insolvency proceedings. States, not limited to developing ones, sometimes reject a rules-based system on the basis that it enriches wealthy states and their outbound traders and investors at the expense of inbound and often developing states and their local industries and consumers. As demonstrated in prior chapters, these issues pose deep-seated challenges in improving current-day regimes regulating cross-border insolvency and corporate restructuring.

Yet, it is important, as Leon Trakman argues, to align the rule of law adopted by sovereign states with the rule of law derived from transnational public policy which overarches the rules of law of individual states.[19] Some might insist on the former before the latter; once nation states have an internal rule of law, then they should accept a rule of law between them. Even if this kind of argument was accepted:

> it would not mean that states could ignore their international obligations – merely that any nation which had violated the rule of law with respect to its own citizens might not be able to rely on an international rule of law to the same extent and standing and, therefore, should only be given to its citizens or their democratic representatives.[20]

The limitations placed on international law in its current form only dilutes the concept of the rules-based system and the rule of law.

A law of cross-border insolvency is especially challenged in the absence of a rule of law in the main place of proceedings and comparably even if not identically, in

19 Leon Trakman, Aligning State Sovereignty with Transnational Public Policy, *Tulane Law Review* 93 (2018) 207. See also Charles Sampford, Reconceiving the Rule of Law for a Globalizing World, in Spencer Zifcak, *Globalisation and the Rule of Law*, Routledge, 2005, 25–26.

20 Ibid., 25–26.

the law in secondary places of proceedings. The application of the rule of law is particularly germane to cross-border insolvency because it relates to a stage of economic stress when a debtor is both economically vulnerable and open to exploitation by others, not limited to creditors. Its fair treatment requirements also protect different classes of creditors in redressing abuses of and delay in distributions, and uncertainty over the fair distribution of assets. The rule of law can also facilitate preferable options to insolvency, such as a restructure under the control of the existing management or as directed by an appointed administrator. Therefore, both debtors and creditors are ordinarily protected by the consistent application of the rule of law and by its applicability across state borders. Its application, arguably, is also beneficial to other parties that are impacted by insolvency and restructuring schemes, such as employees of the entity who are threatened with termination and the absence of termination payments.

The problem is in establishing an international rule of law that is consistent across state boundaries in times of political, economic and cultural conflict among and between states. Dias Varella points to a time when the internationalisation of law accelerated after the Cold War and led to the emergence of a multipolar political and economic order. In the political realm, the shift of the Cold War's bipolar system between the US and the Soviet Union permitted the emergence of various state and non-state actors globally. In economic terms, Varella argues that:

> various powers have ascended, such as the European Union, Japan, and China, along with Brazil, India, and Russia and various nonstate actors. Multinational corporations, which control a growing portion of the global market of goods and services and are interested in global standardization of procedures and ways of doing business, have grown in importance, but so have decentralized networks of economic actors, organized in transnational production chains.[21]

However, the global economic-political order has evolved significantly in 2014, since Varella's comments. Over the last five years and accentuated by the COVID-19 pandemic in 2020, new tensions have arisen, diluting the prospect of an internationalised regime of commercial law that is sustainable and supported multilaterally. Today, the rise of nationalism is visible around the world.[22] It is further compounded by the COVID-19 outbreak in which nation states are taking substantial steps to protect their citizens, especially by closing their international borders to the influx of non-residents on grounds of health, safety, and to protect domestic employment and enterprise. As a result, commercial entities wanting to undertake cross-border restructuring, such as through mergers and acquisitions are being obliged, today more than ever, to follow the foreign investment rules in the takeover entity's state. More specifically, as demonstrated in this book, foreign

21 Marcelo Dias Varella, *Internationalization of Law Globalization, International Law and Complexity*, Springer, 2014, 11.

22 Robert Walters, *National Identity and social Cohesion, in a Time of Geopolitical and Economic Tension: Australia – European Union – Slovenia*, Springer, 2020, 329–356.

investment rules increasingly influence whether a merger or acquisition by a foreign entity will be approved by the relevant domestic regulator. These domestic constraints, including the denial of a hearing and other rights accorded to citizens and residents, have arguably emerged in states like the US, India and to a lesser extent Australia and the UK as an expression of a new nationalist order. The related issue is whether such political and economic restraints on foreign trade and investment, not limited to mergers and acquisitions, are discouraging states from extending rule of law protections to foreign entities and individuals comparably to rule of law protection accorded to nationals. National legislation and case law on foreign investment, elaborated upon in the book, confirms that such rule of law protection is not so accorded to non-nationals and non-residents.

In recognition of this tension between the domestication and internationalisation of commercial law, the book makes a case for the latter. In our view, today more than ever, such internationalisation can only be achieved incrementally. In other words, the days when states engage in a negotiating process and arrive at agreement embodied in a convention comparable to the CISG, may well have receded materially. We call for the establishment of principles, and the ability to strengthen the legal framework, such as by escalating principles to a Model Law, not unlike the Model Law on trans-border insolvency. Our goal is for that Model Law to serve as a framework for an ensuing convention when economic and political conditions better support it.

10.4 Obstacles to Further Internationalising Commercial Law

The internationalisation of commercial law has been far from smooth sailing before the financial tribulations of the 21st century. For an extended period of time, from the 1950s to 2000s, scholars argued that the modern nation state had become outmoded. Particularly, the state had become ill-suited to accommodate the economic, cultural and social demands of globalisation which states largely lacked the means to control. Coupled with this deficiency, as Leon Trakman argued, was the need to acknowledge that globalization in cross-border commercial law was, and remains, pluralistic in nature. Its development is contingent on recognising local variants of it, both in its nature and in its application.[23] The need to accommodate such pluralism has grown, not receded, somewhat in response to global political polarization. The dislocation in trans-border commerce in post-WWII days, ascribed to the Cold War, persist. International Conventions on global trade and investment continue to be conceived and applied differently as the global economic power structure has grown from the US and Russia as dominant world powers to include China. Trade and investment conflicts among these great powers and their allies continue to impede the prospects of reaching multilateral trade and investment

23 Leon Trakman, Aligning State Sovereignty with Transnational Public Policy 93 (2018), 20. See also David Bederman, *Globalisation and International Law*, Springer, 2008, 147.

treaties, including in the sector of trans-border insolvency. The power imbalance between great, middle and developing economies remains, albeit in modified form. Economic demands that were made through gunboat diplomacy in the 19th and 20th century, are now being made tactically through bilateral agreements, notably by China's growing Belt and Road Initiative across Asia and Africa. The reality today is that neo colonialism remains an obstacle that is being resurrected and perpetuated in the developing worlds of Africa, Asia, the Middle East and Latin America. Shepherded by great and middle powers, they remain intact, while being structured and operating a little differently. They are prevalent across the investment sector, including in cross-border banking and commercial insolvency. They are illustrated by preferential deals offered to developing states to allay investment risks to inbound multinational and national corporations emanating from highly resourced Western and Eastern nations.

Central to the continually competing demands within domestic, regional and global economies is the need to embrace new technologies in which the Internet and mobile phones provide services beyond information gathering and sharing that prevailed just a few decades earlier. Technology advancement has gone a long way to standardising functional attributes of transnational business. Illustratively, the use of logistics from shipping to financial servicing are important elements in cross-border infrastructure contracting. These technological innovations have often been gradual, not instantaneous. They have evolved over more than eight decades since WWII. They are now embodied in international instruments implemented by global organisations that have sought to standardise international trade, investment, and finance. In the last several decades, too, state and corporate entities have been aided by technologies to maintain stability and efficiency in the institutional and functional regulation of global commerce. By these means, they have addressed market fluctuations arising from often unforeseen circumstances beyond their reasonable control. Today, these encompass such global threats as pollution and environment degradation along with attendant threats to human health.

However, at both national and international levels, the ability and will of the international community of states and corporate entities to harmonise regulatory regimes is subject to significant economic obstacles. Another factor potentially undermining rather than enhancing the globalisation of trade, is the rise in technology. Information systems operating nationally and internationally are undermining the competitiveness and solvency of business entities, by alleging the inefficiency or lack of competitiveness of such entities and/or by providing IT-based alternatives. The growth of artificial intelligence (AI), as illustrated in the previous chapter, affirms the extent to which AI can predict financial risks and insolvency, even though AI is often poorly adapted to the legal sector generally. AI can also provide inaccurate conclusions that nevertheless precipitate reactions including the race of capital from business ventures which AI depicts as financially at risk. As such, corporate sectors are being displaced or replaced in a global economy in which leading states are negating the benefits of globalisation on grounds of both national security and economic stability. Other states, notably but not exclusively in the developing world, are seeking to maintain globalisation initiatives on converse national security and economic grounds. Adding to the shift away from economic globalisation is the absence of cogent regulatory controls operating internationally. Further extending the reversion to localisation is the lack of physicality associated with economic enhancement achieved virtually. In the absence of tangible movement of goods and services, often intangible technological productivity that is not visualised, is not recognised as a virtue of internationalisation. That critique of economic globalisation is accentuated by distrust for such physical movements in economically and political unstable times, including lockdowns that impede the movement of people and goods across national borders.

The financial servicing sector illustrates these obstacles at work, demonstrating that cross-border finance law and regulation is often complex, cumbersome and inconsistent. While it can take years to develop a fully integrated international regulatory system to govern finance and commerce, the resulting system may also fail at various stages of implementation. The advancement in technology alone may be insufficient to drive reliable implementation processes, including smoothing out transitional obstacles, in regulating trans-border finance and commerce. Information systems may also undermine such internationalisation by predicting insolvency risks based on insufficiently analysed or false information. This can lead to the flight of capital away from an entity that would otherwise not have been as seriously at risk as was portrayed by AI.

The macro-reality is that such internationalisation faces continuing and often expanding global threats that are causes of instability and dissention. These vary from overpopulation, the destruction of the environment, economic underdevelopment, the migration of peoples and international terrorism. In issue, too, are global nuclear threats that are exacerbated by the largely unregulated possession and proliferation of armaments. These risks are attenuated by limited, irregular and inconsistent responses by single nation states and the international community at large to the disclosure of such risks, such as in the construction of a domestic nuclear facility.[24]

An idealised response is through support for the internationalisation of law that is collectively constructed, widely comprehended and, importantly, supported by state and non-state actors alike. A comparable response to nuclear threats is in establishing a transnational legal response to the destabilisation of commerce that arises from local, regional and global militarism. The overriding gain is to encourage multistate and multi-people collaboration through people-to-people contacts, and by bringing countries together rather than dividing them.

Faced with the perceived inadequacy and inconsistency among international regulatory laws, parties to such cross-border dealings can still resort to standardised contracts that are adopted to meet trade or industry requirements. They can draft comprehensive contract clauses that provide, in detail, for staged options in redressing financial risks, debt overload, and the management of ensuing financial stress and crises. They can agree on how to avert or limit those risks, or on their advent, redress them. So too, they can also adopt the non-binding rules and guidelines of

24 Stephan Hobe, The Era of Globalisation as a Challenge to International Law, *Duquesne Law Review* 40 (2002), 655–660.

both trade and legal associations that provide standards and procedures for regulating such risks, and institutionalised dispute resolution facilities to redress them. What parties to insolvency and restructuring agreements cannot do is ensure that, in making choices or law and forum, including resort to domestic courts and international commercial arbitrators, they are able to predict trans-border legal outcomes based on uniform law(s). What they also cannot ensure is that regulators and courts that are responsible for regulating main and secondary proceedings will provide compatible procedures by which to address insolvency and restructuring matters.

A further tension is the idea of creating a borderless world. The quest for and emergence of a 'borderless world' is reflected in global discourse, modelled upon achievements, such as the creation of a borderless EU. However, a tension that remains unresolved is to redress the dysfunctionality between the sovereign nation state as the source of legal harmonisation and coordination across states, and the public international organisations that states create by negotiating comprehensive treaties that purportedly oversee the actions of states.[25] Such dysfunctionality is most readily associated with building consensus among sovereign states that are perceived as sublimating the sovereignty of some states, such as developing states and their subjects, that succumb to treaties that are tailored by developed states to suit their economic needs and those of their outbound investors. These obstacles in public international law are imbedded in state-initiated action under the cloak of the United Nations (UN), that is obscured by intrusive turf battles among state parties to the UN and the sublimation of corporate entities that are seemingly incidental victims of such battles.[26] In significant measure that sublimation is a consequence of COVID-19, in subjecting corporate entities, employers and employees alike, to a multifaceted regulatory apparatus that dictates precisely when, how and where they may function, work and invest. Were such uniform measures applied to cross-border insolvency, it could well result in an international regulatory regime that favours the interests of economically dominant states and their outbound investors at the expense of target-developing states and their vulnerable localised industries.

An accentuating tension is the time and effort required for international treaties and conventions to come to life. They often take years to negotiate, while states often decline to ratify them. Even when treaties and conventions are concluded and ratified, they are often never fully implemented and only spottily enforced.[27] This is evident in relation to commercial conventions and model laws that often take years to negotiate, draft, implement and enforce. Those deficiencies are pronounced in relation to widely touted public international institutions engaged in dispute resolution including the International Court of Justice, human rights and war crimes tribunals, and specialised arbitration mechanisms. However impressive their antecedence may be, they often fail to produce definitive decisions, leading parties to seek other means of settling their disputes.[28]

25 Ibid., 150.
26 Ibid.
27 Ibid.
28 Ibid.

These developments are comparably concerning in relation to international commercial dispute resolution, such as international commercial and investor-state arbitration in which dispute resolution between commercial parties is protracted, costly and where awards are often not enforced in particular states. As this book has demonstrated, these obstacles are readily apparent in relation to the concurrent regulation of insolvency through domestic courts and international commercial arbitration.

For David Bederman, the obstacle to dispute resolution between states is the modern Westphalia nation state system as a purportedly collective instrument for state-to-state dispute resolution.[29] His rationale is that, while this system is under challenge, it has not collapsed. Counter to Bederman's scholarship in 2008 were ensuing drastic economic crises that followed, notably the emergency of the Global Financial Crisis that has not fully retreated for the global arena since its onset. Scholars have more recently, prior to and during the COVID-19 outbreak, began writing about the rise of nationalism again as a purported means of avoiding being ensnared in global financial crises. Then there are ideological reasons for the onslaught of strident nationalism. We are witnessing a widespread rise of nationalism, nationally but also global, that also limits trans-continental spread of goods and services across nations.[30] Nationalist parties proliferate across the Western world, and have been discernible in Western Europe since the 1980s. Elections and referenda in 2016–2017 there highlight the strength of nationalist parties, candidates and propositions.[31] At the same time, they demonstrate a countermovement of progressive increases in popular support for delocalisation to avoid national biases. The issue remains whether nationalism has altered the reaction of states to fundamental changes in global reality, notably the shared benefits of building economic structures and performance capabilities globally, not through the sporadic, insular and duplicative measures adopted by discrete states. Of concern, too, is the explosive potential of national responses to COVID-19, such as through divergent travel and worker lockdowns, to accentuate concomitant constraints on cross-border trade and commerce.

What has emerged from the 2020 outbreak of COVID-19, therefore, is a further manifestation of nationalism, depicted in how nation states have responded differently to its economic effects, based on ideological and political grounds. These reactions are not peculiar to the pandemic; but they do accentuate directional changes, globally, brought about by nationalism. Nor does the impact of directional change wrought by COVID-19 compare to the physical and economic impact of WWI and WWII. The pandemic was not the product of nations going to war, although nationalist tensions had arisen as a consequence of its perceived social and political sequelae. What nationalism is unlikely to produce is a permanent shift away from establishing global patterns of economic behaviour, such as in sustaining access

29 David Bederman, *Globalisation and International Law*, Springer, 2008, 147.

30 Florian Bieber, Is Nationalism on the Rise? Assessing Global Trends, *Ethnopolitics* 17, 5 (2018), 519–522.

31 Ibid.

to foreign financial markets. Florian Bieber makes the pervasive observation that nationalism is deeply engrained in the global system and in most societies around the world. As such, the coronavirus and state responses to it are not going to fundamentally alter this global reality.[32] Given that many citizens are unable to travel today, including from privileged states that have traditionally accentuated open borders to facilitate trade, the appreciation of open borders may well increase over time. For Bieber, a post-pandemic world with more permanent and resilient borders is unlikely to eventuate. However, the opening of closed borders for all citizens will be a drawn-out process, illustrated by expanded nationalistic responses to the pandemic. Both nationalism and globalism were significant motivators in states concertedly reviewing their foreign investment rules. Arguably, those states that, over the past five years (even before the pandemic) have begun to strengthen their foreign investment rules, is a sign that nationalism continues to rise, at a time when more than ever, in our view, there is a need for expanded global trade and investment.

10.5 Bilateralism and Multilateralism

Notwithstanding the previously mentioned, a further impediment to the success of internationalising commercial law, is the rise of bilateralism and divergent multilateralism. While there is nothing new about these two concepts and the benefits they have brought to international trade and investment, their growth is somewhat at the expense of a continued transnational approach to developing commercial law. Bilateralism, for example, provides a platform for 'preferential trade agreements conducted on a bilateral basis, which have become the centrepiece of trade diplomacy'.[33] With multilateral negotiations becoming increasingly complex and protracting business operations, trade deals among selected partners are seen, rightly or wrongly, to hold the promise of quick and comprehensive improvements in access to foreign markets and rules for trade and investment there. Based on this view, bilateralism provides a pathway to homogeneity and consistency, not only between the bilateral state parties, but in global trade more pervasively. Heydon and Woolock opine that:

> Preferential agreements do add complexity to trade, especially given the fact that the various agreements use different rules of origin. But, in some policy areas, agreements concluded between trading partners do not constitute a

32 Florian Bieber, *Global Nationalism in Times of the COVID-19 Pandemic*, Cambridge University Press, Public Health Emergency, 2020, 1–13. See also Roulin Su, Wensong Shen, Is Nationalism Rising in Times of the COVID-19 Pandemic? Individual-Level Evidence from the United States, *Journal of Chinese Political Science, Springer* 26 (2020); Marco Antonsich, Everyday Nation in Times of Rising Nationalism, *Sociology* 54, 6 (2020), 1230–1237; Eric Woods, Robert Schertzer, Liah Greenfeld, Chris Huges, Cynthia Miller-Idriss, COVID-19, *Nationalism, and the Politics of Crisis: A Scholarly Exchange*, Wiley Online, 2020.

33 Kenneth Heydon, Stephen Woolock, *The Rise of Bilateralism: Comparing American, European and Asian Approaches to Preferential Trade Agreements*, United Nations University, 2008–2009, 3.

> preference as such and can facilitate trade. This is the case when agreements promote transparency or regulatory best practice, such as in government procurement or the service sector. PTAs that promote the use of agreed, common international standards can reduce technical barriers to trade. Agreements that provide for enhanced cooperation or consultation can help to remove barriers caused by sanitary and phytosanitary measures. Even in the case of rules of origin, the picture is rather more nuanced than the 'spaghetti bowl' characterization suggests. Rather than innumerable different rules of origin, there are in fact a number of dominant frameworks derived from the United States and European Union that find application in other PTAs. The existence of a limited number of framework rules for rules of origin does not, however, make the task of developing agreed international norms for preferential rules of origin any less intractable.[34]

Thus, on the basis that states are turning increasingly toward bilateralism, the rules of commercial engagement are possibly being diluted internationally, unless those rules of engagement are otherwise expressed or upheld within such agreements. On the other hand, multilateral arrangements have also been on the rise regionally, such as in the EU, Australia and among other Asian and North American states. According to John Ruggie, multilateralism will only ever provide a set of generalised principles of conduct, whereas bilateralism 'differentiates relations case-by-case based principally on a priori particularistic grounds or situational exigencies'.[35] Ruggie wrote in the early 1990s when the EU's regional brand was rising. However, since the 1990s, there has been significant changes in regionalism and multilateralism, including a shift to bilateralism.

Multilateral trade regimes often harbour a substantial bilateral component which operates outside of the multilateral framework which, as Leon Trakman posited, inheres in the proliferation of free trade agreements.[36] The result is two forms of customised multilateralism. The first, as Thompson and Verdier observe, is a multilateral treaty that treats everyone identically but is supplemented with bilateral agreements that accommodate members with particular needs.[37] Under the second form of customised multilateralism, a single instrument institutionalises differential treatment, providing a better opportunity to redress economic inequality among states that may be more appealing to developing countries. A multilateral instrument of this second genre allows states to negotiate as a group, where they stand a

34 Ibid., 5.

35 John Ruggie, Multilateralism: The Anatomy of an Institution, *International Organization* 46, 3 (1992), 561–598.

36 Leon Trakman, The Proliferation of Free Trade Agreements: Bane or Beauty?, *Journal of World Trade* 42 (2008) 367, 388. See also Alexander Thompson, Daniel Verdier, *Multilateralism, Bilateralism and Regime Design*, Department of Political Science Ohio State University, https://politicalscience.osu.edu/faculty/athompson/Lateralisms.pdf, 26. See also, Pasquale Pistone, Coordinating the Action of Regional and Global Players During the Shift from Bilateralism to Multilateralism in International Tax Law, *World Tax Journal* (2014), 26.

37 Ibid.

better chance of resisting pressure from their richer counterparts.[38] However, the effectiveness of institutionalising and internationalising rules and the law in commercial activities impedes this customisation of differential treatment.

As an illustration, the EU has become a standout for embracing regionalism and multilateralism, demonstrating the effectiveness of its harmonisation of commercial law. However, divisions within the EU are ever more readily visible, now with the UK's departure from the EU in December 2020. In contrast, other regions have supported regional partnerships, typified by the Regional Comprehensive Economic Partnership (RCEP) Agreement directed at broadening and deepening ASEAN's engagement with Australia, China, Japan, Korea and New Zealand.[39] Still, the regional objective of the RCEP Agreement is potentially at odds with global convergence and harmonisation of law, such as in recognising Rules of Origin (ROO) that operate beyond the RCEP Rules. Thus, the question arises whether multilateralism expressed through regional agreements will dilute the internationalisation of commercial law.

Applied to the multilateral regulation of international investment law, the lingering question is whether it will reflect the wide consensus of states involved in main and secondary insolvency proceedings; and whether it will facilitate the development of uniform rules and procedures to govern them. Even if a multilateral process is inclusive rather than dictated by wealthy states, the question remains whether uniform rules and procedures are workable globally. In effect, if trans-border insolvency is not between states that are contiguous, but between debtors and creditors in different continents, complex issues arise over their divergent legal traditions, disparate cultural heritages and differences in levels of economic development.

10.6 Transparency – A Concept that Supports the Internationalisation of Commercial Law

The United Nations released a report in 2020, *Recover Better, Economic and Social Challenges and Opportunities.*[40] That report argues that international trade is expected to facilitate technology diffusion among countries.[41] It also acknowledges the high-level rules of data protection established by the OECD, EU and other jurisdictions through core principles and concepts, such as transparency in future legal development. While it is outside of the scope of this chapter to explore transparency in enabling multilateral data protection laws, such laws are instrumental in an international commercial law regime that reflects global needs for cybersecurity and data protection.

More specifically related to this chapter, transparency is salient in resolving trans-border investment disputes, provided for both in bilateral and multilateral investment

38 Ibid.

39 Summary of the Regional Comprehensive Economic Partnership Agreement, 2020, https://asean.org/storage/2020/11/Summary-of-the-RCEP-Agreement.pdf.

40 United Nations, Department of Economic and Social Affairs, *Recover Better, Economic and Social Challenges and Opportunities*, United Nation, 2020, 1.

41 Ibid., 60.

agreements. The 2017–2018 Annual Asia-Pacific Report on Investor-State Dispute Settlement and Transparency accentuates the significance of transparency in the conduct of investor-state arbitration.[42] The notion of greater transparency was reinforced in the October 2017 enactment of the Mauritius Convention on transparency measures, and adopted in the new CIETAC Investment Arbitration Rules.[43] These advances represent direct responses to increasing demands for greater openness, predictability and certainty in investment sectors. Michael Douglas highlights how, at a general level, 'transparency' can be equated with 'openness', namely, in establishing a transparent dispute resolution process that is open to the public.[44] In the context of Investor State Dispute Resolution (ISDS), 'transparency' 'tends to refer to the extent to which the public may be alerted to, gain information about, and perhaps participate in, proceedings organised to adjudicate an investor's claim'.[45] The UNCITRAL Rules on Transparency in Treaty-Based Investor-State Arbitration[46] provide an ideal statement of what transparent ISDS looks like. The value of transparency in ISDS is not only idealized. It is also reflected in the revised Rules of the International Center for the Settlement of Investment Disputes (ICSID) that replaced earlier rules which, Leon Trakman posited, placed 'The ICSID under Siege'.[47]

Douglas elaborates that the UNCITRAL Rules on Transparency provide a useful subject matter for requirements of transparency. Firstly, transparency requires public access to basic information that provides some identity to the dispute. For the UNCITRAL Rules, that information includes the party names, the economic sector involved and the treaty under which the claim is being made. Secondly, transparency requires public access to the tribunal proceedings. Hearings of arbitrations will be public to the extent that an open hearing will not undermine the integrity of the arbitral process or divulge confidential information. Thirdly, transparency requires knowing what the tribunal has decided. This could involve the publication

42 Daisy Mallet, Peter Pether, *Open Up! How Far Should Transparency in International Commercial Arbitration Go?* https://www.kwm.com/en/knowledge/insights/how-far-should-transparency-in-international-commercial-arbitration-go-20180412. See also Ulrich K. Preuß, Transparency in International Law, *International Journal of Constitutional Law* 12, 3 (2014), 820–882. Transparency UNCTAD Series on Issues in International Investment Agreements, 2004, https://unctad.org/system/files/official-document/iteiit20034_en.pdf; Alan Boyle, Kasey McCall-Smith, Transparency in International Law-Making, in A. Bianchi, A. Peters, *Transparency in International Law*, Cambridge University Press, 2013, 419–435.

43 Ibid.

44 Michael Douglas, The Importance of Transparency for Legitimising Investor-State Dispute Settlement: An Australian Perspective, *New Zealand Association of Comparative Law, Hors Series* XIX (2015), Part I: Investor-State Dispute Settlement and UNCITRAL Texts on Transparency, 112.

45 Ibid., 122.

46 Ibid., UNCITRAL Rules on Transparency in Treaty-based Investor-State Arbitration GA Res 68/109, 68th sess, 68th plen mtg, Agenda Item 79, A/68/PV.68, 2013, www.un.org/en/ga/search/view_doc.asp?symbols=A/68/PV.68.

47 Leon Trakman, The ICSID Under Siege, *Cornell International Law Journal* 45 (2012) 603, 665. See also on NAFTA: J. Anthony VanDuzer, Enhancing the Procedural Legitimacy of Investor-State Arbitration through Transparency and Amicus Curiae Participation, *McGill Law Journal* 52 (2007), 681, 687.

of orders, decisions and awards of the arbitral tribunal.[48] In taking the idea of transparency further, Douglas believes that it creates an informal culture of accountability and so could provide the key principles of predictable decision-making. 'Without transparency, the public can never justifiably believe that ISDS is predictable'.[49]

The value of transparency is not limited to general principles of openness and accountability. It also underpins the rule of law as originally developed in Western legal systems. Applied to trans-border commercial dealings, the rule of law is not fully comprehensible unless it is understood as operating transparently. Therefore, this book maintains that internationalising financial law transparency provides a platform for greater certainty and predictability in times of continued uncertainty. Such transparency is especially material to the progressive advancement of cross-border insolvency laws. The next section highlights the international organisations with major roles in further internationalising cross-border insolvency law. It will be argued that the UNCITRAL and UNIDROIT should undertake those roles cooperatively.

10.7 International Organisations

In making the case for further internationalising the law examined throughout this book, there are a number of transnational organisations that all have a level of involvement and input into the legal tools explored. That said, the international framework for liberalising world commercial activity centres on the World Trade Organization, International Monetary Fund, United Nations, United Nations Commission for International Trade Law (UNCITRAL) and International Institute for the Unification of Private Law (UNIDROIT). Additionally, none of the international organisations have a role in developing any future transnational legal framework, such as the Organisation for Economic Cooperation and Development; the Hague Conference on Private International Law; Financial Stability Board; International Monetary Fund; Basel Committee on Banking Supervision; Bank for International Settlements; and World Bank. The International Swaps and Derivatives Association would need to be consulted, particularly in relation to close-out netting provisions within ISDA Master Agreements.

These organisations all share dual roles within the international legal system. The UN and its institutions are empowered to allow for and promote the free flow of goods, services and money across international borders. Contrarily, the UN aims to facilitate global economic activity. The Security Council of the UN has the power to impose economic sanctions against states that violate the UN Charter.[50] The General Agreement on Tariffs and Trade (GATT) and the General Agreement

48 Michael Douglas, The Importance of Transparency for Legitimising Investor-State Dispute Settlement: An Australian Perspective, *New Zealand Association of Comparative Law, Hors Series* XIX (2015), Part I: Investor-State Dispute Settlement and UNCITRAL Texts on Transparency, 112–113.

49 Ibid., 115.

50 Simon Chesterman, Béatrice Pouligny, Are Sanctions Meant to Work? The Politics of Creating and Implementing Sanctions Through the United Nations, *Global Governance* 9, 4 (2003), 503–505.

on Trade in Services (GATS) also empower nation states to impose economic sanctions on another states.[51] The WTO has a more specific role in prescribing rules governing the conduct of states engaged in world trade, including resolving state-to-state disputes through its adjudicative and appellate system.[52] The IMF, in turn, establishes rules to govern the international monetary system, including conduct of states that violate these rules. These institutions collectively also constrain the capacity of one state to sanction the activity of another state unless that sanctioning accords with this international regulatory framework.

An analysis of the regulatory functions of all these institutions is outside the scope for analysis of trans-border finance and insolvency disputes, but these organisations provide a regulatory backdrop for trade and investment generally. They also collectively restrict the power of a state or groups of states from sanctioning the commercial activity of another state to discourage unilateral action by states in the absence of an institutionalised legal basis.

This section will focus instead on the critical functions of the UNCITRAL and UNIDROIT in seeking to harmonise, and stabilise, international trade. The UNCITRAL was established by the General Assembly of the UN in 1966.[53] In establishing the Commission, the General Assembly recognised that disparities in national laws governing international trade created obstacles to the free flow of trade, and it regarded the Commission as the vehicle by which the United Nations could play a more active role in reducing or removing these obstacles.[54] Since its inception, the UNCITRAL has developed international commercial laws (Model Laws and rules) in the areas of insolvency, arbitration, mediation, sale of goods, procurement, electronic commerce, micro enterprises, security, international payments and transport of goods. It is out of scope to examine all of the Model Laws and rules that have been established.[55] However, and as highlighted earlier in this book, notable standouts are the Model Law on Cross-Border Insolvency 1997, and more recently, the Model Law on Enterprise Group Insolvency 2019 and the Model Law on Recognition and Enforcement of Insolvency-Related Judgements 2018.

A successful UNCITRAL legal regulatory framework, arguably, is the Convention on the Sale of Goods 1980 (CISG). The benefits of the CISG cannot be underestimated in providing a 'uniform regime for the settlement of disputes related to the international sale of goods, introducing certainty in commercial

51 Woo-Jun Min, Sukhee Han, Economic Sanctions Against North Korea: The Pivotal Role of US–China Cooperation, *International Area Studies Review* 23, 2 (2020), 177–193.

52 Hercules Booysen, Globalisation and International Trade Law, *South African Yearbook of International Law* 26 (2001), 114.

53 Resolution 2205(XXI), https://documents-dds-ny.un.org/doc/RESOLUTION/GEN/NR0/005/08/IMG/NR000508.pdf?OpenElement.

54 United Nations Commission on International Trade Law, https://uncitral.un.org/en/about/faq/mandate_composition, see also Agenda 88: Progressive development of the law of international trade, https://www.uncitral.org/pdf/english/yearbooks/archives-e/A-6396-E.pdf.

55 Ibid., https://uncitral.un.org/en/texts.

exchanges'.[56] This uniform regime is specifically designed to regulate cross-border transactions in goods, because of the challenges and costs related to sales of goods between parties across jurisdictions, such as challenges attributable to the carriage of goods. The CISG contribution to transnational commercial law is evident in its careful balancing of contractual remedies directed at assisting buyers and sellers to cure deficiencies in performance. Importantly, the CISG subscribes to the principle of preservation of contract in which its objective is to minimise upon any economic loss arising from the non-performance of a contract.[57] This focus of the CISG extends beyond often disparate national laws providing for non-performance designed primarily for short-term transactions.

More pervasively, as Luca Castellani highlights, as its strengths, the:

> CISG has led to greater predictability of the law applicable to the contract for international sale of goods, both in cases where there has been a valid choice of law and in those where there has either been an invalid choice, or no choice at all.[58]

The enhanced predictability provided the CISG cannot be underestimated. The flow on effects to business and government is that, in times of international upheaval and uncertainty, notably through the 2020–2021 pandemic, the CISG provides an important layer of certainty and economic solidity. The CISG's capacity to achieve these objectives was accentuated in its provisions governing hardship and *force majeure* regulating contracts at times of economic instability, notably, COVID-19. Apart from providing an environment and platform of legal certainty,[59] the CISG was depicted as reducing transaction costs, and through it, lowering the prices of imported and exported goods.[60] Arguably, the CISG and the many other legal instruments established under the auspices of the UNCITRAL since 1966, have significantly contributed to stabilising international economic activity across the international business community. The CISG has successfully provided an additional platform for reform to be undertaken by UNCITRAL. That platform includes the CISG operating as an institutional medium by which the community of states has strengthened and further internationalised of cross-border insolvency law.

The UNCITRAL has also assisted in strengthening the framework for resolving international commercial disputes through institutions that replace domestic

56 Luca Castellani, The Adoption of the CISG in Portugal: Benefits and Perspectives: A adoção da CISG em Portugal: Benefícios e perspetivas, *Legal Officer, UNCITRAL Secretariat Outubro* (2013), 3–6.

57 Ibid., 4.

58 Ibid., 4–5.

59 Robert Walters, Bruno Zeller, Is It Time for India to Adopt the Convention on the Sale of Goods? *International Trade Law & Regulation* 26, 3 (2020), 167–169.

60 Luca Castellani, The Adoption of the CISG in Portugal: Benefits and Perspectives: A adoção da CISG em Portugal: Benefícios e perspetivas, *Legal Officer, UNCITRAL Secretariat Outubro* (2013), 5.

courts, notably international commercial institutions that facilitate dispute resolution through arbitration. Trakman notes that 'national, regional and international arbitration centres have become increasingly sophisticated in the range of arbitration services that they provide to an increasingly savvy business clientele'.[61] These centres are driven somewhat by the need to satisfy the interests of an ever-widening array of commercial parties who have ready access to informed sources, including at various sophisticated arbitration websites. International arbitration associations also increasingly respond to competition from *ad hoc* and non-institutional arbitration by providing facilities for *ad hoc* and non-institutional proceedings, while continuing aggressively to market their own arbitration clauses and services.[62] At its core, institutionalised arbitration serves as an expert, transnational and cost- and time-sensitive instrument for resolving disputes across sectors, including finance, banking and insolvency.

The benefits of international commercial arbitration are subject to overstatement, such as whether it is more expeditious over average than litigation before domestic courts. Given its case-by-case operation and the absence of arbitration precedents, sector arbitration is seldom supported by an established jurisprudence based on past decisions. Its strict rules of confidentiality also subordinate transparency, undermining the capacity of parties to finance and banking transactions to conduct their affairs in anticipation of prospective decisions. Still, arbitration is subject to requirements that offset some of these issues of uncertainty, limited predictability and protracted arbitration proceedings. International arbitration institutions provide rules governing arbitration proceedings under their auspices, such as the published rules and procedures adopted by the International Chamber of Commerce (ICC), the International Centre for Dispute Resolution (ICDR) and the London Court of International Arbitration (LCIA). International contracts on finance and banking typically include choice of jurisdiction and law clauses that provide both a law and procedural framework that bind arbitrators in proceedings and rendering awards. International Commercial Arbitration Awards are also enforceable in most jurisdictions that are signatories to the New York Convention of the Recognition and Enforcement of International Arbitral Awards (NY Convention).

The UNIDROIT, formally known as the International Institute for the Unification of Private Law, was established in 1926 as an auxiliary organ of the League of Nations. Following the demise of the League, the Institute was re-established to regulate multilateral agreements through the UNIDROIT statute.[63] The UNIDROIT's primary role is to study needs and methods for modernising, harmonising and coordinating private and in particular, commercial law between States and groups of States; and to formulate uniform law instruments, principles and rules to

61 Leon Trakman, Legal Traditions and International Commercial Arbitration, *American Review of International Arbitration* (2007), 3–6.

62 Ibid., 1–5.

63 Statute of UNIDROIT, https://www.unidroit.org/english/presentation/statute.pdf.

achieve those objectives. The UNIDROIT has undertaken extensive studies and work projects across major commercial sectors in order to highlight and address important legal gaps that have been identified by the international business and legal communities. For instance, this book has demonstrated how the UNIDROIT Principles on Close Out Netting Provisions have raised levels of stability in the banking and finance sectors through both regulatory and self-regulatory measures. The UNDROIT has strengthened the implementation of the CISG through its Principles of International Commercial Contracts adopted a decade ago.

The most recent 2016 version of the UNIDROIT Principles have established a balanced set of rules designed for use throughout the world, irrespective of the legal traditions and the economic and political conditions of the countries in which they are to be applied.[64] The Principles under the UNIDROIT have also demonstrated their flexibility in taking account of the constantly changing circumstances arising from technological and economic developments impacting on cross-border trade practice. The Principles also promote fairness in international commercial relations by expressly imposing a general duty on contracting parties to act in good faith and in fair dealings; and in specific instances, it imposes standards of reasonable behaviour upon them.[65] Moreover, Article 1.1 applicable to the CISG, reaffirms the need to establish an environment of legal certainty, stating that:

> the principle of freedom of contract is of paramount importance in the context of international trade. In other words, the right of business people to decide freely to whom they will offer their goods or services and by whom they wish to be supplied, as well as the possibility for them freely to agree on the terms of individual transactions, are the cornerstones of an open, market-oriented and competitive international economic order.[66]

This right of parties to freely decide on the terms and conditions under which to sell goods under the CISG, as modelled in the UNCITRAL, is indispensable to ensure a stable commercial environment for free trans-border business dealings. Therefore, we are of the view that, even as the world becomes increasingly conflictual with material consequences for international business, the work of the UNCITRAL and UNIDROIT grows ever more valuable. That work, we maintain, is far from finished.

On the backdrop of the aforementioned, it is our specific view that, particularly in the area of cross-border insolvency and restructuring, there is a pressing need for the UNCITRAL and UNIDROIT to consider developing international mechanisms to address ongoing gaps in the law. The next section identifies and

64 UNIDROIT Principles on Commercial Contracts 2016, xxix, https://www.unidroit.org/english/principles/contracts/principles2016/principles2016-e.pdf.

65 Ibid.

66 Ibid., Article 1.1.

recommends specific areas of cross-border insolvency that warrant strengthening and how this can be accomplished through the existing framework of the UNCITRAL and UNIDROIT.

10.8 Pathway Forward and Conclusion

It is our view that transnational cross-border insolvency law and restructuring have both advanced considerably over the past decade. However, it remains largely underdeveloped. Arguably, more work is needed to ensure that cross-border insolvency law can be developed further to satisfy the functional demands of the transnational business community. An important universalist means of doing so is to establish a framework and process in which a financially stressed company can restructure its operations, including in dealing with creditors and debtors located in different jurisdictions. This critical area of law is far from developed, even though most states have adopted schemes of arrangement and comfort letters to address the gap. Now is arguably the time in which to formally develop these vital international legal instruments. This concluding section will highlight key areas of the law, as identified throughout the book, that can be further internationalised or internationalised for the first time.

Transitional trade and investment have grown significantly for more than 50 years, including local entities establishing offices and branches in multiple states. This chapter elaborates further how, in the era of de-globalisation over the past two decades, escalating international economic, social, human health and political uncertainty have all impacted negatively on the solidity of the global economy. The result is an ongoing struggle within the international community to strengthen the universalist approach in applying it to cross-border insolvency law, counterbalanced by states reverting to territorialism. Importantly, too, the nationalisation of the law regulating cross-border insolvency has led some states to adopt a strict punitive legal regime, punishing individuals and entities for their inability to ensure that a debtor company remained solvent. Other national regimes have highlighted the value of law that promotes rescue and rehabilitation of such debtor companies. This has led to a rehabilitative approach in which states have actively provided legal support for corporate restructuring and reorganisation.

This rehabilitative approach, in our view, is an early ethos along a pathway that offers significant economic benefits over the longer term. While the book has highlighted sustainable pathways forward, it has also acknowledged that some of the proposals advocated for the internationalisation of insolvency law will be complex to research and implement without the cooperation of states globally. For instance, letters of comfort, which are used in international insolvency and restructuring, do not have any regulatory backing in any of the jurisdictions examined. The rehabilitative proposal will also be contested both in principle and in its application, with many divergent views being expressed. However, and even though such a proposal might appear to be unpalatable to many, if the world community is serious about providing a strong framework of legal certainty and stability in international commerce, this tool must also be examined more broadly, along with other proposals in this book.

10.8.1 Cross-Border Insolvency

As highlighted earlier, it is our view that the UNCITRAL Model Law on Cross-Border Insolvency, now over 20 years of age, is fittingly due for elevation to the status of a Convention. The view is reflected, in part, in the UNCITRAL's recognition of ongoing deficiencies in the Model Law, from the growing need to respond to the progressively more fraught global landscape surrounding insolvency, and the increased incidence of cross-border insolvencies, complicated by the expansion of international trade and investment.[67] A carefully framed Convention on cross-border insolvency could help to close significant gaps in the Model Law and state practice, such as in addressing choice of law and jurisdictional issues relating to outbound insolvency. Therefore, in our contention a Convention, underpinned and supported by the UNIDROIT Principles, can strengthen the already widening endorsement of a universalist approach to cross-border insolvency. That Convention can also fill gaps in the international law of insolvency, comparable to the achievements of the CISG.

10.8.2 Schemes of Arrangement (SA)

The transition from a territorial approach to cross-border insolvency, or from insolvency in general to a universalist approach, is achievable by enabling indebted entities to restructure or reorganise their businesses. By and large, as evidenced in the SA chapter, they are already subject to national regulation. It demonstrates that they provide an important mechanism for restructuring and insolvency across jurisdictions. Restructuring has become synonymous with a company being able to prevent an insolvency. However, as highlighted earlier in this book, SAs are legal tools and important alternatives to insolvency. They provide a high level of certainty and governance in a restructure. The flexibility of SAs also provides a viable approach to structuring complex transactions within a takeover or restructure. Furthermore, SAs are often viewed positively by courts and offered to shareholders. Their adaptability also extends beyond the sometimes prescriptive and technical regulatory requirements that need to be met under takeover arrangements. Moreover, a scheme of arrangement helps to facilitate the transfer of assets and liabilities, and the issuance of new shares where appropriate. SAs are nationally based, that is, they are regulated or otherwise by national laws. Economically, they support and provide creditors with a formidable tool to ensure that entities experiencing financial stress are able to restructure in a sustainable manner.

67 UNCITRAL, *Model Law on Cross-Border Insolvency with Guide to Enactment and Interpretation*, UNCITRAL, 2013, 20–21.

Viewed in this way, SAs are important alternative tools to insolvency in enabling an entity under financial stress to maintain its business operations. In most jurisdictions the construction and operation of SAs are overseen and approved by national courts. Promoting the wider and more uniform use of SAs nationally, in our view, will also foster its more extensive and productive use during and post COVID-19. However, without evidence of the current use of SAs, further research will be required as the commercial consequences of the pandemic become more evident. Moreover, it will be important for SAs to receive national regulatory backing, and judicial support, to not be subordinated or treated as secondary instruments by domestic courts.

We maintain that the existing evidence demonstrates the growing adoption of SAs nationally and their wider application to cross-border insolvency and restructuring proceedings before domestic courts and through international commercial arbitration proceedings. Moreover, the similarities between how domestic courts in different jurisdictions engage in SAs outweigh their differences. A multi-layered and multi-purpose regulatory regime of SAs is also more likely to gain ground in trans-border proceedings, given heightened international uncertainty and tension arising from global public health and financial crises. We maintain further that these crises render it timely for highly regarded institutions, notably the UNIDROIT or UNCITRAL, to undertake a formal review of SAs. The purpose would be to develop uniform principles based on an internationally agreed scheme of arrangement, or conceivably, a Model Law.

Aggregating tested national mechanisms underlying SAs and raising them to the international level will strengthen market stability and certainty in response to a relentless pandemic and the prospect of further ones arising. Not doing so only weakens and dilutes the overall regulatory framework for cross-border insolvency. It also encourages states to revert to a territorial, and usually insular, approach to insolvency that fails to accommodate the international scope and legal impact of SAs.

10.8.3 Letters of Comfort (LC)

Restructuring indebted entities can assume different forms and dimensions. Restructuring has also emerged as an important alternative to insolvency. Apart from schemes of arrangements, letters of comfort are commonly used to help facilitate such a restructure. There are a number of different types of comfort letters. They can be used for various purposes: for the security of the debtor or creditor(s), as financial guarantees or for regulators to use as a justification for refraining from engaging in further regulatory action. Moreover, letters of credit are, and can be, used by lawyers, liquidators, administrators, accountants or auditors in practice.

The commercial benefit of letters of comfort has been well documented, predominantly to demonstrate their feasibility in areas of commerce where they are most frequently used. As highlighted in the LC chapter, common law countries have used them effectively in managing the restructuring of indebted corporate entities. Yet, letters of comfort are relatively novel instruments in most civil law jurisdictions. In the case of Indonesia, for example, their nature and utility are not clearly established in law. A further and more problematic challenge relates to how state courts will enforce LCs going forward. Generally, common law countries will evaluate the perceived intention of the parties and obligations assumed in the letter of comfort to determine the legality, meaning, scope of application and enforcement of obligations undertaken in the LC. In these respects, the process of regulating letters of comfort will replicate to varying degrees how courts in different jurisdictions apply their laws of contract in construing such letters.

A distinct challenge is that, while letters of comfort are widely used, the law regulating them is often underdeveloped, including not only in emerging economic and financial hubs, but also mature ones. Our view is that, to redress this issue, the UNCITRAL, and likely the UNIDROIT, are well placed to undertake research study to identify gaps in the legal regulation of letters of comfort, notably in the application of national law to them. Based on evidence of the approach towards LCs of most jurisdictions compared in this book, the national regulation of letters of comfort has largely converged. Given the world-wide use of letters of comfort and their acceptance in most states in our study, a set of UNIDROIT Principles would provide continuity and stability to international commercial dealings within and beyond the national laws studied in this book. Uniform Principles governing LCs would aptly address their enforcement in both home states and/or third countries. Even though these letters have no regulatory support at this time, the letter of comfort chapter has demonstrated their importance in negotiations before, during and after insolvency, winding up or restructuring. Therefore, it is our view that consideration should be provided to explore whether such letters can be internationalised, without identified contexts and manageable contexts. They are consensual instruments that enable parties to adapt them to their discrete circumstances; but transnational regulations could determine their legitimate boundaries in the face of abuse, misdirection, error or misunderstanding.

10.8.4 Mergers, Acquisitions – Foreign Investment

A further alternative to insolvency is cross-border restructuring or re-organisation through mergers and acquisitions (MAs). The use of MAs is not directed so much at the manner in which states have developed legal frameworks to facilitate MAs. The focus is rather on whether investment rules underpin and support cross-border mergers and acquisitions. In other words, MAs have emerged as one of the preferred options in maximising cross-border investment and to gain entry to a foreign market. It is well documented that national legal frameworks, rather than encourage new entrants into the MA market, often create obstacles to their entry. This obstacle in promoting MAs is further compounded by restrictions imposed by national foreign investment rules and regional ones for the EU. That, in and of itself, is one of the major hurdles that a jurisdiction will need to assess in determining whether an MA will be approved there. The foreign investment rules have increasingly taken a nationalist approach, which will dilute the ability for MAs to occur in the future, particularly those that are perceived to be a threat to the overall security of the state or supranational polity.

Redressing anti-competitive practices is a significant and complex issue for governments and regulators, including in the finance and insolvency sectors. As highlighted earlier, governments across the globe have recognised that mega-corporations in some sectors, notably technology, have captured the international market. They also have the resources to exclude new entrants, buy them out and discourage the advancement of competitive products. Thus, the legal framework creates a devil and deep blue sea result. Market regulators or the market itself are blessed if they encourage market innovation by preventing monopolists from consuming start-ups. They are dammed if they are perceived to interfere with a free market. While this analogy does not have a direct impact on cross-border insolvency and restructuring, it is an example where predatory practices, in part, avoid predatory behaviour. Thus, competing outcomes based on the perceived benefits and pitfalls of MAs are increasingly complex to resolve. However, in an era of market instability, regulators are under pressure to relax the current rules governing MAs, and to provide platforms for a smoother pathway to acquiring or merging with other companies transnationally. Yet, even though these results have not fully materialised to date, there has been a failure of regulators to constrain MAs that could strengthen monopolistic behaviour and undermine innovation through increased market competition.

Particularly noteworthy are the response of regulators to foreign investment rules pre- and post-COVID-19. As highlighted in the MA chapter, historical attempts were made to regulate foreign investment through Treaties of Friendship, Commerce and Navigation.[68] However, increasingly, sovereign states, except for members states of the EU, have treated foreign investment as an area of regulatory policy, rather than law. Foreign investment rules are conceived more as rules of policy that define, or are defined by, the national identification of the discrete state, or collective states such as the EU. Further expressing this national identity are nationalised conceptions of 'public order', 'public security', 'national essential security interests' that have become synonymous with whether an individual or entity is able to invest in, merge with or acquire a company.

Ultimately, a multi-layered approach to foreign investment rules is complex. On the one side, it promotes competition, including through mergers and acquisitions. On the other side, it restricts as much as it promotes competition, mergers and acquisitions. Arguably, what has eventuated in most jurisdictions, today, is a strong set of rules on foreign investment that exclude mergers or acquisitions in specific sectors, such as energy and defence. Even though this practice will vary amongst jurisdictions, it is likely that rules on foreign investment, in a currently uncertain economic and political climate, could become restrictive in the face of defensive sovereignty. Against this background, attempts to internationalise foreign investment rules are more aspirational than real. Changing that aspiration to reality

68 Carlos Espluhues, Foreign Investment, Strategic Assets and National Security, *Inertia* (2018), 24–27.

would require a gravitational shift away from the now pervasive state territorialism and nationalism to internationalisation that many states consider as threats to their national identities. Under the current approach taken by states, and given the frequency with which economic, social, security and human health shock are impacting the world, there is unlikely to be a global appetite for change. On the other hand, there is scope for jurisdictions to consider developing a transnational response to such issues as the protection of national security, promoting environmental safety, containing money laundering and illegal migration and establishing other measures aimed at fostering legal convergence. Greater convergence could also be achieved through shared regulatory approaches to such issues as the deployment and use of current and future artificial intelligence and redressing biohazards, pests and diseases.

10.8.5 Netting Provisions

A further important area of law to be internationalised is in the UNIDROIT Principles on Close Out Netting Provisions. Given the number of netting arrangements used across financial sectors, general agreement has arisen over the lack of harmonisation of such arrangements across legal systems, a concern that continued until 2013. In responding to legal and policy gaps in close-out netting arrangements, the 2013 UNIDROIT Principles on Close Out Netting Provisions were established. The 2013 UNIDROIT Principles were designed to promote the adoption and application of those Principles in national laws. However, the question now is whether the 2013 UNIDROIT Principles on Close Out Netting remain current. The Netting chapter has demonstrated that the fragmented approach adopted by states to implement and regulate netting provisions had continued to be a major challenge to universalisation. It has also highlighted that, central to building a viable regime of netting principles and provisions within contracts, is recognition of the need for stability, certainty and predictability in protecting billions of dollars committed to large transnational contracts and transactions. The sought-after purpose is to enable a solvent party to close out a contract and agree on a payment that is timely, adequate, efficient and fair to the netting parties.

Viewed at face value, netting provisions appear to be innocuous. However, their future role in the international finance sector cannot be underestimated. As noted in the book, they are widely used in ISDA Master Agreements (see Appendix One). They are also commonly used to govern derivative transactions. The question is how, when and to what extent that can be extended to govern trans-border financial debt, insolvency and restructuring more pervasively.

We have argued, in the Netting chapter, that the normative value of close-out netting in redressing debt and insolvency is contestable. Opponents of close-out netting argue that close-out netting procedures lack transparency, operate inconsistently, have disparate impacts upon participants in financial transactions, and magnify systemic risks by accelerating insolvency and impeding the rescue of troubled institutions. Given these factors, there is a strong case for developing a Model Law on Close Out Netting Provisions as a viable option to address these and other concerns. As highlighted earlier in this book, a further benefit would stem from an incremental approach. That approach would entail the UNCITRAL and UNIDROIT to establish a project that confirms whether, and if so, when to further implement a universal approach to cross-border insolvency. Insofar as that universal approach is confirmed and deemed workable, it would lead to close-out netting principles being raised to a Model Law.

The incremental approach, illustrated in relation to netting, in our view, is the most viable option. It will enable the structure and process of internationalisation to advance incrementally, by taking small but calculated steps forward. However, over time, there will arguably be sufficient reform and interpretation of these principles to develop uniform interpretive measures for the benefit of states in general and the global business community at large. A Model Law could imbed such uniformity, although it is unlikely that states in general will support wholesale change, by raising the Principles or a Model Law into a Netting Convention. While plausible, in our view, at this stage, that is likely to be a jump too far.

10.8.6 Technology – Personal Data

Internationalising technology law to protect personal data remains significantly deficient today. Walters, Trakman and Zeller have demonstrated the need for greater harmonisation and convergence in data protection law internationally.[69] The fragmented approach taken by states reinforces the sovereign and nationalistic regulation of personal data to date. This approach flies in the face of the fact that globalisation of the Internet economy has caused a dramatic increase in personal data being commercialised and now widely traded. Individuals and entities are profiting enormously from this activity.[70] However, the digitisation of this sector of the economy has also created significant complexities in how personal data is collected, used and processed. For instance, the evolution of technology by enabling the collection and collation of personal data through predictive analysis of people's behaviour, is changing the way in which entities not only capture personal data, but also use the data. The result is dominance of a few well-practiced international entities engaging in such data surveillance. In addition, the full extent and commercial activity in the sale and distribution of personal data over the Internet, is far from transparent and only beginning to emerge. A more pervasive issue is in ascertaining the manner in which states are collecting, storing and using personal data. Walters, Trakman and Zeller argue:

> The challenge for governments and regulators, including the community is that regulation will not keep up with these advances in data capture and

69 Robert Walters, Leon Trakman, Bruno Zeller, *Data Protection Law: A Comparative Analysis of Asia-Pacific and European Approaches*, Springer, 2019.
70 Ibid., 424–425.

> use. The law will continue to lag well behind technology development. Therefore, more than ever, a combination of regulatory and non-regulatory approaches is needed to ensure innovation continues to be developed, while maintaining and strengthening the protection of individual's personal data and subsequently privacy.[71]

The authors argue further that this lack of global harmonisation represents a substantial issue for governments and the international business community to address. The reality is that states often develop data protection laws differently, to meet their own economic and social needs.[72]

> [W]hile the EU balances the need for privacy and economic outcomes within the GDPR, the EU places the right to privacy at a higher level to most, if not, all other jurisdictions. On the other side, Singapore has placed the business needs and interests at the forefront of their data protection framework; while, it is our view that Australia sits somewhere in the middle – between Singapore and the EU.[73]

Walters, Trakman and Zeller therefore maintain that a major obstacle to 'legal convergence and harmonisation is for nation states to come together and agree on what level of right(s) should be afforded consistently to privacy through the Internet and its supporting systems and infrastructure'.[74]

At the international level, and unlike schemes of arrangement and letters of comfort, the core principles that have been established by the Organisation for Economic Cooperation and Development (OECD) need to be reviewed to ensure they are still adequate to satisfy current cross-border needs.[75] The starting point is to understand what other principles and concepts have emerged from national laws that need to be placed into the international arena. Arguably, to overcome the hurdles posed by the lack of harmonisation, it could be left to UNIDROIT or UNCITRAL to develop Model Laws. The authors go on to point out that there are two existing reasons that are persuasive in adopting that course of action. First, both organisations are devising instruments directed at legal harmonisation though diplomatic conferences. Second, they are practiced in devising conventions and Model Laws for transnational commercial law.

Viewed against this backdrop, there is a lack of law and a fragmented approach to AI and Cybersecurity Law that needs to be addressed both more expeditiously and homogeneously. Thus, given their global stature and capabilities, UNCITRAL and UNIDROIT have further prospective tasks before these areas of law become ever more fragmented and the prospect for harmonisation recedes.

71 Ibid.
72 Ibid., 428.
73 Ibid.
74 Ibid., 429.
75 Ibid., 441.

10.9 Concluding Remarks

The world is facing significant economic, social, human health and geopolitical challenges. For instance, the Asian Financial Crisis in the 1990s and the 2008 Global Financial Crisis had a significant effect on financial markets. More problematic has been the recent outbreak of COVID-19, which has resulted in economic activity shrinking across the world. The importance of these events has been twofold. On the one side, the financial crisis was largely contained within the financial sector; however, production and trade in goods and services continued unabated. On the other side, COVID-19 has resulted in a production decline. Businesses, large and small, have closed their doors and insolvency is rising geometrically. The economic impact upon the financial sector is also growing daily with inestimable longer-term devastation expected across global financial markets, with consequential impact upon the solvency of sectors across the sector.

In proposing this pathway forward, the book has highlighted the scope of these global financial problems. It has also emphasised the obstacles in meeting these challenges, notably in the fragmentary nature of insolvency law and practice in cross-border financial dealings. A pathway forward is already evinced in a recent study of the Organisation for Economic Co-operation and Development (OECD). The OECD stresses that insolvency and restructuring legal regimes is important to the overall health of the global economy.[76] This book advocates, consistent with the OECD's position, that the further internationalisation of cross-border insolvency and restructuring law, as well as legal tools and mechanisms of maintaining solvency and managing insolvency, are urgently required. The requirement for the harmonisation of insolvency is accentuated when coupled with the economic tribulations of the 2020–2021 worldwide pandemic.

The book has provided an illustration of insolvency and restructuring regulation in India, Indonesia, Singapore and Switzerland. It has emphasised the practical legal mechanisms required for parties to prepare for, engage in and function following insolvency proceedings, such as applying for and enforcing close-out netting provisions and keepwell agreements (letters of comfort). The book has also demonstrated that these measures, used collectively, can protect millions, if not, billions and even trillions of dollars across the world's economy, recognising their spill-over impact upon financial stability. It has proposed building deeper levels of legal convergence and harmonisation than prevail at present. It has also argued for greater acceptance of an existing but evolving international framework to deal with growing global destabilisation associated with trans-border insolvency and compliance with the rule of law.

As a positive sequel to the onset of the global pandemic, many national and international institutions have responded by assisting national governments in

76 Müge Adalet McGowan, Dan Andrews, *Valentine Millot, Insolvency Regimes, Zombie firms and Capital Reallocation Economics Department Working Papers No. 1399*, Organisation for Economic Co-operation and Development (OECD), ECO/WKP, 2017, 31.

responding to financially stressed enterprises. Anika Wolf reinforces the position taken throughout this book that:

> a well-designed legal framework is important for the functioning of financial markets and this is particularly true in times of global financial trouble. The issue of international standards addressing cross-border insolvency is very much at a point of work in progress. There is no such framework yet with regard to cross-border financial institutions, neither at the European level nor at the international level. As a consequence, the interests of domestic and foreign authorities might not be fully aligned.[77]

Arguably more needs to be undertaken by businesses engaged in cross-border trade to develop self-regulatory mechanisms and frameworks in compliance with the evolution of a sustainable international legal regime. Included in that sustainable environment is the stability of corporate entities whose self-regulatory mechanisms are deficient, incompatible, subject regulatory divergence and sometimes, the product of legal absenteeism.

The search for regulatory universalism ought not to be sought in a functional vacuum, nor operate as a mandate on high that directs corporate traffic. The globalisation of trans-border insolvency law should take account of business practice. Multistate initiatives are aptly heralded, accompanied by and supported by contract practices directed at avoiding, preparing for engaging in cross-border insolvency and restructuring proceedings. Such business practice provides at least an indication to states that, if they are to attract international trade and investment, their laws need to be compatible with efficient usages and practices of entities engaged in cross-border trade, including in addressing risks associated with solvency.

A central feature underpinning the way forward in establishing uniform laws to regulate insolvency is through a Theory of Action (TOA). What began as a process of naming and shaming people that would fall into financial stress, has evolved into a preventative and early interventionist framework. Arguably, more needs to be done. A TOA can achieve this. TOAs have already been successfully deployed in health, psychology,[78] primary industries and protect food production, amongst others. It is a critical moment in history for them to be deployed in addressing financial stress in the vulnerable arena of cross-border insolvency.

The debate over the meaning and scope of TOAs is evidenced over its convergence with, or divergence from, Action Regulation Theory.[79] Regardless of the exact definition of a TOA, it is important as a mechanism in enabling regulators

77 Annika Wolf, *A Global Cross-Border Insolvency Framework for Financial Institutions*, European University Institute, MWP 2015/01, Max Weber Programme, 2015, 11–15.

78 Winfried Hacker, Action Regulation Theory: A Practical Tool for the Design of Modern Work Processes?, *European Journal of Work and Organizational Psychology* 12, 2 (2003), 105–106. Hacker refers to an Action Regulation Theory that is not only a description tool but also a normative guide to efficient and humanised work; it became a foundation of international standards in work design.

79 Michael Jones, Action Regulation Theory, Faculty of Business – Papers (Archive), 2014, 405, https://ro.uow.edu.au/buspapers/405.

to manage both business and legal obstacles arising in the internationalisation of cross-border insolvency and restructuring. A TOA has the advantage of offering a holistic approach in analysing the full life cycle of the regulatory framework. Thus, Robert Carkhuff argues that 'a well-developed theory of action acts as a point of reference of all terms is the action of an individual actor or of a collectivity of actors'.[80] In health, a TOA is often referred to as a theory of reasoned action to study the behaviour of individuals.[81] Carkhuff asserts that, a TOA, in offering a standardised approach in ordering business risks, facilitates the removal of the 'internalisation of an organisations culture and narrow focus'.[82] He elaborates that a TOA provides a platform from which to enable the globalisation of culture and business patterns, including to overcome divides with cultural and ideological values. TAOs can provide a theorical foundation that is converted into functional regulatory action.[83] Importantly, TAOs enable culture values, along with international rules based on those values, to be embedded in regulatory action. TAOs also provide incentives for states consider to whether to participate in an action based on a TOA study of individual behaviour. Illustratively, there is a significant benefit for international regulators, along with the international business community, to consider TAOs in addressing the interface between values, ideologies and traditions embodied in Eastern and Western cultures and their influence on cross-border trade practice.[84] The scope of a TAO in arriving at a course of action is illustrated in the following diagram, Figure 10.1.

10.9.1 Diagram – A Theory of Action

This proposed TOA[85] highlights the important policy drivers that inform a universalist regulatory approach directed at further internationalising cross-border insolvency and restructuring. It reinforces the need for the involvement of international organisations that have the knowledge and expertise to developing regulatory tools

80 Robert Carkhuff, *Toward a General Theory of Action: Theoretical Foundations for the Social Sciences*, Routledge, 2017, 4.

81 Henk Staats, Pre-Environmental Attitudes and Behavioural Change, in Charles Speilberger, *Encyclopedia of Applied Psychology*, Elsevier, 2004.

82 Robert Carkhuff, *Toward a General Theory of Action: Theoretical Foundations for the Social Sciences*, Routledge, 2017, 23–24.

83 Anna Azulai, Are Grounded Theory and Action Research Compatible? Considerations for Methodology Triangulation, *Canadian Journal of Action Research* 21, 2 (March 2021), 4–24, DOI:10.33524/cjar.v21i2.485.

84 Robert Walters, *Cross-Border Data Flows – an Evolving Multilayered Regulatory Approach Required!*, Victoria University, forthcoming.

85 Regulation – Organisation for Economic Cooperation and Development, United Nations Commission on International Trade Law, The International Institute for the Unification of Private Law, Hague Conference on Private International Law, Financial Stability Board, International Monetary Fund, Basel Committee on Banking Supervision, Bank for International Settlements, World Bank. The International Swaps and Derivatives Association and World Trade organisation would need to be consulted, particularly in relation to close-out netting provisions within ISDA Master Agreements.

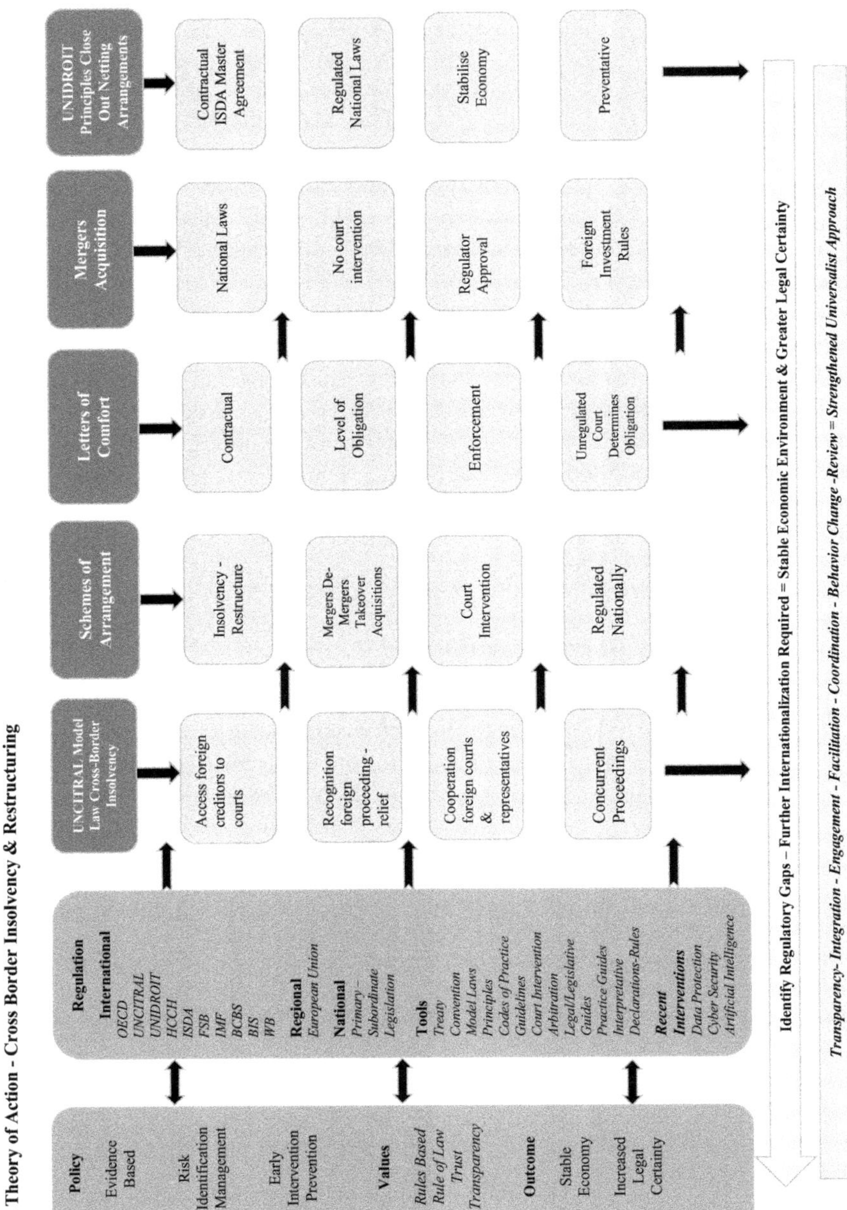

FIGURE 10.1 A Theory of Action

and mechanisms to facilitate cross-border insolvency and restructuring. The TAO identifies its value at the intersection between insolvency-restructuring and data protection, cybersecurity and artificial intelligence in transnational insolvency proceedings. The TOA also demonstrates that mechanisms such as schemes of arrangement, letters of comfort and mergers-acquisitions do not have comparable international standing in business and legal practice as do netting or cross-border insolvency and restructuring values. That said, the TAO identifies that considerable further work is required to internationalise the law of insolvency and restructuring through the tools analysed throughout this book.

In supporting the value of a TAO as a measure of behaviour, the book evaluates how the jurisdictions studied can participate more interactively in supporting the role that international organisations, such as UNCITRAL and UNIDROIT can play in delimiting the rules and procedures that ought to govern transnational insolvency. Their combined contribution to commercial law has been instrumental in providing the platform for nations to harmonise their legal frameworks. Properly utilised, the use of TAOs can strengthen legal instruments that minimise the financial consequences that economic destabilisation has upon discrete and collective markets. TAOs can also provide for a higher level of legal certainty and predictability in support of the enhanced internationalisation of cross-border insolvency and restructuring law(s).

This book has underscored that cross-border insolvency and restructuring is progressively, and alarmingly, more salient in wrestling with massive economic and political upheavals without established templates for future action. The demand for action revolves around human survival that is associated with business survival. An entity is only as sustainable as the health and welfare of those who act as its directing mind, work for and maintain it. Loss of life due to COVID-19 stands at over 2,800,000 at the time of writing. Vaccines are unevenly distributed globally. Unemployment is on the rise in those countries that cannot control the virus. Corporate insolvencies are on the rise especially in the most COVID-threatened sectors. And despite stock market rises, these concerns are not abating even though two and a half years has passed since the pandemic unleashed its devastation upon human life and economic viability.

All these factors make the divide between single-layered and multi-layered regulatory responses to trans-border financial crises that much more daunting. The multi-layered approach that has emerged is complex and cumbersome. This book has depicted the legal mechanisms used to facilitate insolvency and restructuring as multidimensional. Close-out netting provisions are used in finance and other contracts to close out a contract payment. Close-out payments of financially stressed entity led to corporate restructuring, not only to end-of-the-road insolvency.

The complexity of multidimensional solutions, this book has contended, nevertheless has advantages. These include the growth of multiple regulatory measures by which to unify otherwise inconsistent and divergent obstacles to trans-border commerce. Such unification has occurred along institutional lines, such as through international institutions, varying from the UN and the EU, to bilateral trade and investment agreements between states that impact on cross-border trade and investment of their human and corporate subjects. Trade associations in sectors such as finance and business entities that dominant markets, such as mega-IT corporations, further depict the uneven relationship between regulatory proliferation and legal unification.

This book has also evidenced that, notwithstanding significant shifts to regulation under the banner of sovereignty and nationalism, regulatory similarities in navigating between national and supranational laws are emerging. Schemes of arrangement have emerged as multi-purpose legal means for use in trans-border corporate mergers, demergers, takeovers, and creditor and debtor management schemes, amongst others. Letters of comfort have multiple applications transnationally, notwithstanding disparate principles and constructions of the intention of the parties and their nonperformance obligations in the law of contract law and civil law of obligations.

The blessing of diverse legal instruments that are available for use in the cross-border finance and insolvency sectors is also a challenge in achieving greater legal harmonisation in regulatory reform. This challenge is most evident in addressing trans-border mergers and acquisitions that are subject to diffuse national and in the case of the EU, foreign investment rules. These rules have significantly changed since the COVID-19 outbreak, further diluting the ability for cross-border restructuring through mergers or acquisitions. This challenge is not insurmountable if it is subject to reliable analysis to establish, efficiently, harmonised options among the alternatives.

The internationalisation of financial instruments, like MAs, are the lifeblood of corporate enterprise and instruments that can save debtor entities that are financially fraught. MAs often reduce economic inefficiencies and enhance market synergies. The retreat from cross-border MAs on national interest grounds is real, such as in the US. But it is unlikely to be consistently adopted, nor arguably, permanent. Some significant economic leaders, such as Singapore, prioritise a free market in MAs, declining to systemically exclude MAs based on the acquiring person's residence. That approach is likely to become more vital as global trade sanctions and restrictions on foreign investment retreat. What is inextricable importantly now is to redress the economic linkages among state and non-state actors that render the insularity of nationalism into an instrument of self-protection at the expanse of economic progress and market expansion.

A final word reinforces the overall argument and position that has been taken throughout this book. The book has demonstrated the importance of cross-border insolvency in the current era of a global pandemic. It has highlighted how restructuring debts in place of insolvency is an important alternative process that is available to financially stressed organisations that reduces the need for a declaration of insolvency. Prevention is far better than the financial collapse of an entity.

The book has demonstrated that internationalisation has occurred, to varying degrees, across all the areas of the law compared, but not wholly consistently nor uniformly in practice. Cross-border insolvency, close-out netting, schemes of arrangement, comfort letters, the protection of personal data in insolvency and restructuring, have by and large been globalised. Many states have adopted similar positions in using such instruments. However, regulatory differences among states have also grown, not receded. For example, the gap between unchecked and growing data invasions and data protection laws and cybersecurity measures are widening. That divergence represents a continuing threat to businesses and individuals, as to governments themselves. Therefore, to raise their collective status internationally further illustrates their importance in strengthening and retaining high levels of trust in transnational commercial activity.

Nevertheless, these gaps between uniform and divergent regulation are not fully engrained, although those gaps cannot be wholly eradicated. The obstacles in addressing it are long-standing, well preceding COVID-19. Legal responses to market instability and abuse have long post-dated those instabilities and abuses; and a trail of unfortunate business losses have long occupied a littered pathway to effective legal constraints. The pathway towards effective and sustainable finance and insolvency laws epitomises this issue.

Significantly, too, is recognition that states modify their international commercial regimes in response to their own evolving ideological and functional regulatory. China's financing of its massive international belt and road reflects a material shift from its traditionally planned economy to the neo-liberal market orientation that has permeated global commerce since the 1950s. China cannot allow its regulatory order to be static if it is to respond effectively to often unanticipated threats to global finance.[86] Nor can it ignore domestic demands on its finances in deciding how it will assist struggling domestic and foreign entities to sustain their regional and global financial operations including in China. In particular, china cannot ignore the financing needs of its growing elderly population. Nor can it maintain domestic social welfare initiatives if it is to devote itself, unqualifiedly, to its economic outreach into the world economy. In effect, China is realistically motivated to sustain both domestic and international financing initiatives, not to the exclusion of each other, but concurrently and also, sustainably.[87]

Finally, the case for functional legal convergence, notably in trans-border finance and insolvency regulation, is growing into a commercial imperative globally, and well beyond China or any other 'great power'. Effectuating such convergence internationally entails legal convergence and enrichment. The purpose is to promote a higher level of stability, certainty and predictability in an economic order that is truly a 'global village', however much sovereignty association purports to restrict its global dimensions.

86 Leon Trakman, China's Belt and Road: Where to Now, *The International Lawyer* 55(3) (2023) forthcoming.

87 Leon Trakman, *China's Investment Strategies: Where to Post Pandemic?* Journal of Transnational Law and Contemporary Problems 32 (2023) forthcoming.

APPENDIX ONE

ISDA Master Agreements

The International Swaps and Derivatives Association (ISDA) Master Agreements are important contractual legal instruments that are readily used to manage large financial transactions. The ISDA has standardised documentation for counterparties engaging in multiple OTC derivatives transactions that contain close-out netting provisions.[1] Appendix One highlights the number of Master Agreements established by the ISDA. It also briefly provides an outline of key clauses, enforcement arrangements, arbitration and the recent development in technology that has simplified the process for use of these agreements.

Put another way, see Figure A.1[2] for payment obligations with and without close-out netting arrangements. Thus, the process for close-out netting involves three steps: (1) termination, (2) valuation and (3) the determination of net balance. The first step, termination, means that the non-defaulting party puts an end to the obligations under the ISDA Agreement; the step is often called *early termination* because it occurs prior to the scheduled termination dates of the individual transactions.[3] According to Mengle, the second step involves valuation. As part of this process, it is important to determine the replacement cost of each transaction under the contract. The final step is to determine the net balance of the positive value(s) (that is, those owed to the non-defaulting party) and negative value(s) (those owed

1 Nina Hval, Credit Risk Reduction in the International Over-the-Counter Derivatives Market: Collateralizing the Net Exposure with Support Agreements, *The International Lawyer* 31, 3 (1997), 801–803.

2 David Mengle, *The Importance of Close-Out Netting*, 2010, https://www.isda.org/a/USiDE/netting-isdaresearchnotes-1-2010.pdf.

3 Ibid., 2.

DOI: 10.4324/9781003312024-5

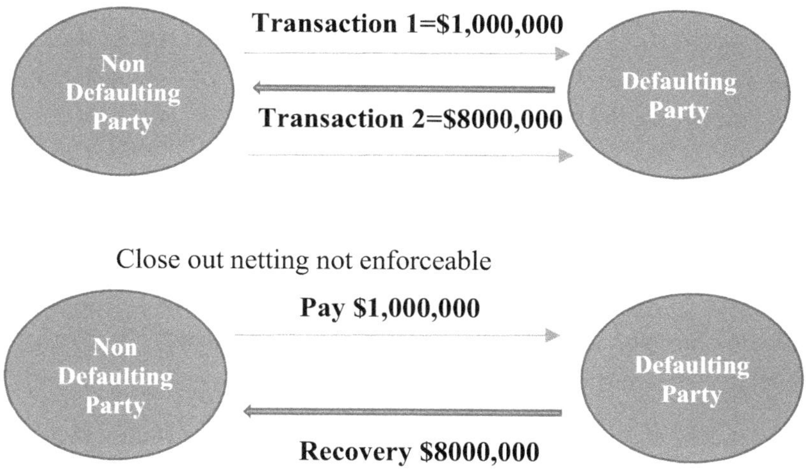

FIGURE A.1 Close-out netting under Section 6 of ISDA Master Agreement

by the non-defaulting party) netted against each other under the single agreement, in order to determine the final close-out amount (Figure A.1).[4]

Thus, to understand close-out netting provisions, it is also important to understand over-the-counter derivative(s) contracts, along with the various ISDA Master Agreements that have now been in place commencing in the 1980s through to 2002.

1987 ISDA Master Agreement[5]

The 1987 Interest Rate Swap Agreement is used to document US dollar-denominated interest rate swaps. It is intended for use with the 1986 Code and incorporates the Code by reference. The 1992 ISDA Master Agreements were prepared to accommodate transactions that could be documented under the 1987 Agreements with their 1989 and 1990 Addenda, as well as other types of OTC derivatives.[6] Additionally, the 1987 Interest Rate and Currency Exchange Agreement[7] for single currency and multiple currency interest rate and currency swaps allows parties to document the derivatives covered within the transaction. Generally, this Agreement is used to document US dollar-denominated interest rate swaps. It enables the use with the

4 Ibid. This amount includes not only the replacement costs at close-out but the costs of unwind such as bid-offer spread as well.

5 1987 Interest Rate Swap Agreement, International Swaps and Derivatives Association, https://www.isda.org/book/1987-isda-interest-rate-swap-agreement/.

6 1987 Interest Rate and Currency Exchange Agreement, https://www.isda.org/book/1987-interest-rate-and-currency-exchange-agreement/.

7 Christian McNamara, Andrew Metrick, The Lehman Brothers Bankruptcy F: Introduction to the ISDA Master Agreement, *Journal of Financial Crises* 1, 1 (2019), 137–150.

1986 Code and incorporates the Code by reference. Yet, and on the other hand, the standard ISDA Master Agreements that are used today are generally the 1992 ISDA Master Agreement and 2002 ISDA Master Agreement. This section discusses these Master Agreements and how they vary between the two.

1992 ISDA Master Agreement (United States)

In an example of a 1992 ISDA Master Agreement that was entered into in 2007 between GMAC Mortgage, LLC and GMAC Bank,[8] Section 2 provides: 'Obligations . . . (c) Netting. If on any date amounts would otherwise be payable: – (i) in the same currency; and (ii) in respect of the same Transaction'. In other words, each party to the other, then, on such date:

> each party's obligation to make payment of any such amount will be automatically satisfied and discharged and, if the aggregate amount that would otherwise have been payable by one party exceeds the aggregate amount that would otherwise have been payable by the other party, replaced by an obligation upon the party by whom the larger aggregate amount would have been payable to pay to the other party the excess of the larger aggregate amount over the smaller aggregate amount.[9]

Section 13, the 'Governing Law and Jurisdiction' provides for, '(a) Governing Law whereby this Agreement will be governed by and construed in accordance with the law specified in the Schedule'.[10] Thus, this Agreement will be governed by and construed in accordance with the laws of the State of New York (without reference to its choice of law doctrine). However, in this example, the ISDA Master Agreement does not include the application of Safe Harbor provisions under the Code. Jurisdiction is another important element of ISDA Master Agreements, and while the parties to this agreement are registered in the US (Delaware-Utah respectively), the chosen jurisdiction is the English courts.[11]

8 1992, International Swap Dealers Association, Inc. Master Agreement, 2007, GMAC Mortgage, LLC and GMAC Bank, https://www.sec.gov/Archives/edgar/data/1332815/000119312509105708/dex1024.htm.

9 The parties may elect in respect of two or more Transactions that a net amount will be determined in respect of all amounts payable on the same date in the same currency in respect of such Transactions, regardless of whether such amounts are payable in respect of the same Transaction. The election may be made in the Schedule or a Confirmation by specifying that subparagraph (ii) above will not apply to the Transactions identified as being subject to the election, together with the starting date (in which case subparagraph (ii) above will not, or will cease to, apply to such Transactions from such date). This election may be made separately for different groups of Transactions and will apply separately to each pairing of Offices through which the parties make and receive payments or deliveries.

10 Ibid., Schedule (h).

11 Ibid., Section 13,

> If this Agreement is expressed to be governed by English law, or to the non-exclusive jurisdiction of the courts of the State of New York and the United States District Court located in the Borough of Manhattan in New York City; if this Agreement is expressed to be governed

2002 ISDA Master Agreement (United States)

In another example under a 2002 ISDA Master Agreement between the Bank of America and LKQ Corporation,[12] Section 2 highlights the obligations of the parties. Moreover, and similar to the previous 1992 ISDA Master Agreement example, this section sets out the netting arrangements to be: *Netting of Payments*, whereby:

> if on any date amounts would otherwise be payable: . . . (i) in the same currency; and (ii) in respect of the same Transaction, by each party to the other, then, on such date, each party's obligation to make payment of any such amount will be automatically satisfied and discharged and, if the aggregate amount that would otherwise have been payable by one party exceeds the aggregate amount that would otherwise have been payable by the other party, replaced by an obligation upon the party by which the larger aggregate amount would have been payable to pay to the other party the excess of the larger aggregate amount over the smaller aggregate amount.[13]

In accounting for single, two or more, or, multiple transactions,[14] Section 2 goes further to provide that:

> [T]he parties may elect in respect of two or more Transactions that a net amount and payment obligation will be determined in respect of all amounts payable on the same date in the same currency in respect of those Transactions, regardless of whether such amounts are payable in respect of the same Transaction. The election may be made in the Schedule or any Confirmation by specifying that 'Multiple Transaction Payment Netting' applies to the Transactions identified as being subject to the election (in which case

---

> by the laws of the State of New York; and (ii) waives any objection which it may have at any time to the laying of venue of any Proceedings brought in any such court, waives any claim that such Proceedings have been brought in an inconvenient forum and further waives the right to object, with respect to such Proceedings, that such court does not have any jurisdiction over such party. Nothing in this Agreement precludes either party from bringing Proceedings in any other jurisdiction [illegible] if this Agreement is expressed to be governed by English law, the Contracting States, as defined in Section I(3) of the Civil Jurisdiction and Judgments Act 1982 or any modification, extension or re-enactment thereof for the time being in force nor will be bringing of Proceedings in any one or more jurisdictions preclude the bringing of Proceedings in any other jurisdiction.

12 2002 International Swaps and Derivatives Association, Inc. Master Agreement, Bank of America and LKQ Corporation, 2011, https://www.sec.gov/Archives/edgar/data/1065696/000119312511118050/dex101.htm.

13 Ibid., 2(c).

14 Ibid.,

> Part 4 Miscellaneous, (i) Netting of Payments. Multiple Transaction Payment Netting shall apply with respect to the following groups of Transactions, but only within such groups, and each such group shall itself be treated separately for purposes of payment netting.

clause (ii) above will not apply to such Transactions). If Multiple Transaction Payment Netting is applicable to Transactions, it will apply to those Transactions with effect from the starting date specified in the Schedule or such Confirmation, or, if a starting date is not specified in the Schedule or such Confirmation, the starting date otherwise agreed by the parties in writing. This election may be made separately for different groups of Transactions and will apply separately to each pairing of Offices through which the parties make and receive payments or deliveries.[15]

Put another way, generally, an ISDA Master Agreement in accordance with Section 2(a)(iii) allows a Non-defaulting Party to suspend its performance, such as making payments, so long as an event of default is continuing and termination of the contract has not been elected. As noted by the ISDA, this provision is intended to provide a means of alleviating transaction issues between the derivative counterparties (posting by a counterparty of an incorrect collateral balance or incorrect payment amount) through a means other than close out, allowing the parties to remedy the situation while providing the non-defaulting party during this period with a suspension of further payments which could increase the non-defaulting counterparty's credit exposure. Section 2(a)(iii) is fundamentally different from close-out netting, which provides for the calculation and payment of a single net termination amount in the event that termination is elected after default.[16] Moreover, in the previous example, Section 13 outlines the governing law and jurisdiction. It states:

(a) ***Governing Law.*** This Agreement will be governed by and construed in accordance with the law specified in the Schedule. (b) ***Jurisdiction.*** With respect to any suit, action or proceedings relating to any dispute arising out of or in connection with this Agreement (Proceedings), each party irrevocably: (i) submits: 1) if this Agreement is expressed to be governed by English law, to (A) the non-exclusive jurisdiction of the English courts if the Proceedings do not involve a Convention Court and (B) the exclusive jurisdiction of the English courts if the Proceedings do involve a Convention Court; or 2) if this Agreement is expressed to be governed by the laws of the State of New York, to the non-exclusive jurisdiction of the courts of the State of New York and the United States District Court located in the Borough of Manhattan in New York City; (ii) waives any objection which it may have at any time to the laying of venue of any Proceedings brought in any such court, waives any claim that such Proceedings have been brought in an inconvenient forum and further waives the right to object, with respect to such Proceedings, that such court does not have any jurisdiction over such party; and (iii) agrees, to the extent permitted

15 Ibid., 2(c).

16 International Swaps and Derivatives Association, Inc., 8, See J. B. Maverick, *Payment Netting vs. Close-Out Netting: What's the Difference?* June 25, 2019, https://www.investopedia.com/ask/answers/062515/what-difference-between-payment-netting-and-closeout-netting.asp.

by applicable law, that the bringing of Proceedings in any one or more jurisdictions will not preclude the bringing of Proceedings in any other jurisdiction.[17]

In other words, to confirm what the governing law is, the usual practice is to look at the Schedule, whereby in this case it states that this Agreement and any and all controversies arising out of or in relation to this Agreement shall be governed by and construed in accordance with the laws of the State of New York (without reference to its conflict of laws doctrine).[18] Therefore, the applicable law that will govern this ISDA Master Agreement will be the law of the State of New York. A feature of the US framework as highlighted next is the provision of Safe Harbors. It reinforces the legal framework of the US by ensuring that the parties to the ISDA Master Agreement considers the Bankruptcy Code and Federal Deposit Insurance Corporation Improvement Act of 1991. It states this Agreement, including any Credit Support Document, is a 'master netting agreement' as defined in the U.S. Bankruptcy Code, and a 'netting contract' as defined in the netting provisions of the Federal Deposit Insurance Corporation Improvement Act of 1991, and this Agreement, including any Credit Support Document, and each Transaction hereunder is of a type set forth in Section 561(a)(1)–(5) of the Code.[19]

Yet, and on the other hand, it must be noted that while these are standard provisions-clauses, they could from time to time vary between ISDA Master Agreements. Today, financial transactions predominantly fall within the 1992 and 2002 ISDA Master Agreements. Nonetheless, in the previous example, Section 6 provides for early termination: close-out netting.[20] Of the two Master Agreements,

17 Ibid., Section 13.
18 Ibid., Schedule (h).
19 Ibid.,

> Schedule, Part 5 (e). (i) This Agreement, including any Credit Support Document, is a 'master netting agreement' as defined in the U.S. Bankruptcy Code, and a 'netting contract' as defined in the netting provisions of the Federal Deposit Insurance Corporation Improvement Act of 1991, and this Agreement, including any Credit Support Document, and each Transaction hereunder is of a type set forth in Section 561(a)(1)-(5) of the Code. (ii) Party A is a 'master netting agreement participant,' a 'financial institution,' a 'financial participant,' a 'forward contract merchant' and a 'swap participant' as defined in the Code, and a 'financial institution' as defined in the netting provisions of FDICIA. (iii) The remedies provided herein, and in any Credit Support Document, are the remedies referred to in Section 561(a), Sections 362(b)(6), (7), (17) and (27), and Section 362(o) of the Code, and in Section 11(e)(8)(A) and (C) of the Federal Deposit Insurance Act. (iv) All transfers of cash, securities or other property under or in connection with this Agreement, any Credit Support Document or any Transaction hereunder are 'margin payments,' 'settlement payments' and 'transfers' under Sections 546(e), (f), (g) or (j), and under Section 548(d)(2) of the Code. (v) Each obligation under this Agreement, any Credit Support Document or any Transaction hereunder is an obligation to make a 'margin payment,' 'settlement payment' and 'payment' within the meaning of Sections 362, 560 and 561 of the Code.

20 Ibid.,

> Right to Terminate Following Event of Default. If at any time an Event of Default with respect to a party (the 'Defaulting Party') has occurred and is then continuing, the other party (the

the varied approach taken is not so much in relation to the respective close-out netting provisions, but rather termination under Section 6. Section 6 allows for the parties in accordance with the respective Schedule to determine whether the party not at fault is required to pay if the net termination amount is worked out to be payable to the party at fault. Alternatively, it also allows for termination values for the transaction, by obtaining quotes from dealers in the market.

However, this only applies to the 1992 ISDA Master Agreement and not the 2002 version. The 2002 ISDA Master Agreement also amended the difference between the market quotation and Loss – the close-out amount. The importance of closing out cannot be underestimated, and closing out becomes exercisable when one or both of the parties may have the right to designate an early termination date in respect of all or some of the outstanding transactions by sending a notice to the other party. A notice designating an early termination date, once given, cannot be withdrawn (Figure 10.3). In some circumstances, the occurrence of an

> early termination date is automatic where 1) the parties have specified in the schedule that automatic early termination (see section on events) is applicable to the relevant party; and 2) one of a limited set of bankruptcy events of default occurs in respect of the relevant party. In such cases, transactions under the ISDA Master Agreement are deemed to be terminated automatically without any requirement to give notice as described above.[21]

'Non-defaulting Party') may, by not more than 20 days notice to the Defaulting Party specifying the relevant Event of Default, designate a day not earlier than the day such notice is effective as an Early Termination Date in respect of all outstanding Transactions. If, however, 'Automatic Early Termination' is specified in the Schedule as applying to a party, then an Early Termination Date in respect of all outstanding Transactions will occur immediately upon the occurrence with respect to such party of an Event of Default specified in Section 5(a)(vii)(1), (3), (5), (6) or, to the extent analogous thereto, (8), and as of the time immediately preceding the institution of the relevant proceeding or the presentation of the relevant Petition upon the occurrence with respect to such party of an Event of Default specified in Section 5(a)(vii)(4) or, to the extent analogous thereto, (8).

21 Legal Guidelines for Smart Derivatives Contracts: The ISDA Master Agreement, 2019, https://www.isda.org/a/23iME/Legal-Guidelines-for-Smart-Derivatives-Contracts-ISDA-Master-Agreement.pdf, 25–26.

The provisions of the ISDA Master Agreement dealing with calculation of the early termination amount payable following close out are complex, particularly where there are many and various live transactions under an agreement. However, there are a few key concepts: • The ISDA Master Agreement provides that the close-out amount is determined by assessing the amount of the losses or costs incurred (or the gains realized) in replacing the terminated transactions or by providing the economic equivalent of the material terms of the terminated transactions. • The early termination amount is a net amount. Where termination values are separately calculated in respect of individual transactions or groups of transactions, they are added to produce the single early termination amount. • The early termination amount is an amount determined by one of the parties, or (in certain limited cases) an average of the amounts determined by both parties. The early termination amount reflects both the value of transaction payments and deliveries that would have been due on or after the early termination date and the value of payments or

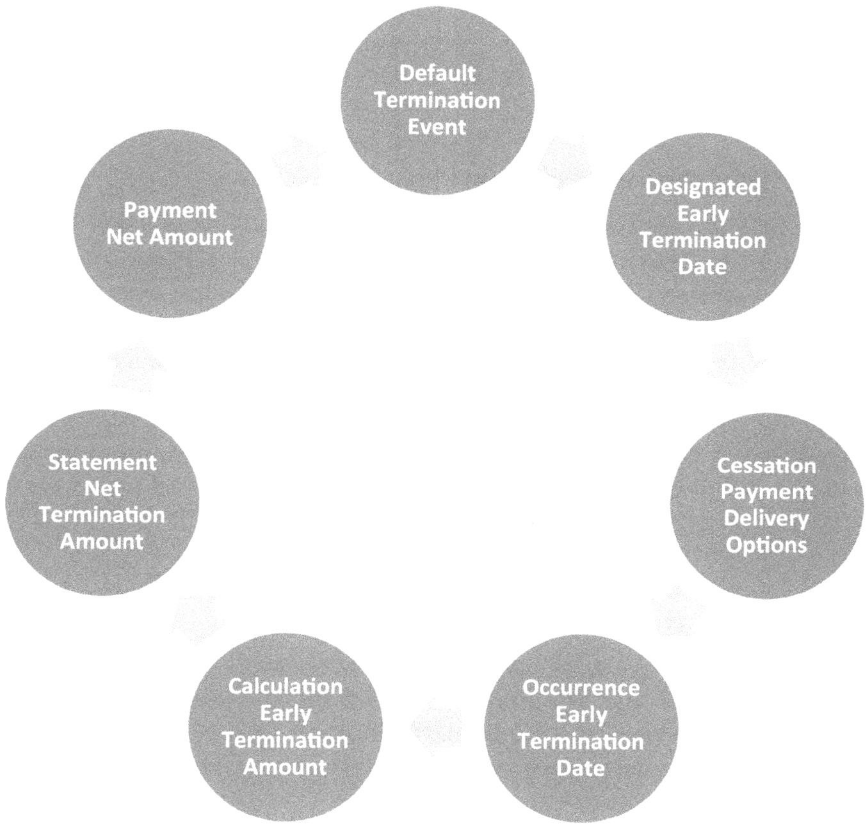

FIGURE A.2 The process of closing out or terminating transactions entered into under an ISDA Master Agreement involves seven steps or elements. Provisions relating to close out are found in Section 6 of the ISDA Master Agreement.[22]

See later for discussion on *Force Majeure*.

The importance of understanding the fundamentals and contents of ISDA Master Agreements ensures policy makers and practitioners have the correct processes in place to ensure any agreement is prepared accurately. Doing so will ensure there is a high level of stability within the financial sector. Apart from providing the framework for large investments, they protect parties in these investments. Viewed

deliveries that were due before the early termination date but remain unpaid/undelivered. • The early termination amount is expressed in a single termination currency, even though individual transactions may specify payments to be made in different contracted currencies and denominate deliveries in different currencies.

22 Ibid.

this way, the ISDA Master Agreement is arguably the standard contract used to govern OTC derivatives transactions. Nevertheless, there are other two forms of Bridging Agreements that have also been established by the ISDA. These include the ISDA, Cross-Agreement and the Energy Agreement.

2001 ISDA Cross-Agreement Bridge

The 2001 ISDA Cross-Agreement Bridge provides parties to an ISDA Master Agreement[23] with the means of achieving cross-product netting. Parties are able, in certain circumstances, to terminate transactions documented under other industry-standard agreements and to incorporate the net close-out amounts calculated in respect of those transactions within the close-out provisions of their ISDA Master Agreement. In addition, it allows the close-out amounts under various industry Master Agreements to be taken into account in Section 6 of the 1992 ISDA Master Agreements as Unpaid Amounts.[24] Although the 2001 Bridge was not prepared with the 2002 ISDA Master Agreement in mind, we do not expect your opinion to differ with respect to whether the 2001 Bridge is utilised with the 1992 ISDA Master Agreement or the 2002 ISDA Master Agreement.

2002 ISDA Energy Agreement Bridge

The 2002 ISDA Energy Agreement Bridge (the '2002 Bridge') (attached at Annex E) was modelled on the 2001 Bridge. The 2002 Bridge is intended to permit a party, upon the occurrence of a designated Bridging Event with respect to the other party, to close out transactions under the ISDA Master Agreement and transactions under other designated agreements.[25] Net close-out amounts under the Bridged Agreements are incorporated into Section 6(e)'s close-out calculation under the ISDA Master Agreement as Unpaid Amounts.

Enforceability

Generally, enforceability of the close-out netting provisions under the ISDA Master Agreement[26] comprises two elements: first, enforceability as a matter of contract law under the governing law of the contract (typically English law or New York law); and second, consistency with the bankruptcy laws of the jurisdiction where the counterparty is located.[27] The ISDA are of the view that the latter is critical since, regardless of the law selected to govern the contract, local insolvency law in an insolvent party's jurisdiction will always override in the event of an insolvency.

23 International Swaps and Derivatives Association, https://www.isda.org/book/2001-isda-cross-agreement-bridge-and-commentary/.
24 International Swaps and Derivatives Association, 12, See M. Konrad Borowicz, Contracts as regulation: the ISDA Master Agreement, *Capital Markets Law Journal*, 16 (1), January 2021, 72–94, https://doi.org/10.1093/cmlj/kmaa026.
25 Ibid.
26 Ibid.
27 Ibid., 3.

Force

In 2020, the world had to grapple with the pandemic of COVID-19. Apart from the human health impact this had on most economies, questions arose as to whether *force majeure* clauses were adequate enough to protect parties to ISDA Master Agreements. As a starting point, it must be noted that, the 1992 ISDA Master Agreement does not contain a standard clause of *force majeure*. Yet, the 2020 ISDA Master Agreements do. The questions arise how under COVID-19 can this event be effectively managed under both Master Agreements? A further accentuating question is whether there are currently provisions within the 1992 ISDA Master Agreement that can be extended to cover such events as pandemics? A starting point is that under both agreements there are provisions that deal with termination, or, put another way, an illegality termination. Under both Master Agreements they can be found in clause 5 (Figure 10.4). However, and more specifically, this section provides just one example for the ISDA Master Agreements that have been established in the US and highlighted earlier in this chapter.

The 2002 ISDA Master Agreement provides a higher level of certainty than its counterpart in 1992, though Section 5 (2)(b)(ii) will be interpreted by the courts differently, depending on the jurisdictions. For instance, in Australia they mean all or nothing, which, in the similar way to the courts in the US, particularly New York, they will be interpreted narrowly.[28] In the example provided, it is not clear whether a pandemic would constitute the use of the *Force Majeure* clause. More problematic, does the clause only pertain to activity undertaken by a state actor, private actor or both? On the one side, careful interpretation under common and civil law systems of the Hierarchy of Events as to whether a pandemic would apply needs to be considered. On the other side, however, when compared to standard international trade and other contracts, there is generally a long and exhaustive list of what would constitute an event-activity to trigger the *Force Majeure* clause. In addition, and outside the *Force Majeure* clause, the courts would be required to interpret and determine what would constitute such an event to trigger this clause and protect the parties. Viewed this way, it could be argued either way that there is an implied provision under the *Force Majeure* Event that would cover a pandemic. However, and on the other hand, it is our view that the ISDA should undertake a review outside of the legal opinions obtained and provide additional certainty to the sector, by amending the *Force Majeure* clause to ensure pandemics are covered as an activity to protect parties (Figure 10.5).

Thus both 1992 and 2002 Agreements provide for termination; however, under a pandemic the 2002 ISDA Master Agreement is specific. In a similar way to the 2002 Agreement, the 1992 ISDA Master Agreement, Section 5 of the Events of Default and Termination Events, apart from not providing for *Force Majeure*, an Event of Default constitutes an Illegality, and it will be treated as an Illegality and

28 Guy Dempsey, Don MacBean, Stanford Renas, *Force Majeure Clauses and Financially Settled Transactions Under the ISDA Master Agreement*, 2020, https://katten.com/.

(b) Termination Events. The occurrence at any time with respect to a party or, if applicable, any Credit Support Provider of such party or any Specified Entity of such party of any event specified below constitutes (subject to Section 5(c)) an Illegality if the event is specified in clause (i) below, a *Force Majeure* Event if the event is specified in clause (ii) below, a Tax Event if the event is specified in clause (iii) below, a Tax Event Upon Merger if the event is specified in clause (iv) below, and, if specified to be applicable, a Credit Event Upon Merger if the event is specified pursuant to clause (v) below or an Additional Termination Event if the event is specified pursuant to clause (vi) below: –

(i) Illegality.[1]

(ii) *Force Majeure* Event. After giving effect to any applicable provision, disruption fallback or remedy specified in, or pursuant to, the relevant Confirmation or elsewhere in this Agreement, by reason of *force majeure* or act of state occurring after a Transaction is entered into, on any day: –

(1) the Office through which such party (which will be the Affected Party) makes and receives payments or deliveries with respect to such Transaction is prevented from performing any absolute or contingent obligation to make a payment or delivery in respect of such Transaction, from receiving a payment or delivery in respect of such Transaction or from complying with any other material provision of this Agreement relating to such Transaction (or would be so prevented if such payment, delivery or compliance were required on that day), or it becomes impossible or impracticable for such Office so to perform, receive or comply (or it would be impossible or impracticable for such Office so to perform, receive or comply if such payment, delivery or compliance were required on that day); or

(2) such party or any Credit Support Provider of such party (which will be the Affected Party) is prevented from performing any absolute or contingent obligation to make a payment or delivery which such party or Credit Support Provider has under any Credit Support Document relating to such Transaction, from receiving a payment or delivery under such Credit Support Document or from complying with any other material provision of such Credit Support Document (or would be so prevented if such payment, delivery or compliance were required on that day), or it becomes impossible or impracticable for such party or Credit Support Provider so to perform, receive or comply (or it would be impossible or impracticable for such party or Credit Support Provider so to perform, receive or comply if such payment, delivery or compliance were required on that day),

1 Ibid.,

> After giving effect to any applicable provision, disruption fallback or remedy specified in, or pursuant to, the relevant Confirmation or elsewhere in this Agreement, due to an event or circumstance (other than any action taken by a party or, if applicable, any Credit Support Provider of such party) occurring after a Transaction is entered into, it becomes unlawful under any applicable law (including without limitation the laws of any country in which payment, delivery or compliance is required by either party or any Credit Support Provider, as the case may be), on any day, or it would be unlawful if the relevant payment, delivery or compliance were required on that day (in each case, other than as a result of a breach by the party of Section 4(b)): (1) for the Office through which such party (which will be the Affected Party) makes and receives payments or deliveries with respect to such Transaction to perform any absolute or contingent obligation to make a payment or delivery in respect of such Transaction, to receive a payment or delivery in respect of such

(c) Hierarchy of Events.
  (i) An event or circumstance that constitutes or gives rise to an Illegality or a *Force Majeure* Event will not, for so long as that is the case, also constitute or give rise to an Event of Default under Section 5(a)(i), 5(a)(ii)(1) or 5(a)(iii)(1) insofar as such event or circumstance relates to the failure to make any payment or delivery or a failure to comply with any other material provision of this Agreement or a Credit Support Document, as the case may be.
  (ii) Except in circumstances contemplated by clause (i) above, if an event or circumstance which would otherwise constitute or give rise to an Illegality or a *Force Majeure* Event also constitutes an Event of Default or any other Termination Event, it will be treated as an Event of Default or such other Termination Event, as the case may be, and will not constitute or give rise to an Illegality or a *Force Majeure* Event.
  (iii) If an event or circumstance which would otherwise constitute or give rise to a *Force Majeure* Event also constitutes an Illegality, it will be treated as an Illegality, except as described in clause (ii) above, and not a *Force Majeure* Event.
(d) Deferral of Payments and Deliveries During Waiting Period.[2]
(e) Inability of Head or Home Office to Perform Obligations of Branch.[3]

FIGURE A.3 Highlights of Section 5 of the Bank of America and LKQ Corporation 2002 ISDA Master Agreement,[4] whereby Section 5 provides for events of default and termination events, that contains the *force majeure* provision

Transaction or to comply with any other material provision of this Agreement relating to such Transaction; or (2) for such party or any Credit Support Provider of such party (which will be the Affected Party) to perform any absolute or contingent obligation to make a payment or delivery which such party or Credit Support Provider has under any Credit Support Document relating to such Transaction, to receive a payment or delivery under such Credit Support Document or to comply with any other material provision of such Credit Support Document.

2 Ibid.,

> If an Illegality or a *Force Majeure* Event has occurred and is continuing with respect to a Transaction, each payment or delivery which would otherwise be required to be made under that Transaction will be deferred to, and will not be due until: (i) the first Local Business Day or, in the case of a delivery, the first Local Delivery Day (or the first day that would have been a Local Business Day or Local Delivery Day, as appropriate, but for the occurrence of the event or circumstance constituting or giving rise to that Illegality or *Force Majeure* Event) following the end of any applicable Waiting Period in respect of that Illegality or *Force Majeure* Event, as the case may be; or (ii) if earlier, the date on which the event or circumstance constituting or giving rise to that Illegality or *Force Majeure* Event ceases to exist or, if such date is not a Local Business Day or, in the case of a delivery, a Local Delivery Day, the first following day that is a Local Business Day or Local Delivery Day, as appropriate.

3 Ibid.,

> If (i) an Illegality or a *Force Majeure* Event occurs under Section 5(b)(i)(1) or 5(b)(ii)(1) and the relevant Office is not the Affected Party's head or home office, (ii) Section 10(a) applies, (iii) the other party seeks performance of the relevant obligation.

4 2002 International Swaps and Derivatives Association, Inc. Master Agreement, Bank of America and LKQ Corporation, 2011, https://www.sec.gov/Archives/edgar/data/1065696/000119312511118050/dex101.htm.

5. Events of Default and Termination Events

(a) Events of Default. The occurrence at any time with respect to a party or, if applicable, any Credit Support Provider of such party or any Specified Entity of such party of any of the following events constitutes an event of default (an 'Event of Default') with respect to such party: –

(i) Failure to Pay or Deliver.
(ii) Breach of Agreement, Repudiation of Agreement.
(iii) Credit Support Default.
(iv) Misrepresentation.
(v) Default under Specified Transaction.
(vi) Cross Default.
(vii) Bankruptcy.
(viii) Merger Without Assumption.

(b) Termination Events. The occurrence at any time with respect to a party or, if applicable, any Credit Support Provider of such party or any Specified Entity of such party of any event specified below constitutes an Illegality if the event is specified in (i) below, a Tax Event if the event is specified in (ii) below or a Tax Event Upon Merger if the event is specified in (iii) below, and, if specified to be applicable, a Credit Event Upon Merger if the event is specified pursuant to (iv) below or an Additional Termination Event if the event is specified pursuant to (v) below: –

(i) *Illegality*. Due to the adoption of, or any change in, any applicable law after the date on which a Transaction is entered into, or due to the promulgation of, or any change in, the interpretation by any court, tribunal or regulation authority with competent jurisdiction of any applicable law after such date, it becomes unlawful (other than as a result of a breach by the party of Section 4(b)) for such party (which will be the Affected Party):

(1) to perform any absolute or contingent obligation to make a payment or delivery or to receive a payment or delivery in respect of such Transaction or to comply with any other material provision of this Agreement relating to such Transaction; or

(2) to perform, or for any Credit Support Provider of such party to perform, any contingent or other obligation which the party (or such Credit Support Provider) has under any Credit Support Document relating to such Transaction;

(ii) *Tax Event*.
(iii) *Tax Event Upon Merger*.
(iv) *Credit Event Upon Merger*.
(v) *Additional Termination Event*.

an Event of Default also constitutes an Illegality, it will be treated as an Illegality and will not constitute an Event of Default.

FIGURE A.4 Highlights of the termination clause in the 1992 ISDA Master Agreement, 2007, GMAC Mortgage, LLC and GMAC Bank[1]

1 1992, International Swap Dealers Association, Inc. Master Agreement, 2007, GMAC Mortgage, LLC and GMAC Bank, https://www.sec.gov/Archives/edgar/data/1332815/000119312509105708/dex1024.htm.

will not constitute an Event of Default. However, there is the ability for those parties that continue to use these Master Agreements to incorporate a *Force Majeure* provision. In the previous example, however, such a clause does not exist. Thus, it is argued that the *Force Majeure* clause from the 2002 ISDA Master Agreement could be incorporated into the 1992 version. The issue for the ISDA is that unlike any other time in history, pandemics are unlikely to go away. It can be argued, and more probable than not, that another pandemic will be experienced by the world in the next two decades. If not realised, regions of the world are likely to see epidemics, which has been the case throughout Asia and Middle East with SARS[29] (severe acute respiratory syndrome) and MERS[30] (Middle East respiratory syndrome coronavirus) over the past decade. These incidents, in and of themselves, are likely to have an economic impact to the financial sector. Therefore, it is increasingly important that these legal mechanisms and instruments be upgraded to address modern-day societal, economic and human health concerns. Yet it must be noted that, while using these examples from the US, there may be likely minor variances to this model. A further accentuating and more pressing issue that has arisen is the possible impact of technology on close-out netting arrangements and ISDA Master Agreements.

Arbitration

Generally, the ISDA Master Agreement contains the parties' choice for the law which will govern the contract and transactions under its terms, as well as a provision specifying which courts can adjudicate upon any disputes about swaps governed by the Master Agreement.[31] The terms dealing with governing law and choice of court were first published in 1987 and underwent revision for the 2002 Master Agreement. Importantly, the ISDA has adopted the internationally agreed framework for arbitration, noting that:

> Agreeing to arbitration allows a party to avoid having to litigate in a jurisdiction in whose courts it does not have confidence, while producing an arbitral

29 World Health Organization, 'Severe acute respiratory syndrome is a viral respiratory disease caused by a SARS-associated coronavirus. It was first identified at the end of February 2003 during an outbreak that emerged in China and spread to 4 other countries', https://www.who.int/health-topics/severe-acute-respiratory-syndrome#tab=tab_1.

30 World Health Organization, MERS is a viral respiratory illness caused by a coronavirus that was first identified in Saudi Arabia in 2012, https://www.who.int/emergencies/mers-cov/en/.

31 International Swaps and Derivatives Association, Inc, 2018 ISDA Arbitration Guide, at 4,

> This Guide provides guidance on the use of an arbitration clause with different forms of the ISDA Master Agreement. It includes a range of model clauses which may be used with either the ISDA 2002 Master Agreement (English/New York law) (the '2002 Agreement') or the ISDA 1992 Master Agreement (Multicurrency – Cross-border) (the '1992 Agreement'). The Guide also includes a model clause which may be used with the ISDA 2002 Master Agreement (Irish law) (the 'Irish Law Agreement'). This Guide is supplemental to and, in relation to Section 13 of the 2002 Agreement and 1992 Agreement, respectively, amends the guidance in the ISDA User's Guide to each of those forms.

award which may have an advantage over a foreign court judgment at the enforcement stage in many jurisdictions. This enforcement advantage arises because of the global regime for the cross-border enforcement of arbitral awards under the New York Convention.[32] There is not yet an international regime of comparable reach for the enforcement of court judgments, although this position may change in time as ratifications of the Hague Convention on Choice of Court Agreements of 30 June 2005 (the 'Hague Convention') increase. The Hague Convention provides for the enforcement in contracting states of judgments in civil and commercial matters rendered in another contracting state pursuant to an exclusive jurisdiction clause.[33]

Therefore, an arbitral award can be enforced against a party or its assets by invoking the coercive power of a court. This can make arbitration particularly attractive for resolving disputes arising out of international transactions. Moreover, a choice of court agreement (a jurisdiction clause) is not always necessary for a court to have jurisdiction over a party or dispute: the court may have inherent jurisdiction by virtue of its rules of civil procedure. On the one hand, when preparing an ISDA Master Agreement, the parties would need to consider the effectiveness of the introduction of arbitration clauses to deal with any disputes. On the other hand, it is well established that arbitration is an effective dispute resolution process, whereby the parties can resolve the issues arising from the ISDA Master Agreement, and arguably would include matters regarding close-out netting arrangements.

Technology

Technology responses to the pandemic have been swift. Public and private entities have both embraced the online world to continue their respective business operations. However, technology often represents a dichotomous dilemma in the source of both accelerating and retreating business initiatives in the arena of the pandemic. Applied to the Fintech sector, on the one side there is an acceleration in the use of technology, while on the other side a significant decline in technology capital

32 Ibid., at 6, there are approximately 160 contracting states to the New York Convention.

33 Ibid., at 9. Note the Guide provides for Model Clauses for ICC Rules (seat, London, New York, Paris).

Model clause for LCIA Rules (London Seat) Model clause for AAA-ICDR Rules (New York Seat) D. Model clause for HKIAC Rules (Hong Kong Seat) 34 E. Model clause for SIAC Rules (Singapore Seat) F. Model clause for Swiss Arbitration Rules (Zurich or Geneva Seat) G. Model clauses for P.R.I.M.E. Finance Rules Part 1 Model clause for P.R.I.M.E. Finance Rules (London Seat) Part 2 Model clause for P.R.I.M.E. Finance Rules (New York Seat) Part 3 Model clause for P.R.I.M.E. Finance Rules (The Hague Seat) H. Model clause for SCC Rules (Stockholm Seat) I. Model clause for DIS Rules (Frankfurt am Main Seat) J. Model clause For DIFC-LCIA Rules (DIFC Seat) K. Model clause for VIAC Rules (Vienna Seat) L. Model clause for LCIA Rules (Dublin Seat).

funding.[34] Yet, and even well before the pandemic, the ISDA had been working towards embracing technology and digitising its system and processors. In its 2020 revised digitisation of definitions the ISDA has taken an initial step to establishing greater industry efficiencies through standardisation, automation and the development of mutualised solutions. Moreover, the ISDA documentation and definitions are the starting point for every trade and every counterparty relationship.[35] The ISDA, in embracing the technology revolution, is also developing a taxonomy and clause library related to the ISDA Master Agreements. IT has developed further tools to assist firms to prepare online platforms for negotiating and contracting. The Standard Initial Margin Model and ISDA Create consist of an online platform for the negotiating terms identified in ISDA documentation. Launched in 2019 to support compliance with the initial margin rules, ISDA Create will extend to other types of documentation, including the schedule to the ISDA Master Agreement.[36] The full transition to the development and management of online ISDA Master Agreements, and subsequent close-out netting arrangements, is under development, although full automation is a longer-term project. Noteworthy too are cybersecurity risks across the financial sector, arising from both state and non-state intrusions, which could be additional further risks to financial instability.

34 Dariusz Wojcik, Stefanos Ioannou, *COVID-19 and Finance: Market Developments so far and Potential Impacts on the Financial Sector and Centers, School of Geography and the Environment*, University of Oxford, 2020, 388–391.

35 International Swaps Derivatives Association, *ISDA® Quarterly*, 6, https://www.isda.org/a/8ALTE/IQ-ISDA-Quarterly-January-2020.pdf.

36 Ibid., 17.

INDEX

For Product Safety Concerns and Information please contact our EU
representative GPSR@taylorandfrancis.com
Taylor & Francis Verlag GmbH, Kaufingerstraße 24, 80331 München, Germany

www.ingramcontent.com/pod-product-compliance
Ingram Content Group UK Ltd.
Pitfield, Milton Keynes, MK11 3LW, UK
UKHW020003200926
475702UK00015B/2444
* 9 7 8 1 0 3 2 3 1 9 1 3 1 *